Frontier Conflict

The Australian Experience

Frontier Conflict

The Australian Experience

Edited by
Bain Attwood
& S G Foster

NATIONAL
MUSEUM OF
AUSTRALIA
CANBERRA

First published 2003 by
National Museum of Australia
GPO Box 1901
CANBERRA ACT 2601
T 61 2 6208 5000
F 61 2 6208 5148
E information@nma.gov.au
W www.nma.gov.au

National Library of Australia cataloguing-in-publication data:

   Frontier Conflict: The Australian Experience

   ISBN 1 876944 11 0

   1. Aborigines, Australian. 2. Cross-cultural studies - Australia. 3. Australia -
   History. 4. Australia - Historiography. I. Foster, S. G. (Stephen Glynn), 1948- . II.
   Attwood, Bain. III. National Museum of Australia.

306.089915

Produced by the Publishing section of the National Museum of Australia
Designed and typeset by msquared design
Printed by Goanna Print
These conference proceedings have been refereed by an independent reader.

Contents

Illustrations

Contributors

Alan Atkinson is Professor of History at the University of New England. He is the author of *Camden: Farm and Village Life in Early New South Wales* (1988), the first volume of *The Europeans in Australia: A History* (1997) and *The Commonwealth of Speech: An Argument about Australia's Past, Present and Future* (2002). He is currently working on the second volume of *The Europeans in Australia* for publication in 2003.

Bain Attwood is Senior Research Fellow at the Centre for Cross-Cultural Research, the Australian National University, and Associate Professor in the School of Historical Studies, Monash University. His books include *The Making of the Aborigines* (1989) and *In the Age of Mabo: History, Aborigines and Australia* (1996). His next book, *Rights for Aborigines*, will be published in 2003.

Geoffrey Bolton is Emeritus Professor and Pro-Chancellor at Murdoch University. He has been publishing intermittently on north Australian history for 50 years. His most recent major book was *Edmund Barton: The One Man for the Job* (2001). He is currently writing a short history of Western Australia before attempting a biography of Sir Paul Hasluck.

Richard Broome is Associate Professor of History at La Trobe University. His books include *Aboriginal Australians* (1982, third edition 2002) and *Sideshow Alley* (1998). He is currently working on a history of Aboriginal people in Victoria from 1800 to the present.

Jan Critchett was Associate Professor at Deakin University and currently holds honorary positions at Deakin University and the University of Tasmania. Her books include *A 'Distant Field of Murder': Western District Frontiers 1834–1848* (1990) and *Untold Stories: Memories and Lives of Victorian Kooris* (1998).

Ann Curthoys is Manning Clark Professor of History at the Australian National University. She has written widely on many aspects of Australian history as well as on national identity and Australian historiography. Her book, *Freedom Ride: A Freedomrider Remembers*, was published in 2002.

Graeme Davison is Professor of History at Monash University. He is the author of *The Rise and Fall of Marvellous Melbourne* (1978), *The Unforgiving Minute* (1993) and *The Use and Abuse* *of Australian History* (2000), and co-editor of *The Oxford Companion to Australian History* (1998). His latest book, *Car Wars: Motorising the Metropolis*, will appear in 2003.

Raymond Evans   is Associate Professor of History at the University of Queensland. His most recent work on Australian race relations is *Fighting Words: Writing about Race* (1999). He is presently working on a dual biography of the Aboriginal sporting identities, Charlie Samuels and Jerry Jerome, with Ken Edwards.

Stephen Foster   is Professor of Museum Studies, Heritage and Collections at the Australian National University and the National Museum of Australia. He is Executive Editor of the eleven-volume series *Australians: A Historical Library* (1987–88), and a past editor of the journal *Aboriginal History*.

Tom Griffiths   is Senior Research Fellow in the History Program of the Research School of Social Sciences, the Australian National University. His books include *Hunters and Collectors: The Antiquarian Imagination in Australia* (1996) and *Forests of Ash: An Environmental History* (2001). He is currently working on a study of key writers and texts in twentieth-century Australian environmental history.

John Mulvaney   is an Emeritus Professor at the Centre for Archaeological Research, the Australian National University. He is the author of *The Prehistory of Australia* (1969, third edition, with Johan Kamminga, 1999), and co-author of *'So Much that is New': Baldwin Spencer, 1860–1929, A Biography* (1985). He is currently working on a biography of Paddy Cahill of Oenpelli, which includes the letters Cahill wrote to Spencer.

Henry Reynolds   is Senior Australian Research Council Research Fellow at the University of Tasmania. His books include the trilogy, *The Other Side of the Frontier* (1981, 1982), *Frontier: Aborigines, Settlers and Land* (1987), and *With the White People* (second edition published as *Black Pioneers*, 2001). He is currently working on a study of north Australia at the time of Federation.

David Andrew Roberts   was awarded his PhD by the University of Newcastle in 2001, with a thesis on the colonial frontier at Wellington Valley, New South Wales. He has published articles in *Australian Historical Studies* and the *Journal of Australian Colonial History*. He is currently researching Aboriginal rock paintings in western Arnhem Land.

Deborah Bird Rose   is Senior Research Fellow at the Centre for Resource and Environmental Studies, the Australian National University. She is the author of *Hidden Histories* (1991), *Dingo Makes us Human* (1992), and *Nourishing Terrains: Australian Aboriginal Views of Landscape and Wilderness* (1996). Her most recent book is *Country of the Heart* (2002).

Lyndall Ryan   is Foundation Professor of Australian Studies at the Ourimbah Campus of the University of Newcastle. Her major publications include *The Aboriginal Tasmanians* (1981, second edition 1996). She is currently writing a biography of her mother, Edna Ryan, a twentieth-century feminist and labour activist.

Keith Windschuttle   is an author and publisher who is a frequent contributor to *Quadrant* and the *New Criterion*. He is author of *The Killing of History: How Literary Critics and Social Theorists are Murdering Our Past* (1994, fourth edition 2000), and five other books. He is publisher of Macleay Press. He is a graduate in history from the University of Sydney and in politics from Macquarie University. He is a former academic who taught Australian history and social policy at the University of New South Wales and other Australian universities.

Preface

This book has its origins in a forum conducted at the National Museum of Australia in December 2001. Many of the speakers who contributed have generously revised or rewritten their papers for the book. An additional chapter has been written by Ann Curthoys, who was unable to attend the forum.

Both the forum and the book express the National Museum's commitment to encouraging public debate on issues of national importance. This role was acknowledged when the Museum was being planned in the 1970s; and it has been vigorously implemented since the Museum opened its doors to the public in early 2001. Through its exhibitions and public programs, the Museum has embraced the function of 'stimulating legitimate doubt and thoughtful discussion', as its planners had intended.

The extent and nature of frontier conflict in Australia have long been subjects of research and matters of debate. The chapters in this book approach the issues from different directions, including case studies of conflict at specific places and times, analyses of different forms of evidence, reflections on how words and memories help shape our view of the past, and discussions of how conflict is represented as part of the national story. As in any historical debate, the authors' perspectives also differ, sometimes sharply, and sometimes influenced as much by their views of contemporary Australia as their research into the past.

I hope this book, together with the Museum's Contested Frontiers exhibit, will contribute to a wider understanding of relationships between Indigenous and other Australians.

Dawn Casey
Director
August 2002

Acknowledgments

The editors acknowledge with thanks the small committee who helped plan
the conference that preceded this publication. Nancy Michaelis and
Harriette Wilson, both from the National Museum of Australia, made large
contributions to both the conference and the book. Michaela Forster and Jeanie
Watson from the Museum's Publishing section prepared the typescript for publication,
which was designed by Maureen MacKenzie-Taylor from **m** squared design.

Key places mentioned in the text

Darwin ■

Gulf of Carpentaria

Forrest River ■

KIMBERLEY   ■ Mistake Creek

■ Rutland Plains

■ Cairns

NORTHERN TERRITORY

■ Barrow Creek

Coniston ■

■ **Alice Springs**

QUEENSLAND

WESTERN AUSTRALIA

Moreton Bay

Brisbane ■

SOUTH AUSTRALIA

Waterloo Creek ■   ■ Myall Creek

NEW SOUTH WALES   LIVERPOOL PLAINS

Perth ■
■ Pinjarra

■ Rufus River

Port Lincoln ■   ■ **Adelaide**

Bells Falls ■■ Sofala
Bathurst ■   *Hawkesbury River*
■ **Sydney**

■ **Canberra**

VICTORIA
WESTERN DISTRICT   **Melbourne**
■ Portland   GIPPSLAND
■ Port Fairy

TASMANIA

■ *Moulting Lagoon*

Map courtesy of the Environmental Unit of Sinclair Knight Merz Pty Ltd

Bain **Attwood** and SG **Foster**

Introduction

In 1968 the eminent Australian anthropologist WEH Stanner, delivering the ABC's Boyer Lectures, spoke of 'the great Australian silence' about the relationship between 'ourselves and the aborigines'. The term has been used a great deal ever since, although its nuances have not always been understood. This silence was not 'a total silence on all matters aboriginal', Stanner remarked, but was instead 'the story of the things we [have] unconsciously resolved not to discuss with them or treat with them about; the story, in short, of the unacknowledged relations between two racial groups'. Rejecting the possibility that such 'inattention' could be attributed to 'absentmindedness', he argued that it should be regarded as 'a structural matter, a view from a window which has been carefully placed to exclude a whole quadrant of the landscape'. It might have 'begun as a simple forgetting', he conceded, but it had 'turned under habit and over time into something like a cult of forgetfulness practised on a national scale. We have been able for so long to disremember the aborigines', Stanner concluded, 'that we are now hard put to keep them in mind when we most want to do so'.[1]

Having surveyed a range of books published between the 1930s and 1960s, Stanner thought historians were largely to blame for this silence. For example, there was a much-reprinted historical textbook, *Australia: A Social and Political History* (1955), edited by Gordon Greenwood.[2] Stanner observed that Aborigines were only mentioned on five occasions: 'twice, quite briefly, for the period 1788–1821; twice again, as briefly, for the period 1820–1850; once, in sidelong fashion, for the period 1851–1892; and thereafter not at all'. (He might have also remarked that they did not rate a mention in the index.) Stanner's comments were borne out by the historian John La Nauze, who observed in 1959 in a survey of Australian historiography over the preceding 40 years:

'unlike the Maori, the American Indian or the South African Bantu, the Australian aboriginal is noticed in our history only in a melancholy anthropological footnote'. Ten years later, most historians were still neglecting the Aboriginal past even though archaeologists and art historians such as DJ Mulvaney and Bernard Smith had already turned their attention to it.[3] Henry Reynolds has recalled: 'In the profession the feeling was that this was a matter of minor importance that you wouldn't get involved with professionally. In fact I was told by the editor of a prestigious historical journal … not to waste time on writing about Aborigines as there was nothing in it'.[4]

'The great Australian silence', as Ann Curthoys notes in her chapter, was primarily a phenomenon of the twentieth century. It had begun around the turn of the century as white Australian nationalism flourished.[5] By contrast, historians in the colonial era, such as John West and George Rusden, chronicled bloody conflicts between Aborigines and Europeans.[6] As historians focused on the making of the newly imagined Australian nation, they increasingly lost sight of the original landowners. By contrast, historians writing regional histories were, as Geoffrey Bolton points out in his chapter, more likely to include the indigenous people in their accounts of place, or at least they were the first to do so after Aboriginal matters began to loom larger in the national consciousness in the 1950s.

The silence was peculiarly 'historical' in another sense. Historians were especially silent about Aborigines, whereas some other narrators of the national story were not. Across the first half of the twentieth century, anthropologists, journalists and campaigners for Aboriginal rights gave accounts of how Aboriginal communities had been dispossessed and destroyed by European colonisation since 1788. The best known and probably the only major historical works devoted to Aborigines to be published in the first 60 or so years were written by the journalists, or former journalists, Paul Hasluck, *Black Australians* (1941), and Clive Turnbull, *Black War: The Extermination of the Tasmanian Aborigines* (1948); novelists such as Eleanor Dark, *The Timeless Land* (1941), and Katharine Susannah Prichard, *Coonardoo* (1943); humanitarians, including EJB Foxcroft, *Australian Native Policy* (1941); and anthropologists, Ronald and Catherine Berndt, *From Black to White in South Australia* (1951). However, a geographer, A Grenfell Price, also wrote *White Settlers and Native Peoples: An Historical Study of Racial Contacts Between English-speaking Whites and Aboriginal Peoples in the United States, Canada,*

Australia and New Zealand (1949). Others in these professions, including Donald Thomson, Mary Bennett and William Morley, Frederic Wood Jones and AP Elkin, told some of the history in speeches they delivered, and articles and pamphlets they wrote.[7] All this history-making suggests that 'the great Australian silence' pertained as much to the act of listening as to that of speaking, which prompts one to speculate whether the questions recently posed by many Australians in the context of reconciliation — 'Why didn't we know?' and 'Why were we never told?' — should not include 'Why didn't we ask?', 'Why didn't we listen?' and 'Why weren't we able to hear?'.[8]

As Stanner also remarked, there had not only been a historical silence but a silencing as well: 'the great Australian silence' had excluded 'the other side of a story', the story which Reynolds, one of a number of young historians to answer Stanner's call to research 'our unexamined history' and do 'another kind of "history"', would subsequently call 'the other side of the frontier'. This history, Stanner asserted, would be 'a world — perhaps I should say an underworld — away from the conventional histories of the coming and development of British civilisation'. At the time he gave his lectures, Stanner knew this history was already emerging: 'Something very remarkable has happened', he wrote, 'the fact that the aborigines having been "out" of history for a century and a half are now coming back "into" history with a vengeance'. He had in mind the recent rise of radical protest among Aboriginal people, but his remarks also refer to a body of scholarly work 'now in course', research which he hoped would ensure that the great Australian silence did not 'survive'.[9]

A new Australian history

By the time Stanner damned 'the great Australian silence', one of his associates, the political scientist and historian Charles Rowley, had already embarked on historical work as part of a larger project on Aborigines sponsored by the Social Science Research Council of Australia. In fact, the principal fruit of this work, a three-volume series, *Aboriginal Policy and Practice,* had been completed by the time Stanner gave his lectures, although these monographs were not published until 1970–71. They were based on Rowley's own historical research as well as the work of other scholars, such as the anthropologist and historian Diane Barwick, who later co-founded the specialist journal, *Aboriginal History*. Like Stanner, Rowley was convinced that Aboriginal affairs were an inherently historical field. In the introductory chapter of the first volume of his trilogy, entitled 'History and Aboriginal affairs', he argued that policy-making in the area had operated 'in some kind of vacuum' and yet it was impossible to understand 'the Aboriginal predicament' unless the 'historical dimension' was grasped. In particular, the history of British colonisation had to be known and acknowledged.[10]

In *The Destruction of Aboriginal Society*, the opening volume of *Aboriginal Policy and Practice*, Rowley attempted to provide a comprehensive survey of what he called the frontier, assuming that it had 'set the pattern of relationships' between Aborigines and Europeans, and had had 'continuing effects' on Aboriginal life. His pioneering work inspired a decade or more of research on frontier relations between Aborigines and Europeans — and it remains a source of fruitful questions for further work. As many historians in Australia began to do 'social history' and recover those people who had been 'hidden from history', a new generation of scholars started to research the frontier. RHW Reece, Henry Reynolds, Raymond Evans, Noel Loos, Lyndall Ryan and Michael Christie published work on New South Wales, Queensland, Tasmania and Victoria, in which they overturned a series of historical falsehoods regarding British colonisation. As a result, the following picture of the frontier emerged during the 1970s: Aborigines and Europeans used the land in quite incompatible ways as pastoralists' cattle and sheep ate, trampled and fouled Aborigines' sources of food and water; Aborigines were forced to steal the newcomers' stock and other property in order to survive and often launched attacks on the colonists; pastoralists and their men wreaked violence on Aborigines, killing large numbers in the course of conflict across the country. These revisionist historians represented colonisation as a matter of invasion, depicted the frontier as a line between conflicting parties, regarded the conflict as war, treated the Aborigines' response as resistance, and explained the violence of frontiersmen in terms of racism as well as other factors.[11]

In some of this early research, although it was much more common in later populist historical works (as Richard Broome observes in his chapter), historians such as Evans paid considerable attention to large-scale killings, often referred to as 'massacres'. For example, the Myall Creek massacre in 1838 was the subject of more than one serious study.[12] It seems some authors thought it was useful to symbolise European violence in this way since it helped convey the fact that the settlement of Australia *was* a matter of bloody conquest. However, historians generally characterised conflict in terms of small-scale warfare, just as they argued that Aboriginal resistance had only a limited impact on the overall pace of pastoral expansion. For the most part, they concluded, Aborigines were overwhelmed because of the small and segmented nature of their communities and the intruders' superior firepower. (Later studies, by David Denholm and Richard Broome, would show that Europeans only truly gained the upper hand in combat in the 1860s, when the technology of firearms improved and they were supported by native police forces.)[13]

In the 1970s, Ryan, Evans, Reynolds, Loos and Christie sought to estimate the human toll of the frontier, and early in the following decade Reynolds and Broome proposed figures for the number of Aborigines and Europeans killed in racial conflicts across the whole continent between 1788 and the 1930s. As Broome explains here, both he and Reynolds recognised this was a difficult task and that one could not be precise, especially with reference to the number of Aborigines killed. They noted that it was a matter of 'estimates' (and when Reynolds reflected on this work several years later, he remarked that it 'was, and remains, little better than an informed guess'). Nevertheless, their work was a departure from Rowley's suggestion that it was 'very difficult even to guess at the *scale* of violence'.[14] At the same time that historians enumerated these death tolls, they argued that European violence was not the biggest killer of Aborigines. The phenomenal decline in the Aboriginal population — it has been estimated that it fell from 750,000 in 1788 to only about 60,000 in the 1920s — was largely the result of introduced diseases, such as smallpox, measles and influenza, as well as venereal and respiratory diseases. (Research by the economic historian Noel Butlin confirmed this, as has a recent study by Judy Campbell.)[15]

This first wave of historical scholarship was not solely focused on what had happened on the frontiers of settlement. Reece and Christie devoted attention to a group of humanitarians who, in the 1830s and 1840s, exerted considerable influence on the imperial and colonial governments. In a strenuous attempt to protect Aborigines, protectorates were established, the rights of Aborigines as British subjects were proclaimed, and colonists were informed of the penalties for harming Aborigines.[16] However, these historians concluded, as Rowley had and as Ryan, SG Foster and AGL

Shaw confirmed in detailed studies, that the humanitarians' impact on what actually happened was quite limited. This was so, they argued, for several reasons: an inherent conflict between the goal of colonising a new country and the rights of indigenous people; the determined pressure from colonists that nothing should get in the way of economic progress; and the practical limits on colonial governments, however high-minded, to enforce their policies in remote regions. Not that local governments were invariably high-minded; sometimes they intervened to ensure the dispossession of Aborigines by providing military forces, as John Connor has recently described in detail.[17]

The other side of the frontier

The pioneering studies undertaken in the late 1960s and the 1970s transformed understanding of relations between Aborigines and Europeans on the Australian frontier. By the late 1970s, however, there was already a sense of diminishing returns; those who had followed Rowley had added much to his overview but they had done so, as one critic remarked, 'quantitatively rather than qualitatively'. Andrew Markus, another historian who recognised this, called for research that would investigate whether Australian frontiers were as 'uniform in character' as the studies completed so far had suggested. He proposed a series of factors that might have resulted in considerable differences according to the time and place of contact.[18]

Over the next decade or so, a growing diversity of approach was evident, contrasting markedly with the rather one-dimensional approach of the 1970s. Many regional case studies of the kind that appear in the opening section of this volume were undertaken. Some of these had already been completed as PhD theses before Markus's review of the historiography, but most were guided by the questions he raised. The most important of these studies were Ryan's *The Aboriginal Tasmanians* (1981) and Loos's *Invasion and Resistance: Aboriginal–European Relations on the North Queensland Frontier 1861–1897* (1982), followed some years later by Jan Critchett's *A 'Distant Field of Murder': Western District Frontiers 1834–1848* (1990). More recently, Evans has also elucidated the ways in which the area he has long studied was both similar and dissimilar to others, as his chapter in this volume demonstrates.

Many of these case studies redressed major weaknesses of the first wave of historical scholarship, such as the absence of Aboriginal perspectives and the denial of Aboriginal agency. When historians first began to pay serious attention to the Aboriginal past, they doubted whether they would be able to see the history of contact from an indigenous perspective and even whether historical sources would enable them to do so. By the early 1980s, Reynolds, among others, had decided they could. He concluded his innovative study, *The Other Side of the Frontier*, by proclaiming that 'the boundaries of Australian historiography [could] be pushed back to encompass the other side of the frontier'. It had become clear, he asserted, that the 'barriers which for so long kept Aboriginal experience out of history books were not principally those of source material or methodology but rather ones of perception and preference'. By researching an extensive range of European historical sources, which included some orally based sources (but few oral histories), and by garnering insights from linguistic, archaeological and anthropological studies, Reynolds sought to explain Aborigines' responses to European settlement from their perspective, in particular, how they treated Europeans in terms of their cultural frameworks.[19]

Reynolds's study influenced a new generation of scholarship. Its turn to the other side of the frontier, and greater focus on Aborigines rather than Europeans, also helped draw into question whether the relationship between Aborigines and Europeans simply comprised conflict. As Bain Attwood notes in his chapter, Reece was one of the most persuasive critics of this emphasis. Reece suggested that historians could learn about relationships of accommodation from the work of historians in other parts of the British world, especially southern Africa, and in his own ongoing research he showed that collaboration occurred between some Aboriginal groups and Europeans, and revealed the continuing importance of inter-Aboriginal conflict after colonisation, which was also the subject of research conducted by Beverley Nance.[20] In a similar vein Marie Fels, in a study of the native police corps in the Port Phillip District of New South Wales, *Good Men and True* (1988), questioned the assumption that Aborigines saw themselves as a common or collective group by reminding us that Aboriginal men engaged in policing duties against their traditional enemies, although the role of the native police in killing other Aborigines was much more important in Queensland, as Evans and Reynolds affirmed at the National Museum's forum.[21] Fels's study, however, was most intent on understanding what it meant to be a native policeman from an Aboriginal perspective and uncovering the dynamics of cross-cultural interactions between the European officers and the Aboriginal policemen.[22]

In doing so, she, along with other historians such as Ann McGrath in her *'Born in the Cattle': Aborigines in Cattle Country* (1987), challenged the concept of a frontier as merely a place of lawless conflict. As Critchett discussed in her 1990 book and does so again in her chapter here, the frontier could also be a place of intimacy.

Aboriginal histories

As students of Australia's frontiers increasingly sought to uncover the historical perspectives and agency of Aboriginal subjects, many turned to 'oral history' — a new body of historical sources created by interviewing people about the past. Particularly in northern and central Australia, where contact between Aborigines and non-Aborigines began much later than in other parts of the country, anthropologists and linguists in the mid-1960s — and historians a decade or so later — started to gather the testimony of Aboriginal people who had witnessed 'the killing times'. Most notably, some of the survivors of a massacre at Coniston station in central Australia in 1928, which followed other killings in 1874 at Barrow Creek, discussed here by DJ Mulvaney, were interviewed. Oral histories compiled by Bruce Shaw, Luise Hercus and Peter Sutton, Peter Read and Jay Arthur, Deborah Bird Rose, and Grace and Harold Koch, as well as historical studies based on oral history, such as John Cribbin's *The Killing Times: The Coniston Massacre* (1984), demonstrated the potential of oral sources. As Rose notes in her chapter, they can be a supplement to, or a corrective of, the written record, particularly when the documentary record provides only a fragmentary account of what really happened.[23]

These scholars were also aware that oral sources can be problematic. Although contemporary written sources are always open to question since they are re-presentations of events rather than the past itself, oral accounts, such as auto-biographies, can have the added problems of distance from the events they aim to record. As a result, they sometimes suffer from serious omissions, inaccuracies and distortions. For example, some Aboriginal people have told stories of Captain Cook being in areas of Australia we know he never visited; some even tell of him being preceded by another significant Australian historical figure, Ned Kelly. On the face of it, narratives such as these have no value whatsoever for the historian who wants to answer conventional historical questions of who did what, when and where. As a result, historians have been reluctant to rely on such sources.

Yet some historians and anthropologists have been loath to dismiss Aboriginal oral sources on these grounds. Since the mid-1980s, they have been using Aboriginal oral sources not so much to recover past events as to discover how these have been interpreted by Aboriginal people since. Oral histories such as Captain Cook stories, Rose and other scholars have argued, can provide rich insights into how Aboriginal people have tried to make sense of the colonial past.[24] In this research the object of study is not so much the past but how individuals and communities develop ways of understanding their past in the present. By using Aboriginal oral histories in this speculative fashion, historians and anthropologists have enabled Europeans to hear Aboriginal perspectives of the past rather than allow a situation where indigenous narratives might be effectively silenced.

Oral histories and oral traditions, that is, stories passed down through generations, are not, of course, the preserve of Aboriginal people. Recently, some historians have explored accounts of frontier conflict that have continued to circulate in rural settler communities. As Tom Griffiths concluded from his research, which he discusses in his chapter, there was evidently a strong current of settler oral testimony about frontier violence in southeastern Australia well into the twentieth century, despite attempts to silence rumours of massacres and poisonings. In an essay first published in 1987, Griffiths considered some of the ways in which Europeans have attempted to remember, or disremember, the frontier past across the nineteenth and twentieth centuries.[25] In a similar fashion, David Roberts has examined an oral tradition in a country town in New South Wales, which claims a large number of Aboriginal people were massacred at Bells Falls Gorge in the mid-1820s. In his chapter, he argues that it would be a mistake to dismiss the possibility that these stories contain elements of historical truth about grim events on the frontier in this area.[26]

New directions

In the last decade or so of the twentieth century, very few historians undertook research about Australia's frontiers; indeed, few major studies of frontier conflict have been published since the late 1980s,[27] as scholarly interest and attention shifted to the post-frontier era and to representations of race and Aboriginality.[28] Recently, however, some historians have revisited the frontier to ask whether the concept of genocide might be applied to the colonisation of Australia.[29] Questions about the possible extermination of the Aboriginal people are not new; indeed, it was one that preoccupied humanitarians in the nineteenth and twentieth centuries. For example, on reading accounts of a spate of clashes in April 1838, James Stephen, the permanent under-secretary in the Colonial Office, wrote: 'The cause & the consequences of this state of things are alike clear and irremediable nor do I suppose it is possible to discover any method by which the impending Catastrophe, namely the extermination of the Black race can long be avoided'.[30]

Inasmuch as there has been any serious consideration of genocide in Australia, it has been dominated, as Dirk Moses has recently observed, by 'the vexed question [of] intention, agency and consciousness ... Does not genocide require an agent, or agents, that makes conscious choices and decisions [with the intention of destroying a people]?'. Where these are lacking, many critics have asserted, 'so is the essential prerequisite of genocide'. But, Moses and others have contended, colonisation 'undeniably had ... a "genocidal *effect*" on Aborigines', and so it would be a mistake to terminate an investigation that might help us better understand this country's colonial past. Moses has recommended greater focus on the processes, structures and contexts of colonisation. Historians, he suggests, should consider 'the gradual evolution of European attitudes and policies as they were pushed in an exterminatory direction by the confluence of their underlying assumptions, the demands of the colonial and international economy, their plans for the land, and the resistance to these plans by the indigenous Australians'.[31] In her chapter here, Curthoys reminds us of the original definition of genocide and discusses how some of its elements might be relevant to colonial Australia, while Evans considers the question of genocide in reference to Queensland rather than Tasmania, the popular site for such discussion, even though Reynolds, among others, has rejected Van Diemen's Land as an example of genocide.[32]

In the end, most non-Aboriginal historians will probably conclude, as Reynolds and Peter Read have done recently and Reece did many years ago, that the most likely examples of genocide on the frontiers of settlement were highly local ones where stockmen and/or police forces were determined to destroy Aborigines. Many Aboriginal historians will probably reach a different conclusion.[33]

Discomforting history

At the turn of the nineteenth and twentieth centuries, historical narratives coalesced into a myth about Australia that celebrated British colonisation of the continent as a peaceful act of discovery and settlement, whereby a progressive people and their venerable institutions were successfully transplanted and the land was transformed, thus resulting in the new nation of Australia.

Research in the field of 'Aboriginal history' has challenged this story in fundamental ways because it amounts to a new Australian history. First, it has challenged its chronology: instead of the two centuries or so since Cook, the history of this land now begins tens of thousands of years ago. This in turn has subverted the foundational events and protagonists of Australian history: the first discoverers, explorers and colonists of Australia have become Aborigines rather than the British. Consequently, the settlement of this country has been rendered as an act of invasion, a process of conquest that dispossessed the rightful owners of the land and resulted in violence, racial discrimination and neglect which destroyed many Aboriginal communities and degraded most Aboriginal people.

Over the last 30 years, this new history's way of understanding Australia's past has become increasingly well known, and Aboriginal history has become central to national discourse and debate, particularly in the context of national reconciliation (led by the Council for Aboriginal Reconciliation), the High Court's 1992 Mabo and 1996 Wik native title decisions, and the Human Rights and Equal Opportunity Commission's 1995–97 inquiry into the separation of Aboriginal children from their parents ('the stolen generations'). This has provoked a crisis of confidence or conscience for many Australians, particularly those born and educated before the 1950s. As David Carter has noted: 'We are not used to thinking of our history ... as contentious, morally compromised or volatile, as dangerous, as, say, Japanese or South African history'. There are probably two reasons for such a crisis. The meanings of nationhood and national identity are primarily formed by, and grounded in, historical narratives about the nation; and histories provide people with a necessary sense of meaning, order and composure. Aboriginal history, by providing a new historical narrative that brings into question the treasured story of how this nation came to be what it purports to be — a country where justice was upheld, democracy nurtured and humanitarianism cherished, and where egalitarianism triumphed — has threatened to deprive many Australians of a familiar and comforting map of the past. The most unsettling aspect of this historical revolution, Curthoys has argued, is that settler Australians have had 'to come to terms with a past in which they were neither heroes nor victims, but rather agents of a colonising ... process that destroyed the lives of many people'.[34]

This, as Curthoys notes in her chapter, has led to denunciations of the creators of the new history. These began in the mid-1980s in the context of Aboriginal people regaining some of their traditional lands and of planning for the forthcoming bicentenary of European settlement. Some conservatives in industry and elsewhere complained that historians were undermining the national story, primarily by their accounts of the colonisation of Australia. It was alleged that Australia's history was undergoing 'an almost uncontested falsification' as historians rewrote 'Australia's past as a story of destruction and persecution'; this threatened to transform Australia 'into a new country unconnected with its past'. History, they seemed to suggest, should perform its traditional task of helping to build the nation and inculcate a spirit of allegiance among its citizens.[35] These criticisms were renewed in 1988 during the bicentennial celebrations but more especially in 1992–93 in the context of the High Court's Mabo decision and Labor Prime Minister Paul Keating's decision to champion the judgment and a republic for Australia, all of which were informed by the new Australian history. Conservatives' fears over Aboriginal assertion of land ownership and sovereignty deepened.[36]

Early in his administration, Keating, advised by his principal speechwriter, historian Don Watson, sought to advance a 'big picture' of Australia's future by casting this in terms of Australia's history. 'Possibly no modern Australian prime minister has uttered the word "history" as frequently', Graeme Davison has suggested.[37] In a series of speeches at historical sites, including Kokoda in Papua New Guinea, Corowa on the Victoria–New South Wales border, and the Australian War Memorial, Keating dwelt on key events and developments in Australia's past, such as Anzac and Australia's relationship with Britain, presenting a view that was in keeping with the new Australian history. At the same time, he sought to promote reconciliation between Aboriginal and settler Australians. In a speech delivered in Redfern, a Sydney suburb with a large Aboriginal population, the Prime Minister asserted: 'many of the problems which

Aboriginal Australians face today are a consequence of ... dispossession ... The past lives on in inequality, racism and injustice'. Most famously, he asserted:

> We took the traditional lands and smashed the traditional way of life. We brought the diseases. The alcohol. We committed the murders. We took the children from their mothers. We practised discrimination and exclusion. It was our ignorance and our prejudice. And our failure to imagine these things being done to us.

Subsequently, Keating represented the High Court's Mabo ruling as 'an historic decision', believing it could create the foundation of 'a new relationship between indigenous and non-Aboriginal Australians'. He saw native title legislation as an act by which the Australian state could 'recognise and make amends for past wrongs' and begin a process that could 'transcend the history of dispossession'.[38]

On the other side of politics, criticisms of Mabo were given credence by one of Australia's most readable and widely read historians, Geoffrey Blainey. He was highly critical of the High Court's decision, particularly its historical basis, alleging that it threatened Australian sovereignty. At the same time, he sought to justify the dispossession of Aboriginal people on the Australian frontier by claiming that '[a]ll over the world, the relatively simple way of life of [Aboriginal] hunters and gatherers was ... bound to be overthrown or undermined'. Yet, as it turned out, Blainey's most telling contribution to the controversy was not so much an argument as a phrase he coined (in an article entitled 'Drawing up a balance sheet of our history') to describe work that 'assailed the generally optimistic view' of Australia's past — 'black armband history'.[39]

Black armbands and white blindfolds

With the election of the Liberal–National coalition government in 1996, criticisms of the new Australian history were renewed as part of a major cultural battle over national identity. During the election campaign, John Howard criticised 'the politically correct brigade', asserted that he would 'like to see [Australians] comfortable and relaxed about their history', and insisted that it was 'very important' that Australians did not 'spend [their] lives apologising for the past'.[40]

Shortly after coming to power, Howard claimed that one of 'the more insidious developments in Australian political life over the past decade or so' had been an attempt by 'self-appointed dietitians' to 're-write Australian history in a partisan political cause'. This 'reinterpretation of Australia's past' had been 'systematic and deliberate' and was 'an abuse of the true purpose of history'. Australians needed 'to understand the past in its own terms' and not according to 'our own contemporary standards'. Moreover, they needed to 'learn from the past' in a way that respected 'the facts'. Later in the year, in another historically minded speech celebrating Sir Robert Menzies as the founder of the Liberal Party, Howard again criticised attempts 'to establish a form of historical correctness as a particular offshoot of political correctness' and insisted on the need 'to restore a sense of balance and perspective'. We must, he emphasised, 'ensure that our history as a nation is not written definitively by those who take the view that Australians should apologise for most of it. This "black armband" view of our past', he claimed, 'reflects a belief that most Australian history since 1788 has been little more than a disgraceful story of imperialism, exploitation, racism, sexism and other forms of discrimination'. Howard took 'a very different view': in his opinion 'the balance sheet of our history is one of heroic achievement and ... we have achieved much more as a nation of which we can be proud than of which we should be ashamed'. Since then, the essence of these arguments has been often repeated, particularly in the context of the Federal Government's criticism of accounts of the stolen generations, most forcibly expressed in March 2000 when it claimed there were no stolen generations because 'only' 10 per cent of Aboriginal children had been separated from their families between 1910 and 1970.[41]

Howard's stance was typically conservative in many respects, especially in its approach to history as a means of celebrating the nation and its founders. More surprising, perhaps, was his view that history is simply comprised of facts. As Davison has observed: 'The idea that history is simply "the facts" and that "interpretation" is something added to them would strike most practising historians as odd. '"Facts", they would say, are constituted in the very act of interpretation. "Just give me the facts"', he points out, 'is something that detectives say but which no historian can really do, for the "facts" are a response to questions, and one person's questions are never quite the same as another's'. Historians similarly found odd the Prime Minister's assumption that history does not involve perspective. As Curthoys has commented: 'The notion of a "balance sheet" implies an independent and objective standpoint from which to decide what was "positive" and what was "negative" about Australia's past'. Was

Howard thinking of Aboriginal people, she asked, when one of his spokesmen claimed that 'the balance sheet of Australian history presents a very positive view'.[42]

From 1998, the magazine *Quadrant* added its voice to criticisms of 'politically correct' history, its editorship back in safer conservative hands after it was wrested from the political commentator and historian Robert Manne (and subsequently 're-launched' in Sydney by the Prime Minister). It increasingly published articles critical of contemporary Aboriginal policy and the histories that purportedly underpinned it. After a well-reported 'seminar' entitled 'Truth and Sentimentality' in September 2000, the magazine's new editor, PP McGuinness, claimed that the 'prevailing fashion in Aboriginal history' was 'crumbling' as 'dissident historians' demonstrated that it was 'the product of invention and exaggeration', merely 'a version of history' advanced by malevolent historians for 'political or other purposes'. Like conservative critics in the 1980s and 1990s, and in keeping with the spirit of Howard's criticisms of 'black armband history', McGuinness accused historians of trying to 'falsify their history' in order 'to bolster the indictment against Australia's white history'.[43]

The 'dissident historian' whom McGuinness most had in mind was Keith Windschuttle. In his address to the *Quadrant* seminar, later published in full as a three-part series entitled 'The myths of frontier massacres in Australian history',[44] Windschuttle alleged that Australian historians had 'constructed a story of widespread massacres on the frontiers of the expanding pastoral industry' that had 'carried off between 5 and 20 per cent of the Aboriginal population on the mainland and up to 70 per cent of the indigenes in Tasmania'. When 'these claims' are 'closely examined', Windschuttle asserted, 'the evidence ... turns out to be highly suspect. Most of it', he argued, 'is very poorly founded, other parts are seriously mistaken and some of it is outright fabrication'. He was particularly critical of historians' estimates of the Aboriginal death toll. The figure of 20,000 had been 'set' by Reynolds and this had determined 'the agenda ever since' because historians have 'colluded in protecting one another from rigorous investigation'.[45]

One senior journalist who reported the *Quadrant* gathering, Mike Steketee, was of the opinion that it risked becoming 'a new attempt to airbrush history'. He detected a 'strident tone' among the speakers and thought that the participants were 'seized by a nostalgia for the nice version of history — the one of intrepid explorers and pioneers and economic development'. Such reports aroused the fears of historians, commentators and supporters of reconciliation, troubled by the ongoing attacks that had been made on so-called black armband history in recent years, especially on the Human Rights and Equal Opportunity Commission's report on the stolen generations, *Bringing Them Home*. They suspected it was just another example of what Henry Reynolds called 'white blindfold history'. Robert Manne alleged that *Quadrant* was 'beginning to drift toward a form of historical denialism of the kind that [the British historian] David Irving has pioneered',[46] while in a more measured response, Andrew Markus, one of the leading scholars in the field of Aboriginal history, contended that there had been 'a radical attempt to rewrite Australian history'.[47]

The *Quadrant* seminar was followed by an afternoon forum convened by Sydney bookseller Bob Gould. This was marked by some fiery exchanges, especially between Windschuttle and McGuinness and members of the audience. A leading anthropologist, Gillian Cowlishaw, observed the proceedings and was troubled by the fact that many 'seemed emotionally committed to a view of the past' and were 'eager to condemn and vilify their own white forebears as deliberately genocidal racists, or perhaps complete fools, [who were] individually and collectively responsible for the dire conditions of the indigenous population, while we today are innocent, exonerated from responsibility by our understanding of the murderous or wrong headed past'. Historians such as Reynolds, she contended, are not responsible for this; but the 'complacent moral fervour, even zealotry, of some who support the Aboriginal cause may be as much a barrier to an understanding of Aborigines and their interests as is the reactionary obfuscation of Windschuttle and McGuinness'. Reflecting on this again more recently, Cowlishaw has pointed out that in order to understand the past we need to comprehend 'its moral complexities and ambiguities'. This means recognising that 'while there may indeed have been heroes and villains then, the vast majority of the population was neither'. What is required, as Alan Atkinson suggests in his chapter, is a historical engagement in moral questions which is neither condescending nor moralising.[48]

In 2001, the focus of contestation between 'black armband history' and 'white blindfold history' shifted following the opening of the long-awaited National Museum of Australia. In keeping with recommendations made many years earlier, the Museum was committed to presenting a social history of the nation and challenging traditional accounts of Australia's history. This included 'Contested Frontiers', described in this volume by Davison. In August, Windschuttle criticised the Museum on several grounds, including the nature of exhibits in 'Contested Frontiers'. He claimed there were two factual errors in captions, detailed in his chapter here and discussed further by Davison, but more significantly he claimed the exhibit featured a story of a massacre at Bells Falls Gorge that was 'a complete fabrication'. These criticisms gained considerable publicity. Subsequently, a two-day conference was held in December 2001 — 'Frontier Conflict: The Australian Experience' — which is the basis of this volume.[49]

A crisis of authority

In recent decades in Australia and many other countries, public interest in the past has boomed and there has been a marked shift to forms of popular cultures, especially film and television, as a means of representing the past. In Australia, the new history has come to be produced and consumed in many forms: genealogy and family history; community history; autobiography and fiction; song, painting, dance and photography; historical re-enactments and pilgrimages; memorials; living history museums and national parks; exhibitions at museums, art galleries, archives and libraries; film, radio, television and the press.[50] As a result of this proliferation and democratisation of history-making, competing accounts of a nation's past jostle for audiences and acceptance more than ever before, and history and historians are no longer necessarily influencing people's knowledge of the past. Indeed, Dipesh Chakrabarty has argued, doubt about the nature of historical understanding has arisen 'precisely because the past is enjoying such a boom in public life in all the democracies of the world'. Consequently, many historians as well as other commentators and critics 'feel that [historians] have lost their public audience and that the discipline no longer enjoys the authority it once commanded'. This has caused a crisis of authority for historians, which has several dimensions, all of which were evident at the National Museum's forum.[51]

This, along with the fact that debates over the Aboriginal past of Australia also reflect a crisis over the moral basis or foundation of the nation, means that the historiographical conflict over the frontier will not be simply resolved by academic historians doing more research, ferreting out truer facts, writing more lucid accounts and so forth (as many of the participants at the Museum's forum seemed to assume, although recent debates over massacres suggest that the reading public expect historians to provide exact and absolute accounts of the past, as if history was a form of science). They also have a role to play, as Davison has argued in *The Use and Abuse of Australian History,* in maintaining 'a watching brief on the varieties of history … that circulate in the larger community'. Historians, he has remarked:

> are sometimes seen, even perhaps see themselves, as policing the past, tramping their beat on the lookout for factual inaccuracies and other offences against the truth. There are indeed issues of truth and error, accuracy and inaccuracy at stake in the debates between historians, but the most serious abuses are usually not just technical breaches of good historical method. Knowing what a history is being used for may be as important as knowing how it has been *argued for.*[52]

Historians in the field of Aboriginal history, perhaps more than other historical sub-disciplines, have been challenged by other history-makers, many of whom either have little concern for history as a discipline or have limited experience in researching and representing the past. (This has led academic historians to criticise 'populist … histories that … merely replace one unsatisfactory past in which we uncritically celebrate the founders of Australia, with another in which we merely "exorcise their disturbing legacy"'.) In recent years, the influence of academic historians has been challenged by 'history-conscious' journalists, such as Bill Bunbury, Les Carlyon, Jonathan King, Stuart Rintoul and Nicolas Rothwell, and there is now something of a struggle over who tells 'the story of the nation'. In this context, some academic historians have challenged the authority of Windschuttle by drawing attention to the fact that he, too, has been a journalist. They have acknowledged that he has an honours degree in history but have questioned his understanding of the methods of historical research, his comprehension of the history of the frontier, his knowledge of Aboriginal historiography, and his grasp of the relationship between theory and history. They have also argued that Windschuttle has often confused popular histories by journalists with scholarly histories by academic historians, unfairly blaming the latter for weaknesses in the work of the former. (As Beverley Kingston remarked at the forum, the recent controversy seems to have shown 'the immense difficulty that historians have in controlling the way in which their work is used'.) At the same time, academic historians have observed that Windschuttle has overlooked the fact that they, too, have been critical of populist and presentist accounts 'marked by silences, distortions and lies'.[53]

WA Cawthorne
A fight at the Murray In the Scene Painting Style, 1844
State Library of New South Wales

Visual representations provide a valuable source of information about frontier conflict, although sometimes they raise more questions than they answer. Cawthorne's watercolour depicts a conflict at the Rufus River, a tributary of the Murray, in 1841. Overlanders, at the right of the painting, and a police party, left, fire on a group of Maraura people, who fight back with their spears. According to an official report, 30 Maraura men were killed and many more wounded.

On the back of his painting, Cawthorne acknowledged that he based the work on a lithograph. However, as Margo Neale demonstrated at the National Museum's forum on frontier conflict, he also drew on a range of other sources to provide an accurate visual description of the event and its location.

Cawthorne's painting in turn provided the basis for an engraving by Samuel Calvert, which was published in the *Illustrated Melbourne Post* in July 1866 with the caption 'Conflict on the Rufus'. Paintings and drawings of conflict were often reproduced as engravings and published in the colonial newspapers and magazines, and in books, pamphlets and journals published in Britain and on the continent. Such images, sometimes accompanied by telling captions or articles, helped shape contemporary attitudes to relations between Aborigines and Europeans.

Historians, journalists and popular writers, however, often have a common approach to history inasmuch as they tend to be wedded to the written word as *the* way of representing the past. Many seem troubled by the fact that an increasing number of people, indeed probably the majority, get their historical knowledge and understanding not from books and the like, but from visual media, most of all from historical films but also institutions such as museums. As a result, they often criticise these accounts of the past for lacking the very qualities found in written histories, and insist that film-makers and museum curators consult with historians and follow their advice. Here, Davison adopts another tack, recommending that critics of forms of history such as museum exhibits should recognise that other history-makers follow different conventions in representing the past. Consequently, historians and journalists should not just apply the standard tests of written history but also ones that are consonant with the forms of historical representation being assessed.

The authority of historians has also been challenged by the practitioners of other disciplines who have cast doubt on the very nature of historical knowledge itself. This challenge, loosely described as 'postmodernism', has troubled some historians. In the field of Aboriginal history, however, as in other areas of Australian history, many scholars have, in the pragmatic manner of most practitioners in the discipline, cautiously adapted some aspects and added these to their traditional methods. In doing so, they have bypassed the concerns that have preoccupied the anxious critics of postmodernism.[54]

Aboriginal voices

The greatest challenge to historians and their authority in the field of Aboriginal history has come not from postmodernism but is instead a byproduct of postmodernity. Aboriginal people themselves are producing histories, principally in the form of autobiographies, life stories, oral histories, documentary and feature films, plays, novels, short stories and poetry, songs and paintings.[55] These representations have been especially 'disruptive', as Rose discusses here, because they often challenge traditional ways of doing history (which have been inherently European). This has given rise, as Chakrabarty notes, to '"relativist" talk about historical facts, divergent perspectives, multiple narratives'. This challenge largely results from the fact that Aboriginal histories are based on memory. One of the crucial intellectual debates in the area of Aboriginal history has been about the similarities and differences between memory and history, and across the political spectrum there are historians, some of them represented in this volume, who are apprehensive about the ways in which memory, in the context of 'identity politics', threatens to displace the authority of history.[56] Some have argued, with Bain Attwood, that historians must defend history 'against an extreme relativism … which denies that some historical accounts are empirically truer than others and rejects the possibility of historical truth of any kind'.[57]

Other practitioners, such as Griffiths and Rose, have been seeking ways of reconciling the different settler and Aboriginal perspectives and representations, so that *both* European and Aboriginal traditions are respected, thus enabling the vital work of cross-cultural communication to occur and on which any hope for reconciliation in a pluralistic democracy ultimately depends. At the Museum forum, however, there were few Aboriginal speakers. There are very few academically trained Aboriginal historians, and even fewer with academic expertise on frontier conflict. Hence there was no obvious way of incorporating their perspectives. This deficiency did not go unnoticed by Aboriginal participants. Trevor Ah Hang, of the Nauo or Nawu people of Port Lincoln, was moved to remark:

> I am honoured … to be among so many historians and learned people but I [regard] … this discussion as two fleas arguing [over] who owns the dog they're on … This [forum] is called 'Frontier Conflict' and yet the conflict we're arguing about … [is] between academics … I see this as a joust with historians, on the shoulders of indigenous people, riding in to do battle … and … I ask … 'Why is it so'. I ask all of you to remember [that] the grounds you base your arguments on are wet with the blood and tears of my people and I ask you to tread with care.

Another Aboriginal participant was enraged by what she saw as the silencing of Aboriginal voices. Wadjularbinna Nulyarimma, an elderly Gulf of Carpentaria woman, was critical of some remarks Windschuttle made about Aboriginal oral history in his paper (which he repeats here), but was more troubled by the broader matter of Aboriginal representation:

> I just want to say to Keith, standing up there and talking about these people, 'How can they remember? How can they remember?'. All of you … [are] on the other side of the fence … How dare Keith get up? He has no knowledge. Keith, have you been in our

> world? ... I would say that you are not in any position to stand up and say what you said this morning ...
>
> Let me speak, because this is all about us ... [H]ow can [I] stay calm when we got all these people saying all this about us and they know nothing about us? They stand there and judge ... There's too much of this 'Be quiet, Aboriginal'. And this is about understanding. I know I'm getting up some people's nostrils here. And I apologise to the people who really care about us and who fight to bring the truth out ... And don't take this personally, but it's to the people who don't know where they stand, who they are, and speaking without knowledge. Absolute fools.[58]

Despite these criticisms, there are signs that the crucial task of listening to and hearing other peoples' histories can be negotiated, so long as there is a will to do so.

Future tasks

Most historians are of the opinion that conservative attacks on the historiography have not advanced historical understanding of the nature of frontier relations between Aborigines and settlers. As the National Museum's forum revealed, historians have found it necessary to recapitulate their work on frontier conflict, much of it undertaken 20 or more years ago, and debate has been forced back onto well-trodden paths with no discernible benefits. It is even questionable whether frontier conflict was — or is — essential to our understanding of the larger picture. In the closing session of the forum, Tim Rowse, who has researched and written extensively in the field of Aboriginal history, challenged the fundamental premise informing the revisionists' criticisms of the historiography as well as the response of academic historians to these. His remarks warrant quoting at length:

> Let us imagine that the scholarly debate that we've just had came to the conclusion that not one indigenous person was ever killed or injured by violence in the service of conquest. Even if that were the best view that one could take on the evidence, there would remain strong grounds for indigenous grievance and for colonists' shame and sorrow, for it would remain a fact that the colonists usurped indigenous ownership and sovereignty. I've heard no one challenge this fact. I'm not aware of anyone dismissing as 'black armband history' the story that says ownership and sovereignty passed from the original owners and sovereigns, without their knowing consent, to uninvited newcomers, who simply assumed a new regime of ownership and sovereignty. In a society in which property and

sovereignty are cherished political values, that story remains a disturbing and challenging one ... So, it is arguable that the current controversy about the extent and causes of frontier violence does not matter much because it is incidental to the really important story that indigenous people lost ownership and sovereignty without ever consenting to that loss. I want to suggest that the grounds for indigenous grievance rest on that uncontradicted story, not on any particular account of ... colonial settlement.

In a similar fashion, Chakrabarty has recently drawn attention to the fact that Reynolds and other historians have placed an emphasis on conquest on the frontiers of settlement whereas another generation of scholars, such as Heather Goodall, has emphasised colonisation, taking this to mean the original dispossession of Aboriginal people as well as the later displacements that repeatedly excluded them from the means of production and prevented their entry into the Australian polity and society.[59]

This said, it remains important to understand the manner in which Aboriginal people were dispossessed on the frontiers of settlement. At the conference, some new directions as well as tasks for future historical research about the frontier were delineated. More work is needed on traditional archival sources, especially relating to parts of Australia where the frontier has not been the subject of historical study. Other bodies of sources, such as the archaeological and visual record, offer potential for further discoveries. Similarly, work presently being undertaken at Griffith University to enumerate frontier deaths will help clarify the level of violence. Yet, empirical work is not enough. As Curthoys has argued, both Reynolds and Windschuttle 'assume that the records speak for themselves, and all that is at stake is how closely we've looked at the records, and how many we've read' (although Reynolds used historical sources in a more interpretive manner in *The Other Side of the Frontier*). Similarly, historians such as Klaus Neumann argue that it is erroneous to presume that 'cataloguing the bones of the dead' will protect historical knowledge of the frontier from conservative users and abusers of Australian history.[60]

According to Alan Atkinson and Tom Griffiths, in their chapters in this volume, the historical work that is required demands not only broad research but also deep thought and analysis, especially of the language of the past and present, if historians are to be able to penetrate the 'past silences' of the frontier. And historians must expand their conventional disciplinary borders so that they encompass Aboriginal remembrance of the past. As Bolton argues in his chapter, historical research in other

Murder of Biddel & two others by the Pt. Lincoln natives. 1848

WA Cawthorne

Murder of Biddel & two others by the Pt. Lincoln natives, 1848

State Library of New South Wales

Cawthorne's watercolour (above) depicts a specific event, details of which are elusive.

A keen observer of Aboriginal society around Port Lincoln in South Australia, he also left a pencil drawing of the incident, which he quite possibly sketched at the actual location. The watercolour is faithful to the sketch, although the artist has added the fence. The published engraving (right) might have been based on either or both images. Either way, the similarities and differences between sketch and painting, on the one hand, and the engraving, on the other, are striking. For example, the painting,

unlike the engraving, suggests that some of the Aboriginal attackers have
been shot during the encounter; and in the engraving the shadowy figure in
the doorway of the hut has become a woman, while some of the Aborigines
now carry shields. An accompanying article described 'this unequal fight'
in chilling detail, including the final assault by 'a horde of exulting
savages'. 'It will be seen from the sketch under what disadvantages our
country people laboured.' An identical engraving in the National Library of
Australia is attributed to Samuel Calvert.

George Strafford (engraver)
Natives attacking shepherds' hut
Illustrated Melbourne Post,
18 May 1864
State Library of Victoria

former British colonies has shown some of the ways in which historians can accommodate the different forms in which indigenous people represent the past as well as the different ways in which they understand the colonial past. His remarks remind us of the value of comparative studies more generally.

Historians must also consider how the past has become the present and how the present relates to the past. Nations rest on such historical consciousness — on a chain of connection between 'them' and 'us' — and so we need histories that create a sense of moral engagement with the past in the present. Studies of the Australian frontier, in common with all historical research, demand what the British philosopher of history RG Collingwood called 'historical imagination'.[61] Without such imagination, our perceptions are blinkered, our vision narrow. With it, we can stretch our horizons, enabling us to perceive the past through the eyes of all its peoples.

The authors wish to thank Peter Cochrane, Paula Hamilton, Maria Nugent, Peter Read, Liz Reed and the anonymous referee for their helpful comments on a draft of this introduction.

[1] WEH Stanner, *The 1968 Boyer Lectures: After the Dreaming*, ABC, Sydney, 1969, pp. 7, 24–5, 53.

[2] By contrast RM Crawford's general history, *Australia* (1952), devoted a chapter to pre-colonial Aboriginal culture, drawing on anthropological studies to provide an enlightened account. He also briefly discussed frontier violence and called for further research on the subject (see Richard Broome, 'Historians, Aborigines and Australia', in Bain Attwood [ed.], *In the Age of Mabo: History, Aborigines and Australia*, Allen & Unwin, St Leonards, 1996, pp. 63–7).

[3] See DJ Mulvaney, 'The Australian Aborigines, 1606–1929: Opinion and fieldwork, Parts 1 and 2' (1958), in JJ Eastwood and FB Smith (eds), *Historical Studies: Selected Articles*, Melbourne University Press, Melbourne, 1964, pp. 1–56; Bernard Smith, *European Vision and the South Pacific, 1768–1850*, Clarendon Press, Oxford, 1960.

[4] Stanner, pp. 22–4; John La Nauze, 'The study of Australian history, 1929–59', *Historical Studies*, vol. 9, no. 33, 1959, p. 11; 'Beyond the frontier: An interview with Henry Reynolds', *Island*, no. 40, 1991, p. 32.

[5] It can also be argued that the 'great Australian silence' owed much to the fact that by 1900 very few Europeans

really met or knew Aboriginal people. Interestingly, the silence started to erode as historians such as Reynolds began to encounter Aborigines. As he has noted of his experience in north Queensland: 'Nothing in my Tasmanian education had prepared me for the realities of race relations in what Rowley called colonial Australia. It was not just the unaccustomed violence and hatred which often grew as lush as guinea grass but the smaller more subtle things — expressions, phrases, jokes, gestures, glances; even silences, which sprang up out of local historical experiences I knew little about' (*The Other Side of the Frontier: An Interpretation of the Aboriginal Response to the Invasion and Settlement of Australia*, History Department, James Cook University, Townsville, 1981, p. 2).

[6] See, for example, John West, *The History of Tasmania* (1852), edited by AGL Shaw, Angus and Robertson, Sydney, 1971; GW Rusden, *History of Australia*, Chapman and Hall, London, 1883.

[7] See *Donald Thomson in Arnhem Land*, compiled and introduced by Nicolas Peterson, Currey O'Neil, Melbourne, 1983, Introduction; Andrew Markus, *Governing Savages*, Allen & Unwin, St Leonards, 1990, Chapters 10–11; Henry Reynolds, *This Whispering in Our Hearts*, Allen & Unwin, St Leonards, 1998, Chapter 11; Fiona Paisley, *Loving Protection?: Australian Feminism and Aboriginal Women's Rights, 1919–1939*, Melbourne University Press, Melbourne, 2000, Chapters 2–4.

[8] See Henry Reynolds, *Why Weren't We Told?: A Personal Search for the Truth About Our History*, Viking, Ringwood, 1999.

9 Stanner, 'Foreword', in Marie Reay (ed.), *Aborigines Now: New Perspective in the Study of Aboriginal Communities*, Angus and Robertson, Sydney, 1964, p. viii; Stanner, *After the Dreaming*, pp. 17, 25, 27, 56.

10 CD Rowley, *The Destruction of Aboriginal Society* (1970), Penguin, Ringwood, 1972, pp. vi, 5, 8–9; 'Dedication', *Aboriginal History*, vol. 11, Part I, 1987, p. 1.

11 Rowley, pp. 2, 34; RHW Reece, *Aborigines and Colonists: Aborigines and Colonial Society in New South Wales in the 1830s and 1840s*, Sydney University Press, Sydney, 1974, Chapter 1; Raymond Evans et al., *Exclusion, Exploitation and Extermination: Race Relations in Colonial Queensland*, ANZ Book Co., Sydney, 1975, Part I; Lyndall Ryan, The Aborigines in Tasmania, 1800–1974, PhD thesis, Macquarie University, Sydney, 1975, Chapters 4, 5; Henry Reynolds and Noel Loos, 'Aboriginal resistance in Queensland', *Australian Journal of Politics and History*, vol. 22, no. 3, 1976, pp. 214–26; MF Christie, *Aborigines in Colonial Victoria, 1835–1886*, Sydney University Press, Sydney, 1979, Chapters 2–3.

12 Reece, pp. 34–42; Brian Harrison, 'The Myall Creek massacre', in Isabel McBryde (ed.), *Records of Times Past: Ethnohistorical Essays on the Culture and History of New England Tribes*, Australian Institute of Aboriginal Studies, Canberra, 1978, pp. 17–51.

13 See David Denholm, *The Colonial Australians*, Penguin, Ringwood, 1979, Chapter 3; Richard Broome, 'The struggle for Australia: Aboriginal–European warfare, 1770–1930', in Michael McKernan and Margaret Browne (eds), *Australia: Two Centuries of War and Peace*, Australian War Memorial/Allen & Unwin, Canberra/Sydney, 1988, pp. 92–120.

14 Reynolds, pp. 98–102; Reynolds, *Frontier: Aborigines, Settlers and Land*, Allen & Unwin, Sydney, 1987, p. 53; Broome, *Aboriginal Australians: Black Response to White Dominance*, Allen & Unwin, Sydney, 1982, pp. 50–1; Rowley, p. 213, his emphasis.

15 Reynolds, *Aborigines and Settlers: The Australian Experience*, Cassell Australia, Melbourne, 1972, Chapter 5; Evans et al., pp. 92, 96–101; Christie, pp. 78, 206–7; Ryan, *The Aboriginal Tasmanians*, University of Queensland Press, St Lucia, 1981, pp. 79, 131, 174–6; Noel Butlin, *Our Original Aggression: Aboriginal Populations of Southeastern Australia, 1788–1850*, Allen & Unwin, Sydney, 1983; Butlin, *Economics and the Dreamtime: A Hypothetical History*, Cambridge University Press, Melbourne, 1993; DJ Mulvaney and J Peter White, 'How many people?', in Mulvaney and White (eds), *Australians to 1788*, Fairfax, Syme & Weldon, Broadway, 1987, p. 117; Judy Campbell, *Invisible Invaders: Smallpox and Other Diseases in Aboriginal Australia, 1780–1880*, Melbourne University Press, Melbourne, 2002. Much more research on disease needs to be conducted, particularly on the inter-relationship between dispossession and disease (see Raymond Evans and Bill

Thorpe, 'Indigenocide and the massacre of Aboriginal history', *Overland*, no. 163, 2001, p. 28).

16 Later work by Reynolds (in *Frontier* and *The Law of the Land* [1987, second edition; 1992]) considered humanitarians and, in particular, the question of whether the imperial and colonial governments had recognised native title in the 1830s and 1840s.

17 Rowley, p. 6; Reece, Chapters 2–5; Ryan, 'Aboriginal policy in Australia — 1838 — A watershed?', *Push From the Bush*, no. 8, 1980, pp. 14–22; SG Foster, 'Aboriginal rights and official morality', *Push From the Bush*, no. 11, 1981, pp. 68–98; Alan Atkinson and Marian Aveling (eds), *Australians 1838*, Fairfax, Syme & Weldon, Broadway, 1987, pp. 301–10, 356–67, 392–7; AGL Shaw, 'British policy towards the Australian Aborigines, 1830–1850', *Australian Historical Studies*, vol. 25, no. 99, 1992, pp. 265–85; John Connor, *The Australian Frontier Wars*, 1788–1838, University of NSW Press, Sydney, 2002.

18 Kerry Howe, 'Review of *Aborigines in Colonial Victoria, 1835–1886*', *Aboriginal History*, vol. 4, no. 2, 1980, pp. 205–6; Howe, 'Review of *The Other Side of the Frontier*', *New Zealand Journal of History*, vol. 17, no. 1, 1983, p. 81; Andrew Markus, 'Through a glass, darkly: Aspects of contact history', *Aboriginal History*, vol. 1, Part II, 1977, pp. 172–3.

19 Reynolds, *The Other Side of the Frontier*, p. 163.

20 See Reece, 'Inventing Aborigines', *Aboriginal History*, vol. 11, Part I, 1987, pp. 15–18; Reece, '"Laws of the white people": The frontier of authority in Perth in 1838', *Push From the Bush*, no. 17, 1984, pp. 2–28; Beverley Nance, 'The level of violence: Europeans and Aborigines in Port Phillip 1835–50', *Historical Studies*, vol. 19, no. 77, 1981, pp. 532–52.

21 In the closing panel discussion of the forum Reynolds commented: 'a great deal of the killing was done by Aboriginal people, both as members of the native police force, which was by far the most destructive force in the whole history of the frontier, but also ... as trackers attached to white parties' (transcript of panel discussion, Frontier Conflict: The Australian Experience forum, Canberra, 14 December 2001, p. 9).

22 See Marie Fels, *Good Men and True: The Aboriginal Police of the Port Phillip District, 1837–1853*, Melbourne University Press, Melbourne, 1988, especially Chapter 4.

23 Bruce Shaw, *My Country of the Pelican Dreaming: The Life of an Australian Aborigine of the Gadjerong, Grant Njabidj, 1904–1977*, Australian Institute of Aboriginal Studies, Canberra, 1981, Chapter 2; Luise Hercus and Peter Sutton (eds), *This is What Happened: Historical Narratives by Aborigines*, Australian Institute of Aboriginal Studies, Canberra, 1986, Part III; Peter and Jay Read (eds), *Long Time, Olden Time: Aboriginal Accounts of Northern Territory History*, Institute for Aboriginal Development Publications, Alice Springs, 1991, Part I; Grace and Harold Koch (comps), *Kaytetye*

Country: An Aboriginal History of the Barrow Creek Area, Institute for Aboriginal Development Publications, Alice Springs, 1993; Deborah Bird Rose, *Hidden Histories: Black Stories from Victoria River Downs, Humbert River and Wave Hill Stations,* Aboriginal Studies Press, Canberra, 1991, Chapters 3–12. (The stories for *This is What Happened* were recorded between the mid-1960s and the mid-1970s, and the interviews for *Long Time* were conducted in the late 1970s.)

24 See, for example, Heather Goodall, 'Colonialism and catastrophe: Contested memories of nuclear testing and measles epidemics at Ernabella', in Kate Darian Smith and Paula Hamilton (eds), *Memory and History in Twentieth-century Australia,* Oxford University Press, Melbourne, 1994, pp. 55–76.

25 See Tom Griffiths, *Hunters and Collectors: The Antiquarian Imagination in Australia,* Cambridge University Press, Melbourne, 1996, Chapter 5.

26 See, for example, Chilla Bulbeck, 'Aborigines, memorials and the history of the frontier', *Australian Historical Studies,* vol. 24, no. 96, 1991, pp. 168–78; Robert Foster et al., *Fatal Collisions: The South Australian Frontier and the Violence of Memory,* Wakefield Press, Adelaide, 2001.

27 Another index of this is the fact that the journal *Aboriginal History* has published few articles on frontier conflict since the mid to late 1980s.

28 See, for example, Markus, *Blood From a Stone: William Cooper and the Australian Aborigines' League,* Allen & Unwin, St Leonards, 1988; Peter Read, *A Hundred Years War: The Wiradjuri People and the State,* Australian National University Press, Canberra, 1988; Anna Haebich, *For their Own Good: Aborigines and Government in the Southwest of Western Australia, 1900–1940,* University of Western Australia Press, 1988; Bain Attwood, *The Making of the Aborigines,* Allen & Unwin, St Leonards, 1989; Heather Goodall, *Invasion to Embassy: Land in Aboriginal Politics in New South Wales, 1770–1972,* Allen & Unwin/Black Books, St Leonards, 1996; Russell McGregor, *Imagined Destinies: Aboriginal Australians and the Doomed Race Theory, 1800–1939,* Melbourne University Press, Melbourne, 1997.

29 See, for example, Reynolds, *An Indelible Stain?: The Question of Genocide in Australia's History,* Viking, Ringwood, 2001; *Aboriginal History,* vol. 25, 2001, which has a special section, 'Genocide?: Australian Aboriginal history in international perspective', edited by Ann Curthoys and John Docker, especially Markus, 'Genocide in Australia', pp. 57–69. Other historians have rejected the suggestion that it might be useful to explore the question of whether genocide has occurred in Australia, see, for example, Inga Clendinnen, 'First contact', *Australian Review of Books,* vol. 6, no. 4, 2001, pp. 6–7, 26.

30 James Stephen, minute for Sir George Grey, 1 November 1838, on Governor George Gipps to Lord

Glenelg, 25 April 1838, CO 201/272, f 397, Public Record Office, London.

31 A Dirk Moses, 'An antipodean genocide? The origins of the genocidal moment in the colonisation of Australia', *Journal of Genocide Research,* vol. 2, no. 1, 2000, pp. 89–92, our emphasis. See also Tony Barta, 'Relations of genocide: Land and lives in the colonisation of Australia', in Isidor Wallimann and Michael N Dobkowski (eds), *Genocide and the Modern Age: Etiology and Case Studies of Mass Death,* Greenwood Press, New York, 1987, pp. 237–51.

32 At the forum, Reynolds asserted, contrary to Windschuttle's allegation that he (Reynolds) has now 'conceded that what happened ... in Tasmania in no way amounted to genocide', that he has never claimed the colony was an example of genocide (Question time, Frontier Conflict: The Australian Experience forum, National Museum of Australia, Canberra, 14 December 2001).

33 Reynolds, *An Indelible Stain?,* pp. 120–1; Read, 'Review of *An Indelible Stain?',* *Aboriginal History,* vol. 25, 2001, pp. 295–7; Reece, 'Aborigines in Australian historiography', in John A Moses (ed.), *Historical Disciplines and Culture in Australasia,* University of Queensland Press, St Lucia, 1979, p. 261.

34 David Carter, 'Working on the past, working on the future', in Richard Nile and Michael Peterson (eds), *Becoming Australian,* University of Queensland Press, St Lucia, 1998, p. 12; Curthoys, History for the nation, or for the world?, address to Museums Australia, Sixth National Conference, 2001, p. 8.

35 See, for example, Hugh Morgan, 'A day to remember realities of history', *Age,* 28 January 1985; Ken Baker, 'The bicentenary: Celebration or apology?', *IPA Review,* vol. 38, no. 4, 1985, p. 181; Peter Coleman, 'The great Australian death wish', *Quadrant,* vol. 24, no. 5, 1985, p. 7.

36 See Attwood, 'The past as future: Aborigines, Australia and the (dis)course of history', and John Morton, 'Aboriginality, Mabo and the republic: Indigenising Australia', in Attwood (ed.), *In the Age of Mabo,* pp. vii–xxxviii, 117–35.

37 See Graeme Davison, *The Use and Abuse of Australian History,* Allen & Unwin, St Leonards, 2000, pp. 2–5.

38 Paul Keating, 'Redfern speech', in Aboriginal and Torres Strait Islander Commission, *1993 International Year of the World's Indigenous People Speeches,* ATSIC, Canberra, 1992, pp. 4–5, 7; *Age,* 29 April 1993; Keating, Address to the nation, 15 November 1993, typescript, pp. 1, 5; *Commonwealth Parliamentary Debates,* 37th Parliament, First Session, 1993, House of Representatives, p. 2880; Keating, 'Dispossessed now out of the shadows', *Australian,* 30–31 July 1994.

39 Geoffrey Blainey, 'Australia: Two peoples: Two

nations?', *Age*, 12 June 1993; 'Mabo: What Aboriginals lost', *Age*, 31 July 1993; 'Land that bypassed a revolution', *Age*, 21 August 1993; 'Drawing up a balance sheet of our history', *Quadrant*, vol. 37, nos 7–8, 1993, p. 15.

40 'An average Australian', *Four Corners*, ABC Television, 19 February 1996.

41 John Howard, Sir Thomas Playford Memorial Lecture, 5 July 1996, typescript, pp. 1–3; Howard, The 1996 Sir Robert Menzies Lecture, 18 November 1996, typescript, pp. 2, 4, 9–10; Federal Government submission to the Senate Legal and Constitutional References Committee, 'Inquiry into the Stolen Generation', March 2000, typescript, p. ii.

42 Davison, p. 6; Curthoys, 'Entangled histories: Conflict and ambivalence in non-Aboriginal Australia', in Geoffrey Gray and Christine Winter (eds), *The Resurgence of Racism: Howard, Hanson and the Race Debate*, Monash Publications in History, Clayton, 1997, p. 119; *Australian*, 26–27 October 1996.

43 'The Prime Minister opens the new *Quadrant* office', *Quadrant*, vol. 44, no. 9, 2000, pp. 2–3; PP McGuinness, 'Truth, sentiment and genocide as a fashion statement', *Sydney Morning Herald*, 14 September 2000; McGuinness, 'Aborigines, massacres and stolen children', *Quadrant*, vol. 44, no. 11, 2000, pp. 2, 4.

44 See Keith Windschuttle, 'The myths of frontier massacres in Australian history', *Quadrant*, vol. 44, nos 10–12, 2000, pp. 8–21, 17–24, 6–20. For Windschuttle's other writings on this subject, consult <www.sydneyline.com>. His criticisms of the historiography have much in common with those of another regular contributor to *Quadrant*, Geoffrey Partington, but Partington's tract, *The Australian History of Henry Reynolds*, published by the Association of Mining and Exploration Companies in 1995, 'sank without a ripple' (John van Tiggelen, 'A whispering in his heart', *Age Good Weekend Magazine*, 13 June 1998).

45 Windschuttle, cited in *Australian*, 11 September 2000.

46 Before making his comment, Manne obtained a copy of the 35,000-word paper Windschuttle had summarised at the conference, the basis, presumably, of articles Windschuttle would soon publish in *Quadrant* ('When historical truths come in dreams', *Sydney Morning Herald*, 18 September 2000).

47 Mike Steketee, 'Off with the armband: Revisionists recast history', *Australian*, 11 September 2000; Manne; Markus, 'The awful truth is out there', *Age*, 30 September 2000.

48 *Sydney Morning Herald*, 15 November 2000; Gillian Cowlishaw, 'The politics of scholarship and the fervour of friends', *Journal of Australian Indigenous Studies*, vol. 3, no. 4, 2002, pp. 20–5. The essence of Cowlishaw's critique dates back some ten years. In an essay

published in 1992, she wrote of histories such as Evans et al.: 'Such chronicles of racist terror and genocidal passions have filled a textual gap about our racial past, but they conceive of racism in such a way that it is not seen to be an organic and ongoing part of colonialism … [H]istorians have created a new silence regarding … this racism … These histories seem to present with ease a view of the past that fills us, as readers, with horror at the same time as it distances us from it. How is it that in reading these accounts we position ourselves on the side of the Aborigines and identify our forebears as the enemy? These violent and racist men could be our grandfathers and they certainly left us something, if not the land they took or the wealth they made from it, then the culture they were developing' ('Studying Aborigines: Changing canons in anthropology and history', in Attwood and John Arnold [eds], *Power, Knowledge and Aborigines*, La Trobe University Press, Bundoora, 1992, pp. 26–7). Klaus Neumann has similarly criticised 'a moralising strategy' in historical work, which, he argues, distances us from '"our" crimes in the past' and so 'effects closure' ('Remembering victims and perpetrators', *UTS Review*, vol. 4, no. 1, 1998, pp. 8–12).

49 Windschuttle, 'When history falls victim to politics', *Age*, 14 July 2001; Angela Shanahan, 'An interpretative dance across history', *Australian*, 7 August 2001; *Drive*, 2CN, 13 August 2001; *PM*, ABC Radio National, 13 August 2001; *Australian*, 13 August 2001; *Radio National Breakfast*, ABC Radio National, 14 August 2001; Windschuttle, 'How not to run a museum', *Quadrant*, vol. 45, no. 9, 2001, p. 19.

50 For a discussion of this in the Australian context, see Davison, *Use and Abuse*.

51 Paula Hamilton, Sale of the century?: Memory and historical consciousness in Australia, unpublished manuscript, 2001, p. 1; Paul Ashton and Hamilton, 'Blood money?: Race and nation in Australian public history', *Radical History Review*, no. 76, 2000, pp. 188–207; Dipesh Chakrabarty, 'Reconciliation and its historiography: Some preliminary thoughts', *UTS Review*, vol. 7, no. 1, 2001, p. 9; Stuart Macintyre, 'History in a new country: Australians debate their past', <www.oslo2000.uio.no/program/papers/s1/s1-macintyre>, 2000, pp. 6, 17; Windschuttle, 'Exposing academic deception of past wrongs', *Sydney Morning Herald*, 19 September 2000.

52 Davison, pp. 18–19, his emphasis.

53 Hamilton, p. 3; Macintyre, 'Review of *The Killing of History*', *Australian Historical Studies*, vol. 28, no. 109, 1997, p. 191; Reynolds, 'From armband to blindfold', *Australian Book Review*, vol. 6, no. 2, 2001, pp. 8–9, 26; Dominick LaCapra, 'Review of *The Killing of History*', *American Historical Review*, vol. 103, no. 1, 1998, pp. 148–9; Daniel Gordon, 'Capital punishment for murderous theorists?: *The Killing of History*', *History and Theory*, vol. 38, no. 3, 1999, pp. 378–88; Ryan,

'Aboriginal history wars', *Australian Historical Association Bulletin,* no. 92, 2001, p. 37; Evans and Thorpe, p. 22; Beverley Kingston, transcript of panel discussion, Frontier Conflict: The Australian Experience forum, National Museum of Australia, Canberra, 14 December 2001, p. 8; Attwood, 'The past as future', p. xxxvii (the passage he cites is from Macintyre, *A History for a Nation: Ernest Scott and the Making of Australian History,* Melbourne University Press, Melbourne, 1994, p. 210).

54 Macintyre, 'Review of *The Killing of History*', pp. 191–2; Davison, 'A premature post-mortem?', *Agenda,* vol. 2, no. 3, 1995, pp. 381–3; Davison, *Use and Abuse,* p. 267.

55 Many scholars in the field of Aboriginal history have also worked with Aboriginal people in producing life stories, oral histories and so forth. For a discussion of this, see Attwood and Fiona Magowan (eds), *Telling Stories: Indigenous History and Memory in Australia and New Zealand,* Allen & Unwin, Sydney, 2001.

56 Davison, for example, has argued: 'Identity history is one of the most powerful forms of history in the contemporary world. But it is also the most dangerous.

While it serves the interests of women's liberation and Aboriginal emancipation, it also serves the interests of ethnic cleansing in Bosnia and Kosovo, and Protestant and Catholic separatism in Northern Ireland. In appealing to sentiments of group pride and solidarity it can also reinforce racial, ethnic, religious and national divisions' (*Use and Abuse,* p. 265). See also Attwood, '"Learning about the truth": The stolen generations narrative', in Attwood and Magowan, pp. 183–212.

57 Chakrabarty, p. 9; Attwood, 'The past as future', p. xxxviii.

58 Transcript of question time, Frontier Conflict: The Australian Experience forum, National Museum of Australia, Canberra. 14 December 2001.

59 Transcript of the panel session, Frontier Conflict: The Australian Experience forum, National Museum of Australia, Canberra, 14 December 2001, pp. 2–3; Chakrabarty, pp. 14–15.

60 Curthoys, 'History for the nation', p. 1; Neumann, p. 15.

61 RG Collingwood, *The Idea of History,* Clarendon Press, Oxford, 1946, pp. 231–49.

Part One

What happened?

Lyndall **Ryan**

Waterloo Creek
northern New South Wales, 1838

Since the early 1970s a generation or more of historians have produced a new body of research that has reframed the dominant narrative of Australian history from that of peaceful settlement of the colonial frontier to one of violent conflict between colonial settlers and Aborigines. This new complexity in Australian history led the best known of this new school of historians, Henry Reynolds, to observe in 1998 that there were now two closely inter-related stories of Australia: those that tell about 'battlers making good in the new world and uniting in praise of equality and a fair go for all', others that tell of the 'fate of the Aborigines [which] casts long, deep shadows over those sunny narratives'.[1]

Not all historians have agreed, however. In a now widely quoted article in *Quadrant* in 1993, Geoffrey Blainey coined the term 'black armband' history to criticise the ways in which recent historical writing in Australia had 'swung from a position that had been too favourable, too self-congratulatory, to an opposite extreme that [was] even more unreal and decidedly jaundiced'. He preferred to focus on the achievements, such as the emergence of a democratic system of government in Australia. While he agreed 'the treatment of Aborigines was often lamentable', he was also disturbed by the 'mischievous statements that the Aborigines' numbers were drastically reduced primarily by slaughter. In fact', he pointed out, 'diseases were the great killer by a very large margin'.[2] His comments were evidently aimed at the work of popular historians who had begun to represent frontier massacres as symbols of shame about Australia's past.[3]

Academic historians of the colonial frontier were also concerned about how conflict was represented, as other contributors to this volume note, but the massacre has taken hold in popular forums. At the beginning of Sydney's Olympic year, Phillip

Knightley, a London-based Australian journalist, compared the fate of the Aborigines
to the holocaust of the Jews:

> It remains one of the mysteries of history that Australia was able to get away
> with a racist policy that included segregation and dispossession and bordered
> on slavery and genocide, practices unknown in the civilised world in the first
> half of the twentieth century until Nazi Germany turned on the Jews in the 1930s.

To illustrate his argument about the bloody dispossession of Australian Aborigines,
Knightley recounted four well-known massacre stories from the colonial frontier
based on published accounts by Australian historians: the Battle of Pinjarra in
Western Australia in 1834; Waterloo Creek in New South Wales in 1838; Forrest River
in Western Australia in 1926; and Coniston Station in the Northern Territory in 1928.
While at least one of his accounts — the Waterloo Creek massacre of 1838 — bore
little resemblance to that provided by historians, the shame of Australia's past was
exposed to world scrutiny.[4]

Enter Keith Windschuttle

Knightley's arresting claim before a global audience provoked a strong response.
Shortly before the Olympic Games, the journalist Keith Windschuttle questioned
whether some of these massacres had ever happened. Emboldened perhaps by
Knightley's aggressive prose, he claimed the historians on whose work Knightley had
drawn had fabricated the past:

> Australian historians had constructed a story of widespread massacres on the
> frontiers of the expanding pastoral industry that carried off between five and
> twenty percent of the Aboriginal population on the mainland and up to seventy
> percent of indigenes in Tasmania. However, when it is closely examined, the
> evidence of these claims turns out to be highly suspect.

Windschuttle converts the term 'widespread violence' used by Richard Broome and
Henry Reynolds into 'widespread massacres', and so transforms the whole
meaning of frontier violence. He then moves to the next step: if some massacres
can be proved not to have taken place, then frontier violence must have been far
less widespread. By implication, the work by historians of the colonial frontier can
be discounted.[5]

To support his claim, Windschuttle examines five well-known massacre stories: the four represented by Knightley and the Myall Creek massacre in northwestern New South Wales in 1838. Of these, he claims only two were genuine massacres — Myall Creek and Coniston — and in the first case the perpetrators were brought to justice and in the second some Aboriginal people survived to tell the tale. The Battle of Pinjarra and Waterloo Creek were legitimate police actions, and the Forrest River massacre was fabricated by the missionary John Gribble.

How does Windschuttle reach this conclusion? He employs a forensic approach to determine whether a massacre occurred on the colonial frontier. He turns each alleged massacre site into a modern-day crime scene. He bestows on himself the retroactive role of a public prosecutor who searches for evidence to construct a case to prosecute the guilty parties or decide that there is not a case to answer. This is how Windschuttle describes his approach:

> Historians should only accept evidence of violent deaths, Aboriginal or otherwise, where there is a minimum amount of direct evidence. This means that, at the very least, they need some reports by people who were either genuine eyewitnesses or who at least saw the bodies afterwards. Preferably, these reports should be independently corroborated by others who saw the same thing. Admissions of guilt by those concerned, provided they are recorded first-hand and are not hearsay, should also count as credible evidence.[6]

There are problems for the historian with this approach. Windschuttle provides no definition of a massacre — how it takes place or how many people need to be killed. Furthermore, often first and second-hand reports of massacres on the colonial frontier are vague because they were prepared long after the event, and eyewitness accounts are often in conflict. So the historian has to rely on other evidence to reconstruct the event.

To demonstrate the limitations of Windschuttle's approach, this essay will analyse one of the massacres Windschuttle claims was a legitimate police action — Waterloo Creek — and compare his account with those of four historians who have researched the colonial frontier. It will conclude, as I have argued elsewhere, that Windschuttle has used this approach selectively for his own political purposes.[7]

What happened at Waterloo Creek?

The 'collision' at Waterloo Creek — to borrow the term used by Sir George Gipps, Governor of New South Wales at the time — took place in 1838. It was the end point of a two-month expedition by a detachment of mounted police sent from Sydney to track down the Namoi, Weraerai and Kamilaroi people, who had killed five stockmen in separate incidents on recently established pastoral runs on the upper Gwydir River area of New South Wales, far beyond the defined boundaries of colonial settlement. In the first weeks of the campaign, the mounted police, consisting of five officers and 20 men and led by Major James Nunn, arrested 15 Aborigines but released all but two, one of whom was retained as a guide while the other was shot attempting to escape. But the main body of Kamilaroi eluded them. So, with the support of at least two stockmen from the area, Nunn and his party pursued the Kamilaroi for three weeks from present-day Manilla on the Namoi River north to the upper Gwydir River. On the morning of 26 January Nunn's party suddenly found themselves under surprise attack.

In the ensuing melée, which lasted for about ten minutes, a spear wounded a corporal and four or five Aborigines were shot dead in retaliation. Then the Aborigines fled down the river. The mounted police regrouped and, over the next hour or two, re-armed and refreshed their horses. Then the main body of mounted police, led by the second in command, Lieutenant George Cobban, set off in pursuit, leaving Nunn behind with the wounded corporal. Cobban's party found their quarry about a mile down the river now known as Waterloo Creek, where a second engagement took place. It is this second encounter or collision that exercised government officials at the time, and has concerned later researchers as to whether it constitutes a massacre.[8]

There are two eyewitness accounts of this second engagement, provided to a judicial inquiry held over a year later. The most detailed account was provided by Lieutenant Cobban. He told of finding a very large group of Aborigines on the other side of the river and how the mounted police tried to cut them off at the front and the rear so that they could be captured. He rode to the rear of the group while the rest of the mounted police drove the Aborigines into the river. Cobban found a large cache of Aboriginal weapons in the bush and secured them. When he returned to the river, he admitted to seeing two Aborigines being shot, trying to escape and at most three or four Aborigines dead. The encounter lasted several hours. No Aborigines were captured.[9]

The second eyewitness account was provided by Sergeant John Lee, who was with the main detachment of mounted police that pursued the Aborigines into the river:

> It was impossible for the party to act in a body; every man had in fact to act for himself; the men spread out so much that it was impossible for any one person to put a stop to the firing at once. From what I saw myself, I should say that from forty to fifty blacks were killed when the second firing took place.

As the mounted police returned to present-day Manilla, stories of their exploits quickly spread around the stock-keepers' huts and finally reached Rev. Lancelot Threlkeld's mission for the Aborigines at Lake Macquarie, south of Newcastle. By then estimates of the death toll from the entire expedition had reached between 120 and 300. It was clear that something out of the ordinary had taken place.[10]

When Governor Gipps received Major Nunn's report of the 53-day campaign in March 1838, he estimated in conversation with Nunn that 'not less than ten or twelve' Aborigines had been killed, 'besides a number wounded'. Gipps reminded Nunn of the new measures in place relating to the violent deaths of Aborigines at the hands of the Queen's officers and sought the advice of the Executive Council. It recommended that a magistrate's inquiry should be held to investigate the circumstances of the 'collision'.[11]

Just as the inquiry was about to begin, however, the magistrate in charge received instructions to investigate the Myall Creek massacre (which occurred in June). The inquiry did not convene until April 1839. By then, the perpetrators at Myall Creek had been hanged and the colonists were deeply divided about the rights of Aborigines in relation to themselves. The inquiry took only five depositions: four from the mounted police officers and one from a stockman. Other key witnesses from the ranks of the mounted police did not appear. Of the five witnesses who provided depositions, only two — Lieutenant Cobban and Sergeant Lee — were present at the second encounter.[12]

On receipt of the report, the attorney-general advised against laying charges on the grounds that it would be impossible to secure a conviction. There were too many inconsistencies in the conduct of the inquiry and it had been held too long after the event. The Executive Council agreed and the matter was dropped. Gipps sent the papers to London in a despatch dated 22 July 1839.[13]

In London the Secretary of State for the Colonies, Lord John Russell, was very critical of the way in which the matter had been handled. He wrote to Gipps:

> The worst feature of the case was, as you properly state, the renewal of the pursuit of the Blacks, and the firing after a pause of about two hours; and, though

you add some reasons in mitigation of this conduct on the part of Major Nunn, I wish without giving you any positive instructions upon the subject to draw your attention to the question how far it is necessary that the Force employed upon similar service should be always entrusted with the use of Fire Arms. In the case before me, the object of capturing offenders was entirely lost sight of, and shots were fired at men, who were apparently only guilty of jumping into the water to escape from an armed pursuit.

Clearly, the Secretary of State did not consider the second encounter a legitimate police action.[14]

How have historians interpreted the 'collision'?

I have found four accounts by historians of the collision at Waterloo Creek. RHW Reece, one of the first of the new generation of historians to research relations between Aborigines and colonists, published a ground-breaking study on New South Wales in 1974. Reece tried to locate the massacre site and place Nunn's campaign in the context of other events on the frontier in the late 1830s. To construct his account he relied on the evidence to the judicial inquiry in 1839, an account by a member of the Legislative Council who visited the site some days after the collision and which was published in the *Sydney Morning Herald* in 1849, information he found in the published papers of Threlkeld, and another account published by the novelist Mrs Campbell Praed in 1885. Armed with these accounts, he visited the area, conferred with local historians and examined the maps of Aboriginal territories and clans by the anthropologist NB Tindale. Reece concluded that the site was at the junction of the Slaughterhouse Creek and the Gwydir River, and that 60 or 70 Aborigines had been killed. But he did not discount Threlkeld's view 'that the number may have been as high as two or three hundred'. He was in no doubt the massacre had taken place but that it had been covered up by the judicial inquiry in the aftermath of the trials of the perpetrators of the Myall Creek massacre. Reece then showed how the colonial government was under enormous pressure in 1839 to contain the public outrage following the conviction of the Myall Creek murderers. Given this environment, he concluded that the few voices of dissent, including that of Threlkeld who had heard about the events taking place on the northwest frontier of New South Wales, should not be discounted. He was also interested in the fact that ten years after the event, the local squatters, who must have known about the collision at the time, began to talk, knowing it was far too late for a fresh inquiry.[15]

The second account is by the military historian Peter Stanley. He based his 1986 interpretation on the evidence in the judicial inquiry of 1839 and Colonel Godfrey Mundy's narrative of his time as deputy adjutant-general to the defence forces in New South Wales between 1846 and 1851. Mundy was told by members of the mounted police about the collision in 1846. In his view the massacre occurred because the mounted police were 'irritated by one of their Sergeants having been treacherously wounded ... they charged into the thick bush, where, out of sight of their officers, they took a fearful revenge on their barbarian foe'. Stanley considered Mundy's account matched that of Sergeant Lee and concluded:

> It seems likely that startled by the sudden appearance of the Kamilaroi, disoriented by the heat and thick scrub and frightened by [the corporal's] screams, the inexperienced young troopers lost their heads and, heedless of their officers, rode up and down the creek, slashing, stabbing and shooting, killing at least fifty Aborigines.[16]

I wrote the third account as part of a chapter for *Australians 1838*, published in 1987. My task was to place the collision in the context of other incidents along the colonial frontier in 1838 and to try to identify the site at Waterloo Creek. I relied on the information provided by Major Thomas Mitchell to Governor Gipps about the possible location, Nunn's evidence to the judicial inquiry, maps from the 1840s and visits I made to the area in 1984. I also used the accounts of events on the frontier in 1838 contained in the British parliamentary papers for 1839. I concluded Snodgrass Lagoon and Waterloo Creek were the same site, a view reinforced by Roger Milliss in an article in the *National Times* in 1985, and commenced my reconstruction of the collision from that point. I considered that Sergeant Lee's estimate of 40 to 50 killed was the most reliable on the grounds he was in the thick of the fray and provided the most convincing story of how the collision took place.[17]

The fourth account is Milliss's *Waterloo Creek,* published in 1992. While he used a vast array of sources, Milliss focused on the evidence about the mounted police campaign provided by Major Nunn. He analysed this account to show how Nunn tried on the one hand to glorify his exploits and on the other to cover up his failure of leadership at Waterloo Creek. Like Reece, Milliss was in no doubt that the judicial inquiry of 1839 was a cover-up and that there were good reasons why other key witnesses in the mounted police were not called. In exploring this theme, Milliss turned to other evidence from the time, including the information provided by Threlkeld. He agreed with Reece's estimate that 60 to 70 Aborigines were killed, based on the length of time of the encounter and the fact the number was cited by a prominent member of the Legislative Council who visited the site a short time after the massacre and saw the remains of Aborigines still in the trees. He also agreed with Reece in suggesting the reader should not discount Threlkeld's estimate of 150 to 300 Aborigines killed, on the grounds he had good contacts with squatters, clergy and Aboriginal people in the area.[18]

Windschuttle's interpretation of the 'collision'

In applying his forensic approach to the 'collision' at Waterloo Creek, Windschuttle finds Waterloo Creek was not a massacre but a legitimate police action in which at most three to four Aborigines were killed in the second encounter. The only account he accepts is the deposition by Lieutenant Cobban on the grounds that as the more senior officer, he was the more reliable witness. Yet Cobban went to great lengths to show that he was on the other side of the river in search of Aboriginal weapons and was not in the thick of the fray described by Sergeant Lee. Windschuttle argues that had 40 or 50 been killed, then evidence in the form of human remains would have been found, even years later. Yet the 1849 account referred to the dead bodies in the trees. Windschuttle dismisses this evidence as hearsay too long after the event. On the basis of Cobban's evidence Windschuttle concludes Waterloo Creek was a 'legitimate police action' that was turned into a massacre by 'the mischievous missionary', Threlkeld, 'who had little compunction about fabricating massacre stories and trying to influence government opinion with them'. According to Windschuttle, Threlkeld had an ulterior motive in fabricating massacre stories: he needed government support for his mission at Lake Macquarie. Windschuttle, therefore, dismisses Milliss's account on the grounds that he accepted the evidence of Threlkeld.[19]

Windschuttle also uses guilt by association to dismiss other historians, in my case because I gave Milliss's book a 'glowing' review. He seems to think that if historians agree that a massacre took place, they must be in collusion.[20]

Where does the evidence lead?

From our research of government archives, parliamentary papers, newspapers and correspondence by squatters and missionaries, Reece and I contended that the rapid spread of the pastoral frontier in 1837 beyond the boundaries of British settlement, and the resistance of the Kamilaroi people to the invasion of their country, led to an extreme situation. Reece focused on the judicial system's initial failure to come to grips with the situation, while I focused on the strength of the Aboriginal response to the arrival of sheep and cattle runs across the frontier of southeastern Australia in 1837. Stanley used military records to examine the collision from the perspective of the mounted police and their exasperation in trying to hunt down such a formidable and elusive foe as the Kamilaroi. Milliss used every record he could find to focus on the key players in the story and, in particular, the character and personality of the man who led the expedition, Major Nunn, whom he believed was searching for military glory after an undistinguished military career.

Windschuttle's account, in contrast, is based on two printed sources: the report of the judicial inquiry held in April and May 1839, and Threlkeld's papers. His finding that the collision was 'a legitimate police action' is based on his belief that the 'foundation of the Australian nation was based on the rule of law and civilised values that abhorred the killing of the defenceless'. In this context, he claims that the alleged massacre at Waterloo Creek could not have taken place because Nunn's expedition was carried out with the sanction of British law. The real point about Nunn's behaviour at Waterloo Creek, however, is that it went beyond the bounds of British law. This is what so disturbed Sir George Gipps in Sydney and Lord John Russell in London.[21]

There are several gaps in Windschuttle's account. First, he does not consider Nunn's original report prepared for the Colonial Secretary of New South Wales, nor the initial deliberations of the Executive Council, nor Lord John Russell's response to the inquiry. Second, he does not adequately address the conflicting accounts of the collision produced at the inquiry. Lieutenant Cobban, who claimed three or four Aborigines were shot in the second encounter, was not with the detachment of mounted police on the other side of the river. This means that no senior officer saw the killings that Sergeant Lee described. Finally, he does not address the fact that a number of witnesses failed to appear at the inquiry and that its conduct did not meet the usual standards of the judiciary. These matters were raised by the attorney-general on receipt of the report. In other words, there are too many unanswered questions about the inquiry to accept its conclusion at face value. In these circumstances, in applying his forensic approach, Windschuttle should have concluded that the collision took place but that it cannot be proved whether it was a legitimate police action or a massacre.

In this situation the historian has to ask, can he or she accept the evidence of Sergeant Lee, corroborated by later accounts? The reasons for doing so are compelling. First, Cobban acknowledged that after the first encounter, the troopers took two hours to refresh their horses and to re-arm, that the second encounter lasted several hours, that no Aborigines were arrested and that he saw the bodies of three Aboriginal men in the river. Second, Major Nunn did not lead his men into what was the most important encounter of the whole campaign and Lieutenant Cobban separated himself from the main party of mounted police on the other side of the river during that encounter. This suggests the two senior officers took care not to be with the main body of mounted police at the second encounter, a point made by Stanley. Finally, the fact that when fully armed, each trooper carried at least two brace of pistols, a sword and a musket, gives a clear meaning to Sergeant Lee's statement that it was every man for himself.

The historian can deduce that no trooper had any intention of arresting possible offenders. Given this, he or she can conclude that the second encounter was an act of mass revenge by the mounted police in retaliation for the wounding of one of their comrades. None of this evidence suggests Waterloo Creek was a legitimate police action. Rather, there is sufficient evidence for the historian to conclude that on 26 January 1838, the mounted police engaged in a massacre — the indiscriminate shooting of people who could not defend themselves. Both the Governor of New South Wales in Sydney and the Secretary of State for the Colonies in London reached this conclusion.

Keith Windschuttle's conclusions about the collision at Waterloo Creek raise serious questions about the quality of his investigation of the past. First, he claims historians of the frontier have to decide whether the foundation of the Australian nation was based on the rule of law and civilised values that abhorred the killing of defenceless people, or whether the nation rests on collusion in the massacre of many thousands of Aborigines who were doing no more than defending their traditional lands. Most historians would not accept either position.[22]

Second, Windschuttle's limited foray into the primary sources reveals little understanding of how the colonial frontier worked. He presents it as if it were a defined battlefield in which the rules of war were carefully followed, and in this arena he places greater weight on the evidence of the senior officer. Instead, it was a shifting, complex and violent site, where the usual practices of British law and order were not consistently applied. In this context, the metaphor of historical research as a courtroom setting does not hold. Windschuttle's forensic approach is an inappropriate tool for understanding the colonial frontier. He would be better served by a more careful reading of all the available sources and a more developed understanding of how the frontier worked. Historians have been engaged in this process for the last 30 years.

[1] Henry Reynolds, *This Whispering in Our Hearts*, Allen & Unwin, St Leonards, 1998, p. 245.

[2] Geoffrey Blainey, 'Drawing up the balance sheet of our history', *Quadrant*, vol. 37, nos 7–8, 1993, pp. 11, 15.

[3] See Bruce Elder, *Blood on the Wattle: Massacres and the Maltreatment of Australian Aborigines since 1788*, Child & Associates, French's Forest, 1988; Al Grassby and Marji Hill, *Six Australian Battlefields: The Black Resistance to Invasion and the White Struggle Against Colonial Oppression*, Angus and Robertson, Sydney, 1988.

[4] Phillip Knightley, *Australia: A Biography of a Nation*, Vintage, Sydney, 2000, p. 107.

[5] Keith Windschuttle, 'The myths of frontier massacres in Australian history, Part I: The invention of massacre stories', *Quadrant*, vol. 44, no. 10, 2000, pp. 9, 13.

[6] *Ibid*, p. 13.

[7] See Lyndall Ryan, 'The Aboriginal history wars', *Australian Historical Association Bulletin*, no. 92, 2001, pp. 31–7.

[8] James Nunn to Colonial Secretary Edward Deas Thomson, 5 March 1838, 'Despatches relative to the massacre of various Australian Aborigines in the year 1838', pp. 22–3, reproduced in *British Parliamentary Papers, Papers Relating to Australia*, vol. 5.

[9] Deposition of George Geddes McKenzie Cobban, 17 May 1839, *Historical Records of Australia*, series I, vol. XX, pp. 253–6.

[10] Deposition of John Lee, 4 April 1839, *Historical Records of Australia*, series I, vol. XX, p. 251; *Australian Reminiscences and Papers of LE Threlkeld: Missionary to the Aborigines, 1824–1839*, edited by Niel Gunson, Australian Institute of Aboriginal Studies, Canberra, 1974, vol. I, pp. 138, 145, vol. 2, pp. 275–6.

[11] Sir George Gipps to Lord Glenelg, 25 and 27 April 1838, *Historical Records of Australia*, series I, vol. XIX, pp. 396, 399.

[12] Enclosures A6–A8, Sir George Gipps to Lord Glenelg, 22 July 1839, *Historical Records of Australia*, series I, vol. XX, pp. 250–7.

[13] Opinion by JH Plunkett on papers re collision between mounted police under JW Nunn and Aborigines, *Historical Records of Australia*, series I, vol. XX, pp. 256–7.

[14] Lord John Russell to Sir George Gipps, 21 December 1839, *Historical Records of Australia*, series I, vol. XX, p. 440.

[15] RHW Reece, *Aborigines and Colonists: Aborigines in Colonial Society in New South Wales in the 1830s and 1840s*, Sydney University Press, Sydney, 1974, pp. 32–4.

[16] GC Mundy, *Our Antipodes: Or, Residences and Rambles in the Australasian Colonies. With a Glimpse of the Gold Fields*, Richard Bentley, London, 1852, vol. 1, p. 169; Peter Stanley, *The Remote Garrison: The British Army in Australia 1788–1870*, Kangaroo Press, Kenthurst, 1986, p. 54.

[17] [Lyndall Ryan], 'At the boundaries', in Alan Atkinson and Marian Aveling (eds), *Australians 1838*, Fairfax, Syme & Weldon, Broadway, 1987, pp. 38–45.

[18] Roger Milliss, *Waterloo Creek: The Australia Day Massacre of 1838, Governor Gipps and the British Conquest of New South Wales*, McPhee Gribble, Ringwood, 1992, p. 189.

[19] Windschuttle, p. 17.

[20] *Ibid*.

[21] Windschuttle, cited in *Sydney Morning Herald*, 17 September 2000.

[22] *Ibid*.

DJ **Mulvaney**

Barrow Creek northern Australia, 1874

Frontier conflict in the Northern Territory during the late nineteenth century offers a fertile research field, one so far not examined as closely as the relations in Victoria, New South Wales and Queensland, discussed in this volume by Jan Critchett, Lyndall Ryan and Raymond Evans. As Ryan has noted, Keith Windschuttle follows sound legal tradition in demanding substantive proof of claims of mass homicide, such as body counts or sworn eyewitness testimony, but neither was readily available under frontier conditions. This, however, does not mean that evidence, especially Aboriginal oral traditions, must be rejected.

It was characteristic of the period that the word of Aboriginal witnesses was discounted as untrustworthy and their evidence excluded from many legal proceedings. Settlers, on the other hand, invariably claimed that Aboriginal deaths resulted from justifiable self-defence during treacherous hostilities initiated by savages. Their word was rarely challenged. In newspapers such as the *Adelaide Advertiser* and *Register* and the *Northern Territory Times*, accounts of assaults on 'innocent' Europeans were given considerable space, with casualties listed in detail. On the other hand, vagueness invariably characterised newspaper reports of settler retaliation, and although Aborigines were rarely arrested the numbers killed during punitive expeditions were rarely provided and then probably minimised. On the occasion of the spearing of Fred Bradshaw, in 1905, the *Register* covered almost two pages with descriptions of most European fatalities in the Top End until that date, but said little about retaliation.[1]

Undoubtedly, many Aboriginal attacks were unexpected and self-defence was vindicated; but it is the uniformity of self-justification and the emphasis on Aboriginal treachery, all without the context of the situation in which they occurred, that suggests innocence is proclaimed too much. In any case, it is hardly surprising warriors reacted to their eviction from their territory or exclusion from a major water supply, or the uncaring violation of their sacred places and the frequent violation of women.

European sources contain hints that the newcomers were neither uniformly innocent victims, nor the indigenes always treacherous and invariably the aggressors. Consider the testimony of Mounted Constable Ernest Cowle, stationed in central Australia between 1889 and 1903. His colleague during his initial Alice Springs posting was Mounted Constable William Willshire, whose documented record of violence and racial vilification is notorious. This background illuminates the sentiments Cowle expressed in letters to his anthropologist friend, Baldwin Spencer, during 1899, by which time Willshire had been charged with murdering Aborigines, declared not guilty, but transferred from the Centre. 'I am not advocating shooting, for a moment, in the so called good old style', Cowle wrote, but he revealed he had terrified a cattle-spearing captive by taking him into the bush: 'I think he felt certain he was going to be shot', Cowle remarked with equanimity.[2]

A fine line was drawn between shooting in self-defence, retaliation on those actually involved and racial revenge. Consider the evidence of another Territorian, Paddy Cahill, whose later record of positive race relations at Oenpelli was outstanding. He was ambushed by Aborigines near the Victoria River in 1895 and, not surprisingly, was enraged when an iron-headed spear passed through his hat. 'I could do nothing but shoot as quickly as I could,' he reported, 'and I can shoot fairly quickly. I don't know how many niggers I shot — I did not stop to count them'. Years later Cahill referred to an 1890s Alligator River 'Shoot-up of blacks by the whites in revenge for the killing of a white man'.[3]

CJ Dashwood, the government administrator, cited Paddy Cahill as one of three sources of information when, in 1899, he told the South Australian Government that during the major cattle drives of the early 1880s, 'the whites, in travelling from Queensland to Kimberley ... shot the blacks down like crows all along the route'. Cahill denied he was a source for Dashwood's claim; as a Territorian, he might have felt obliged to have a flexible memory. In the published letter containing his denial, he also referred to the 1892 spearing of WS Scott, respected manager of Willeroo station, and complained that the Aborigines responsible went unpunished. A week later, WA Millikan, a Wesleyan minister who had worked in the Territory, refuted Cahill's claim: 'He surely knows that at the time two parties of men stirred to anger and well armed started out propossedly [*sic*] to avenge the murder, and were gone some weeks; and was it not an open secret that they made the locality particularly "unhealthy"?' The *Northern Territory Times* report of this episode confirms that two punitive parties, including one of seven white men and five 'blackboys', set out in addition to the police.[4]

Although these general and unquantified episodes do not meet Windschuttle's criteria for authenticity, they involved informed contemporaries and surely exceeded the 'only-shoot-in-self-defence' rubric. The precise details of Europeans killed or injured contrast with the unspecified indigenous casualties. In this regard, the parallel with the Coniston massacre of 1928 is striking. However, Coniston was foreshadowed by the aftermath of an incident at Barrow Creek, which provides a salutary case study for the nature of evidence in outback settlement history.

On the evening of 22 February 1874, possibly 20 Kaytej warriors attacked the Barrow Creek telegraph station, whose staff were relaxing outside the compound. Their motives, although disputed, are irrelevant here, beyond quoting TGH Strehlow's wry observation: the Kaytej 'did only what Europeans living in occupied countries were to do during the 1939–45 war to enemy officials who had usurped the administration of their territories; guerrilla fighters and patriotic individuals made their attacks'. Two postal officers died, a tragic loss on South Australia's vaunted overland telegraph line during its second operational year. Adelaide newspaper editorials revealed fears for the safety of the entire line's staff and that contact with Europe might be cut. These predictions amounted to scaremongering but explain the rapidity and scale of the reaction. The *Advertiser* urged 'swift punishment, and severe as it is swift', adding that England was 'waging war on the West Coast of Africa now to punish crimes not one whit more diabolical than those committed by the blacks at Barrow Creek'. Here, then, was a frontier war in the making.[5]

Trooper Samuel Gason was the only policeman at Barrow Creek. The *Advertiser* hoped he was 'not hampered by too many instructions'. 'We can hardly expect that many arrests will be made', the bellicose editorial continued, 'but a punishment will doubtless be given to the blood-thirsty rascals, which will be remembered for years to come'. Accordingly, EA Hamilton, Chief Commissioner of Police, ordered urgent action to recruit a punitive band, directing that 'a too close adherence to legal forms should not be insisted on'. Although this was intended to speed the swearing-in of special constables, the instruction had a wider application. Popular opinion in Adelaide, and

*Attack by natives on the
Barrow's Creek telegraph
station
Illustrated Australian News for
Home Readers,
25 March 1874*
National Library of Australia

An accompanying report describes the event as a 'serious affray ... The attack was made without the slightest provocation, the sole object of the natives being to get possession of the flour and mutton in the station. The natives had been kindly treated by all accounts, and had received several presents'.

doubtless the 11 men who set out from Barrow Creek a week later, agreed with the *Advertiser* that 'retribution to be useful, must be sharp, swift and severe'.[6]

Gason's party was six weeks in the field, each man receiving five shillings a day, constituting an enormous expenditure of time and money, and indicating that pacification and punishment were taken very seriously in official circles. No prisoners were taken. No questions were asked. Gason acknowledged that 11 Aborigines were shot. Other evidence suggests the number was much higher.[7]

In 1901, Baldwin Spencer and Frank Gillen engaged in several weeks of anthropological research at Barrow Creek. Their chief Kaytej informant was Tungalla, a member of the group that attacked the telegraph station in 1874; indeed, his name was included in the list of eight arrest warrants vainly drawn up by the police, but he escaped capture by hiding in rocks as his pursuers rode by. Spencer was in a sound position, therefore, to collect eyewitness information about these events, but he provided few details and made no criticisms of the punitive expedition: 'they rode out over all the surrounding country, and the natives had such a lesson that they never again attempted an attack'. Spencer's reticence in this case may be explained partly by the attitude of his postmaster partner, whose unusual sympathy for Aboriginal people seems to have been blunted on this occasion by his telegraph connections: he was on duty in the Adelaide office in 1874 and passed messages to Barrow Creek. In retrospect, Gillen reflected: 'In the annals of Native treachery there is no crueller or more unprovoked attack'.[8]

While Spencer and Gillen were taxing Tungalla for ethnographic data, a new informant arrived. This was an Anmatyerre elder, Ulpailiurkna, who also told Spencer of settler violence. Once again, Spencer told less than he learned about an incident at Anna's Reservoir, to the southwest, during 1884, when Aborigines destroyed a homestead and wounded two men. This action possibly was a payback for the wounding of Aborigines by the police. According to Spencer, there were few Anmatyerre people by 1901; they had been 'nearly wiped out, partly by drought and partly by the fact that they had, years ago, been what is called "dispersed" ... with results unfortunate to themselves'. In both these cases, Spencer was clearly referring to violent death or injury.[9]

William Willshire had headed to Anna's Reservoir in 1884 with instructions 'to go out and do as the law provides in such cases' and 'disperse' the Aboriginal people.

His campaign opened with the capture of four Anmatyerre women, from whom he extracted 'useful information'. This led him to an encampment of at least 60 people, where he claimed only to have shot two and wounded three men. Whether any of these victims actually attacked the homestead is unknown. Not satisfied with this punishment, he continued sporadic operations for ten months, at the conclusion of which he boasted proudly: 'all's well that ends well'. This is the bloody background to Spencer's reference to 'dispersion'. It is improbable that only two deaths accompanied this campaign, particularly as Willshire remarked: 'a good Winchester or Martini carbine, in conjunction with a colt's revolver ... are your best friends, and you must use them too'.[10]

Within a few years of Spencer's sojourn at Barrow Creek, another anthropologist, Herbert Basedow, stayed there. He conversed with elders who remembered the retribution, but Basedow only hinted at the consequences: 'The tribe had, of course, since paid dearly for the outrage at the hands of the punitive expedition which included several expert sharpshooters'. In 1918, Barrow Creek was also visited by Skipper Partridge, a missionary who carefully recorded information presented to him. The punitive expedition, he wrote, now 44 years removed in time, 'is said ... [to have] shot every black person they could see for weeks'. This is hearsay, critics might assert, but the phrases used by these three independent recorders — Spencer, Basedow and Partridge — all imply massacres.[11]

The geographic extent of Gason's punitive foray became clearer in 1932, following Strehlow's presence in the region as a patrol officer. Fifty-eight years had intervened, but memories were vivid as two elders led Strehlow to two places devastated by Gason's party in 1874. Significantly, neither place was situated in the territory of the Kaytej, who were responsible for killing the postal officials, but in lands of the southern Anmatyerre people, who were unconnected with the attack. One of these locations, by then suggestively known as Skull Creek, was probably the place where Gason admitted to shooting three men. He claimed they resisted arrest. This was a convenient and well-worn Territory excuse. A variant was used in 1884 by Willshire's partner, Mounted Constable Wurmbrand, who apparently shot three neck-chained men in the back while 'escaping' near Hermannsburg. Strehlow's informants told him that an entire encampment at Skull Creek was 'shot down at sight' although it was situated about 80 kilometres southwest of Barrow Creek and in another group's territory.[12]

At Lukara, 50 kilometres southeast of Barrow Creek, Strehlow was shown the location of a former sacred storehouse in an earth cave destroyed by Gason's posse. Two elders led him to this vandalised place, where fragments of stone *tjurungas* lay scattered in the sand. Even six decades later, the trauma of this desecration was evident to Strehlow in the sadness and actions of his guides. With 'shaking voices' these men told him the oral history surrounding this place. His rendition makes sad reading:

> You have heard of the attack on Barrow Creek a long time ago? The white men had taken the wives of the dark men. They told the husbands of these women to keep away from their wives. The white men did wrong in chasing the dark men from their country and then taking their wives. The dark men surrounded Barrow Creek and speared the whites. The whites shot down our people everywhere. Later on the police came. We still remember their names — Wurmbrand, Willshire and Bennett. They hunted down people like kangaroos. They brought with them dark trackers. They gave them rifles and told them to shoot down their own countrymen everywhere. The trackers sometimes went out while the white men stopped in their camps. When our people saw these trackers coming, they did not run away: they trusted their own relatives.

Strehlow's clear, grammatical exposition suggests that he rephrased his informants' account. That he did not embellish it is indicated by the inclusion of Mounted Constable Bennett's name. In a footnote, Strehlow commented that Bennett 'was stationed at Barrow Creek in 1888' but that he did not know whether 'he was personally involved in any shooting'. He also noted that all the police officers named served in central Australia after the 1880s only, but that 'their zeal in "pacifying" the country was not unnaturally associated [with these particular events] by the natives of the Barrow Creek District'.[13]

Must such oral testimony be derided, simply because it is not accompanied by a solid body of written evidence and conventional footnotes, or because it telescopes events and personalities? Surely the message is clear — that considerable violence occurred.

1 *Register*, 18 December 1905.

2 DJ Mulvaney et al., *From the Frontier: Outback Letters to Baldwin Spencer,* Allen & Unwin, St Leonards, 2000, pp. 128, 117.

3 Unprovenanced newspaper article, 4 September 1901, South Australia State Records, GRS 9/3; C Warburton, *Buffaloes,* Angus and Robertson, Sydney, 1934, p. 144.

4 *Northern Territory Times and Gazette,* 3 August 1900; unprovenanced newspaper article, 4 September 1901; *Northern Territory Times,* 21 October 1892 and 25 November 1892.

5 TGH Strehlow, *Songs of Central Australia,* Angus and Robertson, Sydney, 1971, p. 590; *Advertiser,* 24 February 1874 and 25 February 1874.

6 *Advertiser,* 26 February 1874; EA Hamilton to Chief Secretary, South Australia, 24 February 1874, South Australia State Records, GRG 5/2/1874/260.

7 Gordon Reid, *A Picnic with the Natives: Aboriginal–European Relations in the Northern Territory to 1910,* Melbourne University Press, Melbourne, 1980, pp. 63–5.

8 WB Spencer and FJ Gillen, *Across Australia,* Macmillan, London, 1912, p. 321; FJ Gillen, *Gillen's Diary: The Camp Jottings of FJ Gillen,* Libraries Board of South Australia, Adelaide, 1968, p. 108.

9 WB Spencer, *Wanderings in Wild Australia,* Macmillan, London, 1928, p. 412.

10 WH Willshire, *The Land of the Dreaming,* WK Thomas & Co, Adelaide, 1896, pp. 20, 50.

11 Herbert Basedow, *Knights of the Boomerang,* Angus and Robertson, Sydney, 1935, p. 93; Arch Grant, *Camel Train & Aeroplane: The Story of Skipper Partridge,* Frontier Publishing, Erskineville, 1989, p. 121.

12 Strehlow, pp. 295, 588–93; Reid, p. 118.

13 *Ibid,* p. 592.

Jan **Critchett**

Encounters in the Western District

The Western District of Victoria roughly corresponds with the Portland Bay District, an administrative unit formed to control expansion of pastoral settlement in the southwest extremity of the colony of New South Wales, which then included what we now know as Victoria. The district extends west from the Werribee River to the South Australian border and south from the Great Dividing Range to the sea. In the late 1830s and early 1840s, it established a reputation as one of the two worst areas of racial violence in the colony of New South Wales, the other being the Liverpool Plains, north of Sydney. As RHW Reece has noted: 'The spate of attacks on property and life in these two areas, reaching a climax in 1842–3, was even referred to by some contemporaries as an Aboriginal "rising" in the colony'.[1] In this chapter I consider three questions: what was the most distinctive feature of this frontier; to what extent was there resistance to European settlement; and how violent were relations between Aborigines and Europeans on this frontier?

Charles Joseph La Trobe, Superintendent of the Port Phillip District, found the Western District a difficult area in which to keep the peace. His developing understanding of this frontier can be traced in his responses to an increasingly irritated Governor of New South Wales, Sir George Gipps, during the second half of 1840. First, he pointed out the extended nature of the district: 'settlers had dispersed themselves over an extent of country full 350 miles in length and 150 in breadth'. It was impossible, given the limited number of troops available (two Police Magistrates, one at Melbourne, the other at Geelong, each aided by a small number of mounted troopers and one Crown Lands Commissioner with a 'yet smaller detachment' of border police), to protect those who 'transport themselves to such a distance, and throw themselves in the way of numerous and active tribes'. Later, he elaborated:

Of the very large number of stations now scattered over the face of the country ...

> at a distance of from 50 to 200 miles and upwards from the towns of Melbourne and Geelong, a considerable majority may be considered open to attack from one or other division of the tribes surrounding the district, or comprised within its limits and these attacks ... are seldom to be anticipated.

He expressed despair, admitting the existing police force was hopelessly inadequate to keep the peace. The situation was only marginally improved with the August 1840 appointment of a Police Magistrate to Portland. In November La Trobe reported: 'the peace of the district cannot be preserved by any police force which can be mustered or maintained in the present circumstances of the colony'.[2]

By early 1842, when he replied to a petition from the 'Settlers and Inhabitants of the Port Fairy District' asking for protection against Aboriginal attacks, La Trobe was aware of the most distinctive feature of the Western District frontier:

> situated as you are, it is far easier to deplore your losses than to prevent them. The evils you complain of, are those which have everywhere accompanied the occupation of a new country inhabited by savage tribes. Even under circumstances far more favourable ... for instance, where a well defined frontier or neutral ground could be interposed between the civilised and uncivilised — I need scarcely remind you, how little real security has been enjoyed. Here there is not even such a line; the savage tribes are not only upon our borders, but *intermingled with us in every part of this wide district.*[3]

This one might expect of any area of contact where Europeans invaded land occupied by Aborigines. 'Country' in Aboriginal English, as Deborah Bird Rose has pointed out, 'is not a generalised ... place such as one might indicate with terms like "spending a day in the country"' but a specific place, that has its own 'sacred origins, its sacred and dangerous places, its sources of life and its sites of death'. Each 'country' 'is surrounded by other countries'; 'Aboriginal Australia', she notes further, 'is made up of a series of "promised lands", each with its own "chosen people"'. [4] In a Western District case, for example, the Aborigines ordered Europeans to leave their 'country': 'It was their country, and the water belonged to them', they told the Chief Protector of Aborigines, George Augustus Robinson, 'and if it was taken away they could not go to another country, for they would be killed'.[5]

The frontier, meaning the area of contact and conflict, was the whole district, but it was also true that each settler had local Aborigines either living on or close to what he now called his squatting run. Hence, the frontier was a very local phenomenon, the disputed area being the land each settler occupied. It was represented by the Aboriginal woman who lived nearby and was shared by her Aboriginal partner with European men; it was the group living down beside the creek or river, as they did on many properties; it was the 'boy' used as a guide for exploring parties or for doing jobs now and then; and it was the 'civilised' Aborigine employed as a stockman. The 'other side of the frontier' was just down the yard or as close as the bed shared with an Aboriginal woman. It was this intermingling of the races that determined when and where hostility was shown, for it occurred in response to local conditions. It heightened the anxiety of both Aborigines and settlers and was central to La Trobe's problem of keeping the peace.

In this area, the Aboriginal population was relatively large and settlement was rapid. All of southeastern Australia was experiencing drought at this time but the effect in the Western District, where rivers and streams, even in years of normal rainfall, become a series of waterholes in summer, was particularly severe. Many squatters and their men arrived with as many as 1000 sheep and 200 cattle, all in need of water, and this caused even the earliest settlers to leapfrog over those who had already taken up land in an effort to seize one of the best watered spots further on, places on which the Aborigines were also dependent. This ensured early and close contact between the races across the district. Finally, this was an attractive area for those looking for pasture; by the mid-1840s, with 282 pastoral runs, it was more closely settled than any other part of the Port Phillip District and there was no longer any unoccupied land.

In *The Other Side of the Frontier,* Henry Reynolds argued that black resistance was an inescapable feature of life on the fringes of European settlement from the first months at Sydney Cove, with the intensity and duration of conflict varying widely. Did Western District Aborigines resist European settlement or was there peaceful occupation? If they did resist, what form did it take and what was the intensity and duration of the resistance?[6]

Aboriginal attacks on European men or their sheep, cattle or horses took place from the beginnings of European settlement. The first request in the Western District for government protection against Aboriginal attacks was made in mid-1837 by those who had taken up runs around Geelong. By September 1840, Crown Lands Commissioner Foster Fyans, returning from his first tour of the district, reported that 'every gentleman's establishment' had been 'molested by the natives'. The duration of 'outrages' varied across the district. There was little conflict east of the Hopkins River (half-way across the district) after 1842, while west of the Hopkins attacks continued well into 1847.[7]

Thirty-five Europeans were killed by Aborigines between 1834 and 1848, invariably one or two at a time. An analysis of the details surrounding the death of the Europeans killed by Aborigines suggests that it is likely these individuals had been singled out for specific reasons. Murder, however, was not the outrage of which most settlers complained. It was stealing, sometimes of cattle, calves and horses but usually sheep, all expensive and hard to replace in this period. It is difficult to be sure why Aborigines stole sheep. Some were taken and eaten, others were driven long distances and kept in fenced yards until they were needed, others were left behind crippled and no longer of value, their hind-legs having been dislocated. There is some evidence that the aim was to remove the Europeans from their country. At Niel Black's Glenormiston station, near present-day Terang, where the massacre of Aborigines allegedly by Frederick Taylor was followed by attempts to keep away those who had survived, the 'remnants of the tribes' frequently came 'in a body of twenty and thirty at a time threatening to murder the [shepherds] unless they left them the place'. Joseph, a shepherd employed by Thomas Learmonth at Buninyong, reported that the Aborigines repeatedly told him in their own language 'to go or they would kill me'. Home stations were attacked as well as isolated shepherds and hut-keepers. Patrick Codd, overseer and book-keeper for the Wedges, for example, told the Assistant Protector of Aborigines of an attack by 18 to 20 Aborigines on the Wedges's head station on the Grange River. The swivel gun mounted there indicated such an attack was not unexpected. The Manifold brothers, first to take up the land near present-day Camperdown, had their homestead twice burnt down by the Aborigines before a third, built of stone, survived. Aborigines also deliberately burnt off grass close to Europeans.[8]

The year of greatest racial conflict was 1842. In August, the *Portland Mercury* reported: 'the country might as well be in a state of civil war, as few but the boldest of the settlers will move from their home stations'. The petition of the 'Settlers and Inhabitants of the Port Fairy District' provides an indication of the seriousness of attacks. Over what they claimed was a two-month period, 25 properties had been attacked and the Aborigines had stolen or killed more than 4000 sheep, 10 horses, 23 cows, 4 bulls and 150 calves, as well as robbing a number of huts, killing four men and wounding eight. Foster Fyans's list of squatters who suffered from Aboriginal attacks between December 1841 and June 1842 confirms the large number of properties attacked.[9]

What distinguished Aboriginal actions of this time and later is that those who are named as leaders — Koort Kirrup, Cold Morning, Jupiter, Cocknose, Charley and Mr Murray — had considerable experience of European ways, sometimes having lived and worked as a trusted employee on a station. Furthermore, as James Blair, Police Magistrate at Portland, wrote to La Trobe, there was 'a general move among the aborigines'. Virtually the whole area west of the Hopkins River was caught up in a wave of attacks destructive of sheep, cattle, buildings and equipment. Many more lives were threatened than earlier. Previously Europeans had complained that the Aborigines used guerrilla tactics: they attacked and disappeared. Now Aborigines 'closed with their antagonists'. Formerly they had attacked during the winter months. Now they did so throughout the year. This, one might argue, was an attempt by the Aborigines to remove the Europeans from their country. While there is no evidence of cooperation among Aboriginal groups across the district, the wave of attacks came at the same time and there is some evidence of nearby clans joining together in attacks.[10]

How violent was this frontier? Does the evidence from this region support Reynolds's contention that 'settlement occasioned mass violence. It grew out of the barrel of the gun'? Or does it support Keith Windschuttle's claim that massacres 'were unusual events, "rare and isolated", with their own specific causes', and the 'picture of the Australian frontier as a war zone where whites could kill blacks with impunity … a myth'?[11] In the 1980s, I examined the official records and concluded that approximately 300 Aborigines were shot or poisoned before 1850. But, if one adds up what would appear to be conservative numbers for those incidents that were widely acknowledged in the district at the time, although not necessarily officially recorded, a figure of at least 350 Aborigines killed seems likely.[12]

Recently, Lyndall Ryan referred to my count as an example to illustrate the difficulty of estimating the numbers of Aborigines killed on the frontier. The problem, she argued, is not lack of evidence. 'Rather it is a case of working out how many Aborigines could have been killed in each encounter. In the end the historian relies on her own judgement and knowledge of the field.' An examination of three depositions regarding the same incident reveals the discrepancies one finds. In this case, the depositions are taken on different days with the individuals interviewed on different properties. They concern a 'collision' in late June 1840 between Aylward, Knolles (Knowles) and Tulloch, and a group of Aborigines. The Aborigines had stolen sheep and the men looking for them came across a large party of Aborigines. Aylward estimated the Aborigines to number nearly 300, Knolles more than 150, and Tulloch about 500. The Europeans, on horseback, fired on them and then retreated; the Aborigines followed them; as soon as the three men had reloaded their guns, they charged again with the Aborigines fleeing before them. The 'engagement' lasted quarter of a hour. Aylward reported that 'there must have been a great many wounded, and several killed ... saw two or three dead bodies'; Knolles reported: 'Some of the Natives must have been wounded, but I saw none dead'. How many should one add to Aylward's report of those killed? I added five.[13]

In listing individual incidents in an appendix to my book A *'Distant Field of Murder'*, I supplied the varying numbers of those killed taken from different sources, but in reaching a total I added the number at the minimal end rather than the top end of the estimates, unless there was overwhelming evidence supporting the upper figure. I now believe it would have been helpful had I suggested a possible range for my count — that is, to have provided both a lower and an upper figure, with all the supporting documentation.

Although some of those who died in massacres were members of large groups, I recorded only 11 incidents for which there are official records in which eight or more Aborigines were killed. The native police were responsible for two of these. There were only three incidents in which over 30 Aborigines were killed: an encounter about 1833–34 between whalers and Aborigines over a beached whale on a part of the coast near Portland, called thereafter the Convincing Ground; the Murdering Gully massacre of 1839, in which a party of Europeans led by Frederick Taylor, superintendent on Glenormiston station, in the vicinity of present-day Terang, killed between 35 and 40 men, women and children in retaliation for taking sheep; and the Fighting Hills massacre of March 1840, in which between 30 and 51 Aborigines were killed after sheep were stolen from the Whyte brothers' run, Konongwootong, near Coleraine.[14]

The most common kind of incident involved the death of one or two Aborigines. In Ian Clark's detailed study of massacres and killings in the Western District, 53 out of the 107 entries are of this kind. Windschuttle has argued that massacres were rare and isolated but Reynolds has never claimed anything else. On the contrary, he has remarked that it 'has been obvious to anyone who has worked in the field' that most Aborigines were not killed in massacres but in ones and twos.[15]

The number of Aborigines killed in conflict with Europeans was, I now believe, far larger than my previous estimate. I have several reasons for asserting this. Clark's *Register* reveals how few *recorded* 'massacres and killings' there are in some areas of the district. Take, for example, the Girai wurrung and Djargurd wurrung — whose territory stretched from Warrnambool east to Lake Corangamite, and from the coast north to Lake Bolac, Derrinallum and Cressy — an area in which it was widely believed that killing Aborigines was necessary. Niel Black, for example, wrote to his partner: 'A few days since I found a Grave into which about 20 must have been thrown. A Settler taking up a new country *is obliged to act towards them in this manner* or abandon it.' As for Aboriginal women, 'it is no uncommon thing for these rascals to sleep all night with a Lubra — and if she poxes him or in any way offends him perhaps shoot her before 12 next day'. It is also the area about which the editor of the *Hampden Guardian* commented that its history would never be written for it 'would be such a long record of oppression, outrage, wrong, and cold blooded murder on the part of the "superior race" that it dare not be, and, therefore, never will be written'. Yet the *Register* lists three entries only.[16]

Second, one would expect many casualties in the district, since the response of the squatters and their men was to ask for government protection and to deal with matters themselves when it was not provided. (Aborigines in the Portland Bay District did not see a military force before 1842.) In such circumstances, settlers could not be expected to behave in a disinterested manner. In early 1842, La Trobe warned Police Magistrate Blair of the need for vigilance:

> The passions of men, circumstanced like the settlers in this colony, are easily
> excited; and even with regard to the superior education and standing of many of
> them, I need not remind you how very liable the mind of man is to be moulded by
> the position in which he may find himself placed, and especially in circumstances
> so materially affecting his interests.

Hunting parties were still dealing with attacks around Dunmore to the east of Mt Eeles in 1845 despite the presence of border police and native police for part of each year. At this time, William Campbell implored the Government to send a force to protect the settlers, arguing that it should be placed under the control of the magistrates or

James Dawson's memorial
obelisk to the Aborigines
Australasian Sketcher,
7 April 1886
National Library of Australia

In Camperdown in Victoria's Western District, James Dawson, friend and
guardian of the Aborigines, erected a monument 'In memory of the Aborigines
of this District ... The date 1840 at the top of the column is the commencement of
the extinction of the local tribes; ... and at bottom, 1883, the date of their total
extinction'. Dawson suggested that 'extirpation' was a more appropriate term
than 'extinction'. Dawson sought donations to the memorial from local
landowners, but with little success. One wrote: 'I decline to assist in erecting a
monument to a race of men we have robbed of their country'.
(Quoted in Tom Griffiths, *Hunters and Collectors*, p. 113.)

other gentlemen in the neighbourhood, to be ready to be called out when needed. 'At present', he wrote, 'the settler had a very difficult [path?] to sustain. He may be obliged to have recourse to bloodshed, in defence of his life and property'.[17]

Third, there is clear evidence that squatters in this district tried to conceal information about actions taken against the Aborigines. Niel Black and other highly respected squatters fabricated a story to protect the men who shot several Aboriginal women and a child sleeping in ti-tree scrub at Muston's Creek; and Annie Maria Baxter, wife of Captain Andrew Baxter of the pastoral run, Yambuck, failed to report an incident in which a local European had shot two Aboriginal children, killing one and seriously wounding the other, even though she was sympathetic to Aborigines.[18]

Was it true whites could kill blacks with impunity? These cover-ups suggest they were not entirely sure that they could. Some no doubt thought so, especially in the years before 1842. There were then few officials to observe their actions. The small number of police has already been noted. Even the Port Phillip Protectorate officials, Chief Protector Robinson and Assistant Protector CW Sievwright, were slow to move into the district: Robinson did not begin his work in the region until early 1841; Sievwright, although ordered 'to take the field' in March 1839, only arrived at Mt Rouse, in the heart of the district, in February 1842. But La Trobe reacted strongly, for example, when there were allegations by a Wesleyan missionary of the continued wanton destruction of the natives by the settlers in the district. He sent Police Magistrate Blair 'to investigate whether men went out on the Sabbath, professedly to shoot kangaroo, but in reality to shoot natives in cold blood'. He also made it clear he was outraged at the murder of the women and child shot sleeping in the scrub at Muston's Creek, calling on settlers to clear their names from suspicion of involvement and asking them to come forward and provide him with the names of the murderers.[19]

The squatter Tom Browne, whose run was located in Nillan gundidtj country, expressed the squatter's dilemma:

> We could not permit our cattle to be harried, our servants to be killed, and ourselves to be hunted out of the good land we had occupied by a few savages.
>
> Our difficulty was heightened by its being necessary to behave in a quasi-legal manner. Shooting blacks, except in manifest self-defence, had been always held to be murder in the Supreme Courts of the land, and occasionally punished as such.

Most escaped without punishment. Only five men from the Portland Bay District were tried for shooting Aborigines and just one, John Stokel, was found guilty — and then not of murder, but of the lesser charge of inflicting grievous bodily harm. He was imprisoned for only two months. Few men were brought to trial, partly because those who were collecting evidence did not reach the area for a considerable time. This gave the perpetrators time to flee to another colony. Yet, one could not guarantee that one would not be prosecuted. Stokel, for example, went to prison.[20]

The Western District frontier was relatively brief but an abundance of evidence suggests that settlement occasioned considerable violence and that this was one of the worst areas of frontier conflict in the colony of New South Wales. The frontier's most distinctive feature was the fact that Aborigines and pastoralists were in close contact right across the district. The result of this intermingling was violence since their interests, as the surveyor and pastoralist John Helder Wedge stated, were 'directly opposed to each other' and both had 'much at stake'. In fact, for the Aborigines and some pastoralists *everything* was at stake. Aboriginal attacks began soon after settlement and persisted across the district until in each case the local clan accepted the futility of continuing their resistance given their violence met with its equal and considerably more. This took several years longer in the area west of the Hopkins River but by 1848 peace had been achieved. Dispossession was complete.[21]

1 RHW Reece, *Aborigines and Colonists: Aborigines and Colonial Society in New South Wales in the 1830s and 1840s*, Sydney University Press, Sydney, 1974, p. 23.

2 CJ La Trobe to Colonial Secretary, 28 August 1841, House of Commons Sessional Paper, Aborigines (Australian Colonies), Return to an Address, *British Parliamentary Papers*, vol. 34, 1844, p. 133; La Trobe to Colonial Secretary, date unknown, headed Report, No. 3, Aborigines (Australian Colonies), Return to an Address, *British Parliamentary Papers*, vol. 34, 1844, pp. 138–9; La Trobe to Colonial Secretary, 21 November 1840, Aborigines (Australian Colonies), Return to an Address, *British Parliamentary Papers*, vol. 34, 1844, p. 139.

3 La Trobe to the Gentlemen signing a Representation without date, 26 March 1842, Aborigines (Australian Colonies), Return to an Address, *British Parliamentary Papers*, vol. 34, 1844, p. 214, my emphasis.

4 Deborah Bird Rose, *Nourishing Terrains: Australian Aboriginal Views of Landscape and Wilderness*, Australian Heritage Commission, Canberra, 1996, pp. 7, 9; David Turner, 'The incarnation of Nambirrirrma', in Tony Swain and Rose (eds), *Aboriginal Australians and*

Christian Missions: Ethnographic and Historical Studies, Australian Association for the Study of Religions, Bedford Park, 1988, p. 479.

5 George Augustus Robinson to La Trobe, 30 December 1843, Aborigines (Australian Colonies), Return to an Address, *British Parliamentary Papers*, vol. 34, 1844, p. 282.

6 Henry Reynolds, *The Other Side of the Frontier*, Penguin, Ringwood, 1982, p. 61.

7 Michael Cannon (ed.), *Beginnings of Permanent Government, Historical Records of Victoria Foundation Series*, vol. 1, Victorian Government Printing Office, Melbourne, 1981, p. 220; Foster Fyans to La Trobe, 20 September 1840, Aborigines (Australian Colonies), Return to an Address, *British Parliamentary Papers*, vol. 34, 1844, p. 89.

8 Niel Black to Gladstone, 5 August 1840, Letterbook, La Trobe Library, MS 8996; T Learmonth's shepherd, deposition dated 27 July 1838, Victorian Public Record Office, VPRS 109; Statement by Patrick Codd, 6 March 1840, Aborigines (Australian Colonies), Return to an Address, *British Parliamentary Papers*, vol. 34, 1844,

p. 142; Rodney Hall, *JS Manifold:
An Introduction to the Man and his Work*, University of
Queensland Press, St Lucia, 1978, p. 12.

9 *Portland Mercury*, 31 August 1842; Aborigines
(Australian Colonies), Return to an Address, *British
Parliamentary Papers*, vol. 34, 1844, pp. 213–14; *Geelong
Advertiser*, 4 April 1842; Foster Fyans, Itinerary for
March to June 1842, Victorian Public Record Office, VPRS
19, 42/178 enclosed in 42/2364.

10 James Blair to La Trobe, 29 January 1842, Aborigines
(Australian Colonies), Return to an Address, *British
Parliamentary Papers*, vol. 34, 1844, p. 202; Acheson
French to La Trobe, 8 August 1842, Letterbook, 1 October
1841–10 October 1842, La Trobe Library, MS 10053; James
Hunter to La Trobe, 1 September 1842, Aborigines
(Australian Colonies), Return to an Address, *British
Parliamentary Papers*, vol. 34, 1844, p. 234.

11 Henry Reynolds, 'Foreword', in Ian Clark, *Scars in the
Landscape: A Register of Massacre Sites in Western
Victoria*, 1803–1859, Aboriginal Studies Press, Canberra,
1995, pp. ix, x. Keith Windschuttle, 'When history falls
victim to politics', *Age*, 14 July 2001.

12 See Jan Critchett, *A 'Distant Field of Murder':
Western District Frontiers 1834–1848*, Melbourne
University Press, Melbourne, 1992, pp. 242–55, 130–1.
Despite the undeniable loss of life in encounters
between Aborigines and settlers, this was not the only,
or even the most significant, cause of the decline in the
size of the Aboriginal population. Aborigines killed
other Aborigines and large numbers died from the
effects of European-introduced diseases.

13 Lyndall Ryan, 'The Aboriginal history wars',
Australian Historical Association Bulletin, no. 92, 2001,
p. 37; Critchett, p. 124.

14 The figure of 51 was given by a neighbour, John G
Robertson. See Robertson's letter in Thomas Francis
Bride (ed.), *Letters from Victorian Pioneers: A Series of
Papers on the Early Occupation of the Colony, the*

Aborigines etc. (1898), Lloyd O'Neil, Melbourne, 1969,
p. 164. For more detail on the massacres, see Clark and
Critchett.

15 Clark, p. 9; Reynolds, 'Black deaths: The evidence
abounds', *Age*, 28 September 2000.

16 Cited in Margaret Kiddle, *Men of Yesterday: A Social
History of the Western District of Victoria*, Melbourne
University Press, Melbourne, 1962, pp. 121–2, my
emphasis; *Hampden Guardian*, 12 September 1876.

17 La Trobe to Blair, 12 February 1842, Aborigines
(Australian Colonies), Return to an Address, *British
Parliamentary Papers*, vol. 34, 1844, p. 204; William
Campbell to La Trobe, 22 July 1845, Victorian Public
Record Office, VPRS 19, 45/1370. Sometimes the hunting
parties consisted simply of squatters and their men. The
squatters sometimes joined parties led by a police
magistrate, a local JP or the Crown Lands Commissioner.
The native police were sometimes accompanied by
others, and the commandant of the native police
occasionally authorised squatters to lead the force
against Aborigines involved in 'outrages'.

18 See Critchett, pp. 118–19, 137–9.

19 Evidence of La Trobe's strong handling of the claim
by the Wesleyan missionary can be found in Aborigines
(Australian Colonies), Return to an Address, *British
Parliamentary Papers*, vol. 34, 1844, pp. 183–93; La Trobe
to the Gentlemen signing a Representation without
date, 26 March 1842, Aborigines (Australian Colonies),
Return to an Address, *British Parliamentary Papers*,
vol. 34, 1844, pp. 214–15, provides his response to the
Muston's Creek murders.

20 Rolf Boldrewood, *Old Melbourne Memories* (1884),
William Heinemann, Melbourne, 1969, p. 57. All of Tom
Browne's work was published under the pseudonym
Rolf Boldrewood.

21 Aborigines (Australian Colonies), Return to an
Address, *British Parliamentary Papers*, vol. 34, 1844,
p. 119.

Raymond **Evans**

Across the Queensland frontier

Travelling through central Queensland in early 1862, a French representative of the Geographical Society of Geneva, Edouard Marcet, described himself and his party as *'arme jusqu'aux dents'*, that is, 'armed to the teeth' with carbines, pistols and knives against the threat of Aboriginal attack. On a journey from Logan Downs to the coast, he was wary of lighting camp fires for fear of attracting hostile attention and kept a gun at hand on all occasions. Stumbling on a group of Aborigines for the first time while circumventing a bushfire, his first reaction was to gallop his horse into their midst, firing off six shots from his 'pistolet' and scattering them in panic in all directions.[1]

A decade later, a British migrant, Augustus Cutlack, recalled how his first encounter with an Aborigine on the outskirts of Brisbane had terminated with his drawing a 'long sheath knife' on the man after the latter had remonstrated with him for matches. In late 1873, Cutlack joined an expedition of surveyors, government officials, police and navvies sent to open the port of Cooktown for the Palmer gold rush into the Cape hinterland. Four months later, there were 60 vessels riding at anchor in the Endeavour River, disgorging miners and supplies. Cutlack wrote: 'Many were the shooting parties formed and as there was no game to kill, it consisted of making repeated attacks on the blacks. Each day a shooting party was out somewhere and all *armed to the teeth'*.[2]

Both the Frenchman in 1862 and the Englishman in 1873 found themselves on frontiers which, from both sides, bristled with weaponry. The passions of fear, anxiety and vengeance were running high in these regions and European attitudes towards Aborigines as the hated and despised 'other' were intense. 'The aboriginals', Cutlack wrote, 'are a low, savage, treacherous looking race of people ... [They] are the most degraded race on the face of the earth. They are dirty, lazy ... specimens of human beings'.

Both frontiers were suffused with acts of violence and terror, a consequence of both a single-minded determination to dispossess and a spirited indigenous defence.[3]

In 1862, as Lorna McDonald has commented, central Queensland was arguably the centre of Australian 'pioneer warfare', beginning with the Mt Larcom tragedy in December 1855 where six station workers were killed by the Darumbal; leading into the Hornet Bank killings of October 1857 where 11 whites had perished at the hands of the Jiman; on to the rape and murder of Fanny Briggs, a former Sydney barmaid, in Rockhampton by native policemen in November 1859; continuing with the slaughter of two parties of Europeans at Castle Creek and Clematis Creek in the lower and upper Dawson, respectively, in early 1860; and culminating in the unprecedented massacre of 19 settlers out of a party of 22 by the Kairi at Cullin-La-Ringo, south of Emerald in October 1861. In four of the above six incidents, white women had perished as well as men; and in three of them, the women were also raped. European retaliation was incendiary and ungovernable. Following the loss of some 40 European lives, 'untold hundreds' of Aborigines perished in payback campaigns of mass destruction involving white vigilantes and native police. Perhaps 500 or more were killed in total, and the Jiman, Wadja, Kairi, and Darumbal peoples were reduced to small groups.[4]

By the early 1870s, when Augustus Cutlack travelled north, the scene of major carnage had shifted to the Cape York region, and especially to the coastline and hinterland between Cardwell and the Endeavour River. Violent reprisals seem to have become particularly intense following the wreck of the *Maria* on Bramble Reef, when a dozen or so shipwrecked New Guinea gold-seekers were killed by the Djiri in late February 1872. Reprisal raids by native police, marines, local settlers and vigilantes from Sydney continued for many months.[5]

Charles Heydon, who had come north on the *Governor Blackall* to search for or avenge the missing men, was sickened by what he observed. During early 1874, he wrote to the *Sydney Morning Herald*:

> I heard white men talk openly of the share they had taken in slaughtering whole
> camps, not only of men, but of women and children. They said that the gins were
> as bad as the men, and that the picaninnies, all their tribe being killed, would die
> of starvation if not also put out of the way.

Heydon wrote, however, specifically to protest at activities then occurring on the

Endeavour River, to which Augustus Cutlack was also witness. 'Private persons go out to kill blacks and call it "snipe-shooting"', Heydon alleged:

> Awkward words are always avoided you will notice. 'Shooting a snipe' sounds better than 'murdering a man'. But the blacks are never called men and women and children; 'myalls' and 'niggers' and 'gins' and 'picaninnies' seem further removed from humanity … What right have 'myalls' to exist at all — mischievous vermin with their ignorance, and their barbarism, and their degradation and their black skins?

Heydon later became a New South Wales supreme court judge and attorney-general in the 1890s. Writing in support of his son's charges, Jabez Heydon told FW Chesson of the Aborigines' Protection Society in London: 'Nothing short of English interference will avail … [against] this deplorable state of things … Public opinion in Queensland is all against the Blacks'.[6]

Summing up the ongoing conflict in February 1877, a correspondent to the *Cooktown Courier* stated:

> This district has been settled over three years; armed police to a considerable number have been waging war with the blacks, and private individuals have been doing a good deal of shooting among them … [and yet] we can only be secure in patches … no man can put a reasonable limit to the bloodshed and expense that will be necessary under our present system, before we reckon on security equal to that enjoyed in central and southern Queensland.[7]

These arresting images from northern and central Queensland over a 20-year period raise questions about the nature of colonial frontiers which continue to reverberate: Was the taking and settlement of Queensland more conflict-ridden and violent than that of other Australian colonies? And just how conflict-ridden and violent was it?

Following the news of mass settler reprisals after the Wills massacre of 1861, Rev. John West, Australia's foremost colonial historian, asked in mock astonishment of Queensland, 'Is it a part of Her Majesty's domains?', and went on to charge that its government was complicit in a policy of 'extermination'. Three years later, Gideon Scott Lang told a Melbourne audience that whereas in Queensland:

> there has always been more destruction of the blacks in occupying new country than in any other colony … within the last few years it has been wholesale and indiscriminate and carried on with a cold blooded cruelty on the part of the whites quite unparalleled in the history of these colonies.

Lang did not speak as a soft-hearted humanitarian. In fact, he had himself utilised the native police against the Mandandanji people when he had held squatting runs covering 400,000 hectares of the East Maranoa region of southwestern Queensland in the 1850s.[8] In response to any suggestion that Lang might be embellishing his case by alleging that eradication was being accomplished with 'no more compunction or responsibility than if [the Aborigines] were vermin', a British Colonial Office official ventured in January 1866:

> I believe it to be by no means easy to exaggerate the recklessness with which blacks
> have been destroyed (in some cases by strychnine like foxes) in Queensland. But
> the Home Government can but hold up its hands. There is no effectual power to
> interfere in their cause.

Here was a striking recognition, from the highest official sanctum, of Queensland's uniqueness in delivering its 'special treatment' to indigenous peoples, as well as an equally arresting admission of the imperial government's powerlessness to intervene since colonial self-government had been granted in 1856 and Queensland had become a separate colony in 1859.[9]

In early 1868, in response to press reports of a native police massacre of unoffending Aborigines at their camp on the Morinish goldfield, inland from Rockhampton, Chesson of the Aborigines' Protection Society argued that the level of official neglect and culpability concerning 'barbarous outrages' was unexampled in the colonies. 'Many of the leading journalists and public men of Australia have given utterance to strong feelings of indignation at the shocking state of things in Queensland', he concluded. Yet the Colonial Office continued to register its impotence 'beyond raising their voice' in verbal protest at the colony's excessive behaviour.[10]

'Putting it in plain English this is what we Queenslanders do', the editor of the *Cooktown Courier* commented a decade later: 'we set the Native Police on [the Aboriginal inhabitants] to make them "quiet". This is effected by massacring them indiscriminately'. In a series of well-researched, sensational disclosures in the *Queenslander* in mid-1880, entitled 'The way we civilise', editor Gresley Lukin and an anonymous journalist, since recognised as Carl Feilberg, concurred that settler behaviour in Queensland 'fell far below British standards'. Of all the colonies, its editorials contended, 'we alone have descended to the "kinchen lay" of extermination ... a process which would shame us before our fellow-countrymen in every part of the

British Empire'. In response to 14 editorials written in this vein, a wide range of squatters and other old pioneers wrote long, detailed accounts of witnessed or reported atrocities, virtually all agreeing, either with profound regret or brazen acceptance, that a 'war of extermination' was going on.[11]

The dissemination of this forum in pamphlet form throughout the colonies and Great Britain led Sir Arthur Gordon, then Governor of New Zealand, to impress on Prime Minister William Gladstone in April 1883 Queensland's 'special unfitness' for colonial governance (and thus helped thwart its imperial ambitions in Papua). Gordon referred to an amplified 'tone of brutality and cruelty in dealing with "blacks" [in Queensland] which is very difficult for anyone who does not know it, as I do, to realise'. Another prominent colonial historian, GW Rusden was also prompted by 'The way we civilise' to mount a searing indictment of Queensland's frontier relations in his *History of Australia*, published in 1883. The very 'air of Queensland', he charged, 'reeks with atrocities committed and condoned'. Yet actions by perpetrators, government functionaries and their supporters to suppress evidence of happenings, much talked about yet less commonly recorded, threatened to see this history of excesses 'wither out of men's knowledge unexposed'.[12]

Rusden's fears were partially realised during the following century as less and less was spoken about Queensland's sanguine past. Hints of dark deeds still persisted in the popular media and in private white reminiscences, as well as in the sequestered oral cultures of Aboriginal people themselves. In 1900, for instance, the Brisbane *Worker,* then one of the most explicitly racist journals in Australia, could still comment in passing: 'We Queenslanders' ... treatment of our aboriginal races is, perhaps, the most shocking and callous on record'.[13] Yet, for the most part, for the next five or six decades, there would be mainly obfuscation, elision and silence on the subject.[14]

More recent academic histories of the frontier have tended to restore to Queensland the unenvied crown of having the most troublesome story of all the Australian colonies. In 1970, Charles Rowley ventured that Queensland's pastoral expansion and 'decades of attack on Aboriginal social gatherings' had dismembered these societies far more rapidly than in the Northern Territory or Western Australia. Living in north Queensland from the mid-1960s first activated Henry Reynolds to face the serious history of frontier violence and racism in Australia, much as living in southern Queensland did for me. In his recent work, *An Indelible Stain?*, Reynolds asks, 'was Queensland guilty of genocide?' and answers, 'there is certainly much evidence available for retrospective prosecution'. He does not move towards so forceful a conclusion in the case of the other colonies. Similarly, Pamela Lukin Watson concludes, based on her study of the Channel country: 'The kill ratio was higher in Queensland than elsewhere'. Lorna McDonald and Gordon Reid, investigating central Queensland, arrive at similar findings. By 1870, McDonald contends, 'Central Queensland pioneering warfare had exceeded in ferocity' all regions but Tasmania. Reid believes that the Europeans' 'terrible revenge' after Hornet Bank and Cullin-La-Ringo was of 'a scale bordering on genocide'.[15]

Younger historians, such as Dirk Moses and Alison Palmer, are even more trenchant. Moses views Queensland's frontier as 'the purest incarnation of the colonisation project'. In the nineteenth century, he writes:

> the use of government terror [via the Native Mounted Police] transformed local genocidal massacres by settlers into an official state-wide policy ... Nowhere in Australia did the objective and inherent implications of colonisation become so consciously embodied.

Palmer, in her recent comparative history, *Colonial Genocide,* agrees that 'the role of the Queensland Government was crucial'. It 'actively condoned the ongoing slaughter', she writes, 'and made no attempt to bring it to an end'. Instead it 'entertained a general, implicit policy to aid and encourage the destruction'. Such devastation was 'societal-led', as indicated by a wide range of private statements and actions 'to exterminate' indigenes, augmented by the native police which, by and large, functioned as 'a death squad aimed at eradicating Aborigines'. '[R]ecurrent, piecemeal massacres' culminated in 'large-scale decimation'.[16]

There are growing stockpiles of primary data, even from exclusively non-Aboriginal sources, to give such propositions considerable weight. How do we explain all this? And how do we arrive at a reasonable appreciation of the degree of violence that ensued?

There is much about the Queensland frontier experience that is as epic as it is gothic. Its racial conflict spreads across a vast temporal and geographical canvas. This arguably begins between white and black as early as William Jansz's rough intervention into Wik society on Western Cape York Peninsula in 1606.[17] It petered out a little more than 300 years later in the 1910s in roughly the same region. In September 1910,

Frank Bowman, a pastoralist of Rutland Plains on the southwestern Cape, was speared by a mission Aborigine following a protracted history of Aboriginal child theft, the forceful concubinage of women, and unpunished murders and floggings by Europeans in the region.[18] Around eight years later, a man named McKenzie was apparently killed by the Kaiadilt after a shooting and raping spree on Bendinck Island in the Gulf.[19] Small native police patrols in the Gulf country and the Cape persisted after Federation and into the early years of World War I; but the last official investigation of a native police massacre was at Moreton in northern Cape York in 1902, after troopers shot and killed four peaceable Aboriginal men from three different groups during a patrol.[20] Police Inspector James Galbraith also reported from Normanton around this time: 'the blacks are often dispersed by the station hands. Of course, such dispersals are not reported to the police'.[21] John Dymock has similarly recorded an Aboriginal massacre at Flick Yard station in the southwestern Gulf country in 1904. Killings around the Northern Territory–Queensland border seem to have continued beyond this date.[22]

Queensland frontiers covered a vast extent of territory, a landmass of 1.73 million square kilometres, almost one-quarter of the Australian total and two-and-a-half times the size of Texas. They ranged over temperate, sub-tropical and tropical zones, regions of heavy rainfall and great aridity: rainforested uplands, the 'extensive mudflats' of the Gulf, 'boulder-strewn highlands' of the southeast, the dry interior lowlands of the Great Artesian Basin, and 'massive sand barriers', continental and reef islands, numbering more than 1000, scattered along a coastline of more than 1000 kilometres.[23] Pervasive settlement over tens of thousands of years by scores of Aboriginal societies — numbering, it is now believed, more than 200,000 people — was confronted from the 1820s by permanent, largely British intrusions, which also penetrated this enormous region more thoroughly than in the other larger colonies of South and Western Australia.[24] With the beginning of pastoral occupation around 1840, the frontier did not merely spread; it galloped. By 1859, the year of separation from New South Wales, there were 1300 squatting stations, covering one-quarter of the new colony and grazing millions of sheep and tens of thousands of cattle, pigs and horses. In late 1862, Queensland's first Governor, Sir George Bowen, estimated that 'the tide of colonisation' was advancing by 200 miles or 320 kilometres each year.[25]

From 1858, mining frontiers, notable for their large, sudden population influxes and material rapacity, began opening alongside pastoral ones. They denuded forests, commandeered watercourses, killed off the fauna, introduced few domestic animals as compensation and rarely employed Aboriginal people — a recipe for intense Aboriginal resistance and human wastage. The Palmer, Hodgkinson, Mulgrave and Etheridge gold rushes into barely penetrated Aboriginal territories involved many thousands of Asians as well as Europeans and led to savage clashes.[26] The pastoral and mining rushes, which occurred in three great waves, had monopolised most of the Queensland landmass by the late 1880s, bordering a period of some 50 years of intense dispossession. By the 1890s, the migrant population had expanded by a factor of 13 on its size at separation and the rural population had increased almost 20-fold. Whereas this incoming society had grown from a handful of convicts and military in 1824 to around 400,000, the Aboriginal population had disastrously shrunk to approximately 25,000, a demographic slump of some 90 per cent, owing to a combination of disease, starvation, a rapidly falling birthrate and overt violence.[27]

Frontier expansion had therefore proceeded across the widest ambit of territories and landscapes over a long period, bringing massive disruption via a considerable range of developmental processes: penal, pastoral, agricultural, maritime and mining. Large populations over enormous areas had been brought into conflict, and, overall, these combined populations contained the broadest racial and ethnic diversities in Australia. It was also a highly masculine frontier, with male to female newcomer ratios as high as nine to one in far western Queensland.[28] It was the only colony where pastoral, mining, maritime and plantation frontiers were advancing simultaneously; and all this occurred as Western racist theories, grouped around polygenism and social Darwinism, were peaking in their certitude and influence. AT Yarwood and MJ Knowling write of Queensland's intellectual situation as special in this regard, as respectable scientific ideas gave rise to racial attitudes, values and behaviours 'in their most concentrated form'. Ideas that allowed indigenous people to be leached of their humanity rendered them vulnerable to all manner of ill treatment. As a Ravenswood miner, David Cormack, wrote to his sister in November 1880, 'I have knowen [sic] plenty of men in this Country that will shoot the poor things for Sport ... same as we used to shoot rabbits'.[29]

But if scientific respectability provided succour for racial excesses, so too did Queensland legislatures, which effectively sanctioned violence through the medium of the native police corps. This force of up to 150 non-Aboriginal officers utilised around

1000 troopers over its lifespan, and from May 1849 it performed as a military unit to suppress indigenous resistance.[30] Many of its activities were routine and non-destructive, but its essentially decentralised structure allowed for maximum local autonomy and discretion in the deployment of force. White officers, leading squads of well-armed 'foreign' Aboriginal fighters, numbering usually between 6 and 12, were engaged in continual monthly patrolling of troubled frontier zones. Such patrols led to frequent 'collisions' and 'dispersals' in which large numbers of local Aborigines — and sometimes native police officers and troopers themselves — died. The force's official foundations and procedures remain murky. Essentially, it operated within a legal twilight zone between normal policing activities and unsanctioned military engagements, with a strong bias towards the latter. Thus it fought what was essentially a war without the necessity of declaring one, thereby freeing itself from any of the obligations military law demanded. At its most lethal, it cut a bloody swathe through Aboriginal communities, often wiping out whole clans, especially in central, north and western Queensland. Its operations peaked as Western technology transformed the gun from a weapon barely a match for the spear-thrower to a repeating rifle capable of considerable destruction. By the early 1870s, the force was equipped with Snider carbines, and by the early 1880s it was using Martini-Henrys. Other technologies, such as the telegraph, the steamboat and the railways, were just as vital to the force's efficiency. The horse alone was not responsible for its remarkable mobility.

Despite pessimistic assertions that most native police records are unavailable due to destruction or intense secrecy, the principal contours of the corps' work is gradually being pieced together through a painstaking trawling of archival files, newspaper runs and manuscript collections. Many thousands of vital documents are now coming to light, especially in the records of the Queensland Justice Department, Colonial Secretary series, Police, Attorney General, Crown Solicitor's Office, Governors and Executive Council papers. Broadly speaking, it appears that the force operated at its most destructive on the Cardwell to Port Douglas coastal strip, the Cairns–Cooktown–Palmer goldfields triangle, the Gulf country, far western Queensland and the Maryborough to Mackay region of central Queensland, although its presence was painfully felt by most Aboriginal people — even on certain occasions those actually working on pastoral runs — from Brisbane to Birdsville, from Goondiwindi to Somerset.

Civilization in Queensland
Queensland Figaro,
January 1885
John Oxley Library

This double page spread and the accompanying article tell the story of a murder and kidnapping by native police at Irvinebank, inland from Cairns, in October 1884. Artists and writers often blamed the native police for frontier violence. Here, however, *Figaro* also takes aim at the Queensland Government, suggesting that it had trained black troopers in 'a career of murder and rape'.

Although the native police corps was the singularly most destructive institution, private settlers, alone or in vigilante parties, undoubtedly killed many more Aboriginal people. A ratio of two to one between settlers and the corps may be suggested. Aborigines fought back with all the tenacity they could muster. On the basis of research Bill Thorpe and I have conducted on the Moreton Bay penal settlement (1824–41), we have estimated that 38 whites were killed and a dozen or so wounded by Aborigines. From 1842 until 1859, another 250 white deaths were contemporaneously enumerated; and, by 1866, the Queensland Executive Council would minute Lord Carnarvon, Secretary of State for the Colonies, that 'at least six hundred Englishmen [sic]' had now perished.[31] Noel Loos lists another 435 likely migrant deaths from frontier violence in north Queensland between 1867 and 1897. There were several other newcomer deaths beyond this date.[32] Additional to this tentative total of 1075, Clive Moore has recently traced Queensland's maritime frontier as it moved beyond the colonial landmass into Torres Strait, the southeast coast and eastern archipelagoes off New Guinea and eastward into the near Pacific. He has found more than 724 deaths of newcomers to the north of Cape York and in excess of 684 other foreign deaths in the Melanesian Pacific, that is, above 1400 more deaths in 584 ascertainable frontier incidents.[33]

The indigenous death and wounding rate can only be guessed. Contemporaries usually adopted a ten to one ratio, but Chief Protector of Aborigines for Southern Queensland, Archibald Meston, who interviewed members of 60 to 70 'tribes', suggested it could have been as many as 50 to 1. A vast primary data bank presently being compiled at Griffith University now claims to trace around 10,000 violent Aboriginal frontier deaths with supportive documentation. That is, these deaths are no longer a matter of mathematical projection or speculation. They can be known of, it is suggested, as most things in history are known, with relative certainty. Yet what can be projected from this new knowledge base is that the real death rate was possibly double this number.[34]

Among the biggest casualties on this frontier were veracity and justice. Despite all the slaughter, the rapes, the child theft and the general brutality that occurred, no European was successfully prosecuted for any crime against an Aboriginal person until 1883, when a Townsville man was sentenced to life imprisonment for the rape of an Aboriginal child.[35] Otherwise, the tragic events of a period variously described by contemporaries as 'the great fear', 'the wild time', 'the red, shocking years' and 'a "war" of sad ingloriousness' unfolded, challenged but unabated.[36]

[1] Edouard Marcet, *'Notice sur la partie de l'Australie recemment colonisee', Tiree des Memoires de la Societe de Geographie de Geneve,* tome III, Geneva, 1864, pp. 37, 47, 52, 58–61.

[2] AJ Cutlack, Four Years in Queensland and New South Wales, Rhodes House, Oxford University, mss Aust. r. 1, 1875, Chapters 5, 17 (unpaginated), my emphasis; Queensland Legislative Assembly, *Votes and Proceedings,* 1874, vol. I, p. 34.

[3] Cutlack, Chapter 4 (unpaginated).

[4] Lorna McDonald, *Rockhampton: A History of City and District,* University of Queensland Press, St Lucia, 1981, pp. 183–97; Gordon Reid, *A Nest of Hornets: The Massacre of the Fraser Family at Hornet Bank Station, Central Queensland, 1857, and Related Events,* Oxford University Press, Melbourne, 1992, pp. ix, 41, 65, 119; A Laurie, 'The Black War in Queensland', *Royal Historical Society of Queensland Journal,* vol. 1, no. 1, 1959, pp. 155–73.

[5] *Sydney Morning Herald,* 9 March 1873; A Hillier, 'If you leave me alone, I'll leave you alone': Geographical sketches, reports and incidents from the Myall war of the Queensland Native Mounted Police Force, 1860–1885, unpublished manuscript, p. 156; Raymond Evans and Bill Thorpe, 'Indigenocide and the massacre of Aboriginal history', *Overland,* no. 163, 2001, p. 28.

[6] *Sydney Morning Herald,* CG Heydon to the editor, 15 January 1874; *Queensland Journals of the Legislative Council,* 1875, vol. XXII, part 2, pp. 907–9; JK Heydon to FW Chesson, 20 March 1874, Public Record Office (UK), Queensland, no. 6302, CO234/34, XC/A/59034.

[7] *Cooktown Courier,* 21 February 1877.

[8] See PJ Collins, *Goodbye Bussamarai: The Mandandanji Land-war, Southern Queensland, 1842–1852,* University of Queensland Press, St Lucia, 2002, Chapters 9, 12.

[9] *Sydney Morning Herald,* 12 December 1861; GS Lang, *The Aborigines of Australia: In their Original Condition, and in their Relations with the White Man,* Wilson and McKennon, Melbourne, 1865, pp. 45–6; J Rogers, Colonial Office Minute, 29 January 1866, Public Record Office (UK), CO 234/13, 57283.

[10] Chesson to the Duke of Buckingham, Secretary of State for the Colonies, 15 January 1868, Public Record Office (UK), CO 234/21, 57510; Colonial Office minutes, 21 January 1867, Public Records Office (UK), CO 234/16, 57333.

[11] *Cooktown Courier,* 10 January 1877; Anon., *The Way We Civilize: Black and White. The Native Police,* G and J Black, Brisbane, 1880; *Queenslander,* 3 July 1880.

[12] GW Rusden, *History of Australia,* vol. 1, Chapman and Hall, London, 1883, pp. 239, 249.

[13] *Worker* (Brisbane), 2 June 1900.

[14] See Raymond Evans. 'Blood dries quickly: Conflict study and Australian historiography', *Australian Journal of Politics and History,* vol. 41, 1995, pp. 88–9.

[15] CD Rowley, *The Destruction of Aboriginal Society* (1970), Penguin, Ringwood, 1972, p. 186; Henry Reynolds, *An Indelible Stain?: The Question of Genocide in Australia's History,* Viking, Ringwood, 2001, pp. 117–18; Pamela Lukin Watson, *Frontier Lands and Pioneer Legends: How Pastoralists Gained Karuwali Land,* Allen & Unwin, St Leonards, 1998, p. 107; McDonald, p. 187; Reid, p. 138.

[16] A Dirk Moses, 'An antipodean genocide?: The origins of the genocidal moment in the colonisation of Australia', *Journal of Genocide Research,* vol. 2, no. 1, 2000, pp. 99, 102–3; Alison Palmer, *Colonial Genocide,* Crawford House, Adelaide, 2000, pp. 19–20, 49, 58, 62, 193.

[17] See NA Loos, 'Aboriginal–Dutch relations in north Queensland, 1606–1756', *Queensland Heritage,* vol. 3, no. 1, 1974, pp. 3–8.

[18] See Bruce A Sommer, 'The Bowman incident', in Luise Hercus and Peter Sutton (eds), *This is What Happened: Historical Narratives by Aborigines,* Australian Institute of Aboriginal Studies, Canberra, 1986, pp. 241–64. Bowman was speared by Jimmy Inkerman of Trubanaman Mission (later Kowanyama), who in turn was shot and killed by James McIntyre, a stockman accompanying Bowman.

[19] See Roma Kelly and Nicholas Evans, 'The McKenzie massacre on Bendinck Island', *Aboriginal History,* vol. 9, part 1, 1985, pp. 44–5. McKenzie and others raped numerous women and killed approximately 11 of the Kaiadilt, representing some 10 per cent of their number.

[20] See J Richards, 'Moreton telegraph station 1902: The native police on Cape York Peninsula', in Mike Enders and Benoit Dupont (eds), *Policing the Lucky Country,* Hawkins Press, Annandale, 2001, pp. 96–106.

[21] Inspector (and Aboriginal Protector) James Galbraith, 25 April 1901, quoted in William Roth, Report of the Northern Protector of Aborigines for 1902, Queensland Legislative Assembly, *Votes and Proceedings,* 1903, vol. II, p. 23.

[22] J Dymock, *Nicholas River Southern Gulf of Carpentaria: Wanji and Garama Land Claim,* Australian Government Publishing Service, Canberra, 1994, pp. 10, 44–5.

[23] D Wadley and W King (eds), *Reef, Range and Red Dust: The Adventure Atlas of Queensland,* Queensland Department of Lands, Brisbane, 1993, pp. viii, 66.

[24] William J Lines, *Taming the Great South Land: A History of the Conquest of Nature in Australia,* Allen & Unwin, St Leonards, 1991, p. 109. Lines places the pre-

contact indigenous population within 'the range of 750 000 to 900 000 people' (pp. 10–11). Noel Butlin places it inferentially at above 1 million (*Our Original Aggression: Aboriginal Populations of Southeastern Australia, 1788–1880,* Allen & Unwin, Sydney, 1983, p. 175). See also 'How many people?' in DJ Mulvaney and J Peter White (eds), *Australians to 1788,* Fairfax, Syme & Weldon, Broadway, 1987, pp. 115–17, where the authors conclude 'that an estimate of about 750,000 people is a reasonable one'.

25 George Bowen to Duke of Newcastle, Despatch 67, 3 November 1862, Queensland State Archives, Gov/23.

26 Noel Loos, *Invasion and Resistance: Aboriginal–European Relations on the North Queensland Frontier 1861–1897,* Australian National University Press, Canberra, 1982, pp. 62–87; Palmer, pp. 92–102.

27 JC Caldwell, 'Population', in Wray Vamplew (ed.), *Australian Historical Statistics,* Fairfax, Syme & Weldon, Broadway, 1987, pp. 26, 41; B Davidson, 'Agriculture', in Vamplew, p. 72; Palmer, p. 114.

28 Watson, p. 88.

29 AT Yarwood and MJ Knowling, *Race Relations in Australia: A History,* Methuen, North Ryde, 1982, pp. 192, 220–2; D Cormack to A Cormack, 24 November 1880, 'Australian Aborigines — Queensland', Mitchell Library, DOC 3167, quoted in T Bottoms, A history of Cairns: City of the South Pacific, draft manuscript, 2000, p. 43.

30 Henry Reynolds, *With the White People,* Penguin, Ringwood, 1990, p. 50; Palmer, pp. 60–1; Hillier, *passim.*

31 Maurice French also draws attention to Captain Wickham's listing of 174 whites killed in southeast Queensland by Aborigines between 1842 and 1853 (*Conflict on the Condamine: Aborigines and the European Invasion,* Darling Downs Institute Press, Toowoomba, 1989, pp. 112, 154).

32 This covers Loos's list from 1867 until 1897. It must be emphasised that the total figure remains speculative. It could be inflated because 'missing' colonists were often believed to have been killed by Aborigines when they were not. It could also be an under-estimate because of presently uncited sources; under-reporting of white deaths on stations due to pastoralists' fears that replacement workers might be deterred; and general European apathy about the violent deaths of non-Europeans killed by Aborigines. It might be more accurate, instead of arriving at a 'rough figure', to indicate a 'reasonable range': for instance, in this case, of 900–1100.

33 Raymond Evans, 'The Mogwi take Mi-an-jin; Race relations and the Moreton Bay penal settlement, 1824–1842', in Rod Fisher (ed.), *Brisbane: The Aboriginal Presence,* 1824–1860, Brisbane History Group Papers, vol. 11, 1992, pp. 7–30; Evidence of Captain John Coley to

Select Committee on Native Police, 14 May 1861, Queensland Legislative Council, *Votes and Proceedings,* 1861, vol. I, pp. 424–5; Bowen to Carnarvon, Despatch 61, 12 November 1866 (Enclosure 1), Queensland State Archives, Gov/24; Loos, *Invasion and Resistance,* pp. 199–247; Clive Moore, Explaining violence, unpublished manuscript, 2000, pp. 1–2.

34 Archibald Meston, 'Report of the government scientific expedition to the Bellenden–Ker Range (Wooroonooran) north Queensland', Queensland Legislative Council, *Votes and Proceedings,* 1889, vol. II, p. 1213. The Hon. Boyd Morehead, a future Queensland Premier, claimed in 1880 a death ratio of ten to one (*Queensland Parliamentary Debates,* vol. XXXII, 1880, p. 666). On the other hand, Rev. JE Tenison Woods wrote in early 1882, 'Ten lives for one would, I think, be very much below the truth' (*Queenslander,* 25 February 1882). Yet, if Edward Curr's estimate, based on his questionnaire to fellow pastoralists, of 'from fifteen to five and twenty percent' falling 'by the rifle' were applied, the violent Aboriginal death rate would be much higher than 20,000 in Queensland alone (*The Australian Race: Its Origin, Language, Customs,* Government Printer, Melbourne, 1886–87, vol. 1, p. 209).

35 Gary Highland, 'Aborigines, Europeans and the criminal law: Two trials at the Northern Supreme Court, Townsville, April 1888', *Aboriginal History,* vol. 14, part 2, 1990, pp. 182–96.

36 David Denholm, *The Colonial Australians,* Penguin, Ringwood, 1979, pp. 38–42, 44–5; French, p. 104; Dymock, p. 44; Watson, p. 89; Palmer, p. 133.

Part
Two

How do we know?

Henry **Reynolds**

The written record

Since the late 1960s, many historians have conducted research on the nature of relations between Aborigines and Europeans on the Australian frontier. From time to time our findings have been questioned, most recently by writers such as Keith Windschuttle. To respond to their criticisms, I begin with four propositions:

1   Overt, armed conflict occurred in all parts of Australia for well over 100 years from within a few weeks of the arrival of the British at Sydney Cove until the 1930s when frontier settlers pushed into the surviving areas of Aboriginal-controlled territory.

2   The conflict was characteristically small scale, scattered and sporadic, differing in nature, intensity and duration according to both time and place. It is easier to mark the beginnings of conflict than to determine when it concluded.

3   It accompanied Australian life for well over half the history of white settlement. The fact that it normally took place on the outer fringes of an ever-receding frontier does not diminish its significance.

4   It was one of the most written about — and likely talked about — subjects throughout the nineteenth and early twentieth centuries. The evidence for this is both vast and various. But how do we find it?

There are literally thousands of accounts of conflict in the written record. It would take one person many years of persistent reading to absorb it all. One can only summarise the more obvious sources for this information:

• There is the voluminous official archive, much of it printed in reports of royal commissions and select committees produced by legislatures in Great Britain and each of the colonies; there are the hours of parliamentary debates from the same source.

- There are hundreds of dispatches exchanged between the colonial office and the colonies between 1788 and 1856 in the east, and between 1829 and 1890 in Western Australia.

- There are many unpublished letters from officials and from settlers to assorted government departments.

- Reference to conflict can be found in the private letters, journals, diaries, drafts of sermons and speeches of many colonists. There are also books by visitors or by the colonists themselves: travel books, autobiographies, memoirs and histories.

There are relevant news items, editorials and letters in newspapers printed in all the capital cities and many provincial towns: Geelong, Launceston, Maitland, Roebourne, Port Augusta, Broome, Darwin, Toowoomba, Bundaberg, Maryborough, Rockhampton, Mackay, Bowen, Townsville, Cairns, Cooktown, Herberton, Charters Towers, Croydon and Thursday Island. Queensland had by far the largest number of provincial newspapers published in towns when frontier conflict was still raging in the immediate hinterland.

The letters from correspondents provide the most interesting, varied and vivid material for the researcher. There are many from men out on the frontiers working on pastoral stations, in minefields, on pearling and *bêche-de-mer* luggers and on small farms, who were actively involved in conflict of one sort or another or who wrote about it in the recent past. There are letters from old drovers, bullock drivers, explorers and prospectors, from townsmen and teachers and clergymen. Many letters relate stories of conflict, often in great detail. Practically everyone who wrote them was concerned about the morality of frontier conflict, of killing Aborigines, of taking their land, of the whole colonial project. It would be possible to compile a large anthology of these letters that would make compelling reading for a modern audience.

But what in particular can we learn from this vast collection of written material? More specifically, what can be counted? We can find specific references to Europeans who were killed, wounded or harassed. Eventually it will be possible to compile a list of every such reference in the written record. It will never be definitive but it will provide us with an approximate count of settler casualties.

We could compile a much more fragmentary and incomplete account of loss and damage of European property occasioned in conflict with the Aborigines: cattle, sheep and horses killed, wounded or run off; huts, tents, houses, drays and wagons broken into, ransacked, burnt down. We could, if we really wished, calculate the volume of stolen goods mentioned in the records: pounds of flour, twists of tobacco, guns, shot and powder, axes, knives, blankets.

Having done all that we could assess the total impact of Aboriginal resistance. Economic historians could undoubtedly put a price on it. But it would not be an easy task. It would take a team of researchers countless hours to compile the statistics. It may, therefore, never be done. Historical research into Australia's overseas wars has always attracted funding from governments, but as a society Australia has shown little desire to deal in a similar manner with frontier skirmishing.

Fortunately, contemporaries occasionally compiled lists of colonists killed or attacked and property lost on the frontier. Sometimes settlers in a troubled district listed their losses as they appealed to distant governments. This was the case of settlers at Port Fairy in the Port Phillip District of New South Wales in 1842. In a petition to the government, they detailed their losses over a two-month period including: 3600 sheep, 176 cattle and ten horses killed or driven away; ten settlers killed or wounded; eight huts or stations attacked.[1]

Officials on the frontier also compiled lists to underline the intensity of conflict in their district. A good example was provided by the report of the Commissioner for Crown Lands in Maryborough (Queensland) in 1855. He listed the incidents that had taken place over a two-month period:

November

7   Mrs. White's house robbed of a quantity of flour.

9   Mr. Palmers stores robbed of tobacco.

12 Cahills dray robbed of 200 lbs of flour.

12 Hughes dray robbed of 200 lbs of flour, and a quantity of rations.

18 Mr. Melvilles house robbed of 60 lbs sugar.

19 Jas. Frectius house robbed of tea, sugar and flour.
    Thos. McCrudden robbed of 100 lbs of sugar and 48 lbs of Flour.

22 J. Church robbed of wearing apparel and rations.
    Mrs. Gadd — laundress robbed of linen, clothes, etc.

25 Mr. Reid's dray robbed of 70 lbs of Flour.

26 Two of Mr. Reid's bullocks speared.

27 Dowdle (?) speared by the Blacks. Denny and (?) beaten and ill used by
    the Blacks and robbed of Blankets clothing 145 lbs of Flour, 45 lbs of
    Beef, 50 lbs of Sugar, 2 lbs tea and a quantity of cooking utensils.

28 Jas. Western robbed of 4 sovereigns and beaten.

December

2 Walsh's dray robbed.

5 George Furber and Jos. Wilmshurst murdered and a large quantity of
   rations blankets clothing and Tomahawks stolen.

6 Michael Joyce nearly murdered being left for dead and his hut robbed of
   rations, clothing etc.

7 Dowzer and (?) store broken into and robbed.

8 Mr Uhr's house and garden robbed.

9 Comm. C. Lands garden robbed.

10 Herberts dray robbed of 800 lbs of sugar and 600 of Flour.

11 Martins house entered.

17 Mr. Landrigans house entered and robbed at night.

18 J. Arthurs carrier dray robbed of a quantity of sugar and flour.

19 J. Leitchs house entered and robbed during the night.

20 Mrs. Bennett assaulted and head cut with a Tomahawk.

21 Mr. Uhrs store attempted to be broken into.

22 Powers store entered and robbed.[2]

An even more comprehensive list was prepared by the official Aborigines Committee in Tasmania detailing the 'atrocities committed by the natives' during the so-called Black War of the late 1820s and early 1830s. There are pages of references to settlers killed and wounded, of animals destroyed, stores stolen and huts torched. Building on the detailed and meticulous records kept by the administration of Colonel George Arthur, NJB Plomley compiled a statistical study entitled *The Aboriginal/Settler Clash in Van Diemen's Land 1803–1831,* published in 1992. He provides tables of many types of incident: settlers killed, wounded or harassed; huts set on fire and plundered; cattle, sheep and horses killed. In the period of most intense conflict between 1824 and 1831, there were 706 'incidents'; 369 settlers were killed or wounded and a further 225 were harassed.[3]

In his 1982 study of frontier relations in north Queensland between 1861 and 1897, Noel Loos sorted through a vast body of material — official records, newspapers, diaries

The Aborigions of Van Demondsland endeavouring to kill Mr John Allen on Milton Farm in the District of Great Swanport on the 14th December 1828

Unknown artist
The Aborigions of Van Demonds land endeavouring to kill Mr John Allen on Milton Farm in the District of Great Swanport on the 14th December 1828
State Library of New South Wales

and letters — to build up a list of Europeans killed or wounded as a result of Aboriginal attack. He included such non-European settlers as Chinese, Pacific Islanders, Japanese and Aboriginal stockmen and police troopers. He concluded that the Aborigines had killed between 410 and 470 settlers. Parallel work at the same time on southern and central Queensland resulted in a figure of about 450 deaths. More recent research has suggested that as many as 1000 were killed. Given what we know of casualties in regional studies there may have been, as Raymond Evans discusses in his chapter, a further 700 or so settler deaths.

We can find out a great deal about the impact of Aboriginal resistance on colonial society and much of it can be documented. But what can we know about the other side of the frontier?

Many Europeans wrote about what was happening to the Aborigines. They had varying degrees of experience with frontier conditions. Some were directly involved in conflict. A significant number — settlers, travellers, missionaries, policemen and government officials — attempted to estimate the Aboriginal death rate. They often suggest a proportional relationship between black deaths and white, though the range suggested was wide — anywhere between 5 to 1 and 50 to 1. There are numerous accounts in the records of settlers coming upon Aboriginal bodies, sometimes partly burnt, sometimes not; sometimes piled up in one place; on other occasions scattered about. Police and military officers often reported the killing of Aborigines, but how honest the accounts were is impossible to say. Some were no doubt more accurate than others. But, as other authors in this volume discuss, many more reports adopted a well-understood euphemistic code, their reports referring to punishment, chastisement and dispersal.

As well as official operations there were innumerable private expeditions. They varied in size and the length of time they were out 'after the blacks'. How effective, or how ruthless, they were is difficult to determine. Participants had even less reason than police officers to account for what had been done beyond talk of 'customary chastisement', 'a brush', 'a battle', 'a thumping', 'a warm time', or most commonly 'a dispersal in the usual way'.

We also know that for much of the time men on the frontiers were usually well armed and that their guns were much more efficient in the second half of the nineteenth century. Contemporaries had no doubt what the guns were for. They were purchased, maintained, carried and loaded in order to provide protection by intimidating and, if necessary, shooting Aborigines.

It is far harder to quantify what happened to the Aborigines. In 1995, Ian Clark published *Scars in the Landscape,* a register of massacre sites in western Victoria resulting from conflict with Europeans between 1803 and 1859. Eventually similar work will be done in other parts of the country. While compiling his register of settler deaths in north Queensland, Noel Loos gave much thought to what was happening to the Aborigines and came to this conclusion:

> To suggest that at least ten times as many Aborigines were killed for every intruder
> killed seems very conservative when one considers that Aborigines were often killed
> to drive them from runs and river valleys and for merely disturbing or killing

cattle and horses, let alone killing or wounding settlers. One has to remember that Native Police detachments were constantly involved in punitive raids and dispersals from 1861 to 1896 in North Queensland and that the settlers were unrestrained in their use of force throughout this period. Thus to suggest that at least 4000 Aborigines died as a result of frontier resistance in North Queensland between 1861 and 1896 is probably so conservative as to be misleading.[4]

There was much regional variation in the relations that developed between incoming settlers and resident Aborigines but few contemporaries doubted that conflict took place and that given their superior weapons and, above all, the mobility provided by their horses, many more blacks died than did whites.

We are aware from many discussions in newspapers that the contentious question was not whether blacks were being killed, but whether the carnage was justified or not, avoidable or not. These questions were debated over and over again throughout the nineteenth century and in every region of the continent. In November 1870, the editor of the *Rockhampton Bulletin* argued:

> No way of treating them, except as belligerents when they commit outrages, has yet been found efficacious in the back tracks. They may be tolerated and treated kindly so long as they refrain from mischievous acts, but when they rob, steal or murder, they must be treated as enemies to the state and shot down with as little compunction as soldiers shoot each other in battles amongst civilised men.

Fifteen years later, the editor of the *Queensland Figaro* observed: 'Out on the very borders of civilisation, where absolutely new country is being opened up, and where blacks are brought into contact with whites for the first time, the use of the rifle is undoubtedly necessary'.[5]

Well-informed contemporaries had no doubt about the extent, intensity and consequences of frontier conflict. They said so in speeches, letters and books. The police magistrate at Muswellbrook, ED Day, gave evidence in 1839 to a New South Wales Legislative Council Select Committee on the Police about the situation on the troubled northern frontier. He explained that the whites:

> seemed to feel that they were in an enemy's country, and were afraid to move out of their huts without firearms ... [The Aborigines] were repeatedly pursued by parties of mounted and armed stockmen, assembled for the purpose and that great numbers of them had been killed at various spots, particularly at Vinegar Hill, Slaughterhouse Creek and Gravesend, places so called by the stockmen, in commemoration of the deeds enacted there.[6]

In southern Queensland the experienced Commissioner of Crown Lands William Wiseman observed that after 15 years on the frontiers of settlement, he was of the opinion that:

> no tribes will allow of the peaceable occupation of their country but, following the counsel of the boldest and strongest men amongst them, will endeavour to check the progress of the white men by spearing their sheep and murdering the shepherds. This I have known to be invariably the case … some solitary murder may occasionally occur owing to the wicked and foolish conduct of the white labouring man in his relation to the blacks … but the greater number of murders which I know of in these districts I should attribute to the determination of the natives to pillage and murder till they can drive out the white man.[7]

Similar views were expressed by John L Parsons, the Government Resident in the Northern Territory, in 1887. While discussing the intensity of frontier conflict he wrote:

> In nearly all cases the early results of the white man's intrusion is a permanent feud between the blacks and whites. The blacks frighten and spear the cattle and hold themselves in readiness to attack boundary riders and stockmen, or to make a raid upon outstations or the store room. The whites look well to their Winchesters and revolvers, and usually proceed on the principle of being on the safe side. It is an affectation of ignorance to pretend not to know that this is the condition of things throughout the back blocks and the new country Australia.[8]

Even weightier authority was provided by John Forrest during a debate in the West Australian Legislative Council in 1886. Drawing on his own wide experience he declared:

> We went amongst them with our sheep and our cattle, and we found them in an altogether uncivilised state, and hostile, and we had to defend our lives and property, not by the strong arm of the law, but by force. That occurred on every station on the outskirts of civilisation in these colonies.[9]

One could go on quoting similar passages from prominent and experienced colonists from all parts of Australia and throughout the nineteenth century. The former squatter Edward Curr provided the most authoritative account of frontier conflict. After corresponding with a large number of settlers all over the colonies, he came to this conclusion:

> In the first place the meeting of the Aboriginal tribes of Australia and the White pioneer, results as a rule in war, which lasts from six months to ten years, according to the nature of the country, the amount of settlement which takes place in a

neighbourhood, and the proclivities of the individuals concerned. When several squatters settle in proximity, and the country they occupy is easy of access and without fastnesses to which the Blacks can retreat, the period of warfare is usually short and the bloodshed not excessive. On the other hand, in districts which are not easily traversed on horseback, in which the Whites are few in number and food is procurable by the Blacks in fastnesses, the term is usually prolonged and the slaughter more considerable …

Hence the meeting of the White and Black races in Australia, considered generally, results in war. Nor is it to be wondered at. The White man looks on the possession of the lands by the Blacks as no proper occupation, and practically and avowedly declines to allow them the common rights of human beings. On the other hand, the tribe which has held its land from time immemorial and always maintained, according to native policy, the unauthorised digging up of one root on its soil to be a *casus belli*, suddenly finds not only that strangers of another race have located themselves permanently on their lands, but that they have brought with them a multitude of animals, which devour wholesale the roots and vegetables which constitute their principal food, and drive off the game they formerly hunted. Besides this, the tribe finds itself warned by the more merciful settler, that as cattle will not remain on a run about which Blacks seek their daily food in the usual way, as they are alarmed at their very smell, they must give up that practice, or take the consequence and be shot down whenever met. The tribe, being threatened with war by the White stranger, if it attempts to get food in its own country, and with the same consequences if it intrudes on the lands of a neighbouring tribe, finds itself reduced to make choice of certain death from starvation, and probable death from the rifle, and naturally chooses the latter.[10]

How then do we know about frontier violence? Because the written evidence is both vast and various, and convincing. To pretend otherwise is to indulge in an affectation of ignorance.

1 Petition of Port Fairy Settlers to Superintendent, Port Phillip, Aborigines (Australian Colonies), *British Parliamentary Papers*, vol. 34, no. 627, 1844, pp. 213–14.

2 Annual Report of Crown Lands Commissioner for 1855, Wide Bay and Burnett, 1855–57, Queensland State Archives, 30/11.

3 Aboriginal Tribes in British Possessions, *British Parliamentary Papers*, vol. 44, no. 617, 1834, pp. 156–8; NJB Plomley, *The Aboriginal/Settler Clash in Van Diemen's Land, 1803–1831*, Queen Victoria Museum and Art Gallery, Launceston, 1992.

4 Noel Loos, *Invasion and Resistance: Aboriginal–European Relations on the North Queensland Frontier 1861–1897*, Australian National University Press, Canberra, 1982, p. 190.

5 *Rockhampton Bulletin*, 8 November 1870; *Queensland Figaro*, 31 May 1885.

6 Select Committee on the Police, New South Wales Legislative Council, *Votes and Proceedings*, 1839, p. 224.

7 *Ibid.*

8 WH Wiseman, Letterbook, 5 January 1856, Queensland State Archives, CCL 7/61.

9 West Australian Legislative Council, *Parliamentary Debates*, vol. IX, 1886, p. 588.

10 Edward Curr, *The Australian Race: Its Origin, Language, Customs*, Government Printer, Melbourne, 1886–87, vol. 1, pp. 100–3.

Richard **Broome**

The statistics of frontier conflict

Violence was a hallmark of the Australian frontier, but we will never know exactly how many people died in conflicts between Europeans and Aborigines. The historical record is always fragmentary, and records of the frontier doubly so. The evidence of violence is scarcer still, owing to a natural secrecy or reticence to discuss what has occurred. Scholars only began to estimate fatalities in the 1960s; the *Australian Encyclopaedia,* for instance, gave several regional estimates in its 1963 edition.[1]

Charles Rowley produced the first continental approach to Aboriginal history and fathered a new genre of history with his *The Destruction of Aboriginal Society* (1970). While describing white violence as 'commonplace over wide areas and long periods', Rowley believed it was 'very difficult even to guess at the scale of violence'. By the 1980s, however, much more research had been conducted and estimates were produced. In his *The Other Side of the Frontier* (1981), Henry Reynolds asked what was the cost of warfare that was fought sporadically across the continent over 150 years. He claimed it was a question 'white Australians have rarely posed and never satisfactorily answered'. The development of Aboriginal history in the 1970s, which produced regional studies, meant that Reynolds could now attempt what Rowley did not. He set about adding up detailed death counts by Lyndall Ryan, Michael Christie, Malcolm Prentis, Neville Green and his own work with Noel Loos, which together covered five regions: Tasmania, Victoria, northeastern New South Wales, southwestern Western Australia and Queensland. On the basis of this partial coverage, Reynolds estimated that 'somewhere between 2000 and 2500 Europeans' were killed in the frontier clashes across the continent.[2]

But how did he approach the count of Aboriginal deaths through violence? Reynolds understandably found this extremely difficult, but decided that to ignore the question was to slip back into the 'great Australian silence' about the history of European relations with Aboriginal people. To estimate Aboriginal deaths, Reynolds again turned to the regional studies. From these, he suggested that 'for the continent as a whole it [was] reasonable to suppose that at least 20,000 Aborigines were killed as a direct result of conflict with the settlers'. He implicitly, rather than explicitly, used a method of applying a 10 to 1 fatality ratio of black-to-white violent deaths. He pointed to discrepancies in regional death tolls, especially between Tasmania, where the ratio was about four black deaths to every white death, and Queensland, where his own work suggested it was 10 to 1. Reynolds noted that settlers in Tasmania, unlike those on northern frontiers, lacked horses, and breech-loading and multishot weapons. In his 1987 book, *Frontier,* he estimated that perhaps '3000 settlers died and 3000 were wounded in Australia as a whole', up from '2000 to 2500' in his earlier book. Of Aboriginal deaths he maintained his earlier 'informed guess' of 20,000, adding that it might be 'too low'.[3]

My own work, *Aboriginal Australians* (1982), in press at the time *The Other Side of the Frontier* was first published, argued that the European death toll 'was probably somewhere between 1000 and 1500'. Using Reynolds and Loos's 10 to 1 Queensland ratio,[4] I suggested the Aboriginal deaths might have been 'about 20 000, yet it could be much more'. In 1984, apparently after much debate, the Council of the Australian War Memorial agreed to include a chapter on frontier war in a book that was edited by Michael McKernan and Margaret Browne, *Australia: Two Centuries of War and Peace* (1988). I wrote a continental overview of the frontier clashes, entitled 'The struggle for Australia', which surveyed fighting in broad regions and time zones across the continent in order to assess changing military tactics and technology, engage with the face of frontier fighting, and count the cost of the violence. Regarding European deaths I was able to find close counts for eight regions: the five Reynolds used (somewhat refined), and for incomplete areas of northern Western Australia, western Northern Territory, and New England in New South Wales. To this tally of 1280 I added estimates of 120, 150 and 150 for South Australia, and the remainder of New South Wales and the Northern Territory, respectively, making 1700 in all. I suggested it could be 1800, allowing for unrecorded deaths of about one in 20. I commented that further research might verify a 'total around 2000'. I then discussed the scope of regional black–white death rates around the country, ranging from 4 to 1 in sparsely populated Tasmania, through 10 to 1 in the heavily black-populated Queensland, to 40 to 1 in sparsely populated Gippsland. I decided that 10 to 1 was a likely average ratio. Noel Loos claimed his 10 to 1 ratio in heavily Aboriginal-populated north Queensland might be 'so conservative as to be misleading', and yet there were ratios in other regions which seemed to be 'well below 10 to 1'. Thus I concluded that a 10 to 1 ratio gave 'an Aboriginal death toll of 18 000 to 20 000'.[5]

I then made another calculation — which Keith Windschuttle recently stated was an 'extraordinary' mathematical formula of 'how to reach the figure of 20 000' — in order to understand if the figure of '18 000 to 20 000' was at all possible. It was a check not a formula, indicated by my asking, 'Is this figure feasible?'. I pondered what 20,000 deaths meant on average for each group in terms of anthropologist Norman Tindale's estimate of 586 Aboriginal cultural-linguistic groups in Australia at first contact. The average of 34 deaths per group did not suggest that 20,000 was a wild estimate.[6]

No other historians of Aboriginal history have attempted a continent-wide analysis of the frontier fatalities. Some journalists and popular writers have made inordinate claims, which are quite unsubstantiated since they do not draw on any serious historical research; for example, Bruce Elder claims 'tens of thousands' of Aborigines were killed. The lack of new estimates is not 'collusive' or an orthodoxy inspired by Reynolds, as Windschuttle asserts, but is due to the lack of additional exact regional counts to refine the estimates. Richard Kimber has given a rough figure of 500–1000 deaths in the Northern Territory between 1871 and 1894, but it is not as yet a close count. Clearly there are great difficulties with such continental estimates without more studies and in the light of the problems of the sources indicated above.[7]

I will now seek to demonstrate that historians of the frontier neither 'collude' nor 'make up figures'. Where they 'guess', these are educated by the known facts, the context and by deep and extended reading of the sources, and the 'guess' is clearly identified as such. The following Victoria case study will also test Windschuttle's claim that 'fabricated and exaggerated Aboriginal massacres have become accepted as historical fact because of the sloppy work of Australian historians'.[8]

In 1979, Michael Christie published an important regional study of colonial Victoria that, among other achievements, ended the myth of a peaceful European penetration of Victoria and Aboriginal passivity. He revealed significant frontier violence but failed to cover the equally important cultural resistance and accommodation practised by Aboriginal people. He also assumed Aboriginal motivation and over-emphasised the power of the muzzle-loading rifle. And, despite Christie's impressive archival work, when he attempted a tally for frontier violence, he avoided a grassroots count because he believed there was a significant under-reportage of frontier killings. Instead, Christie accepted the estimate of Edward Curr, a former pastoralist and author of *The Australian Race* (1886–87), an ethnographic work, that between 15 and 25 per cent of Aboriginal people had died through white violence across Australia. Taking the higher level without justification, Christie claimed 2000 Aborigines in Victoria died from white violence, based on an 8000 total loss of life in the frontier period from all causes. Christie also claimed in his thesis that 200 whites were killed on the Victorian frontier.[9]

In a review of this book in 1980, I criticised Christie's figures of Aboriginal deaths on the grounds of method, since it was derived from the top end of Curr's estimate and not from the archives Christie had scoured. I also suspected the estimate was too high. The following year, Beverley Nance published an important article that explored the Aboriginal motives for violence which Christie had found unproblematic. Nance counted European deaths at 59, which she claimed was a very reliable figure. She wondered, given that there were about 200 *inter se* deaths, why Aborigines killed more Aboriginal people than whites. Her answer is a fascinating exploration of the Aboriginal connection between deaths and sorcery, a chain of connection between Aboriginal people of which Europeans were not a part. Nance also claimed the number of Aboriginal deaths was about 400, one-fifth of that claimed by Christie. However, Nance does not say how she came to that figure. Her fine MA thesis, on which her article was based, was somewhat misnamed as 'The Aboriginal response to white settlement in the Port Phillip District, 1835–1850', as it was about Melbourne and central Victoria. Therefore it is not authoritative on Gippsland, the Western District and northwestern Victoria. As such, Nance's claim of 400 Aboriginal deaths for Victoria is not based on sufficient historical research.[10]

Research on the Western District from the late 1980s has refined the findings of an earlier pioneering study by Peter Corris in which he counted 159 Aboriginal deaths and over 20 European deaths. Jan Critchett's *A 'Distant Field of Murder': Western District Frontiers 1834–1848* (1990) listed 257 known deaths (although Windschuttle claims she only 'counts a total of 200 Aborigines' killed by whites). To this, she added legitimate

ST Gill
The marauders
undated watercolour
Mitchell Library, State Library
of New South Wales

The titles of these two undated images suggest that they are part of a
single story, separated in time only by the waxing of the moon. The
marauders have stolen sheep and speared to death a shepherd. The
avengers await their moment. Gill leaves it to the viewer to speculate
on how many Aborigines will die and whether the dead will include
women and children.

ST Gill
The avengers
undated pencil sketch
Mitchell Library, State
Library of New South Wales

estimates for the known mass killings at the Convincing Ground and by both Frederick Taylor and the Whyte brothers, and several other incidents, arguing that 330 or possibly 350 Aborigines were killed, as opposed to 35 Europeans. It is more than interesting that this careful count produces a ratio of about ten black violent deaths to one white death, the ratio accepted by Reynolds and myself for our continental estimates.[11]

In this study Critchett argues that only five Europeans faced trial for the 68 incidents listed. However, Windschuttle naively asserts that 'ever since they were founded in 1788, the British colonies in Australia were civilised societies governed by both morality and laws that forbade the killing of the innocent'. This may have been the aspiration and possibly the actuality in the towns, but the frontier was different despite good government intentions. A study of the law in Port Phillip by Suzanne

Davies has revealed how European prejudice, the inadmissibility of Aboriginal evidence, the language barrier and cross-cultural misunderstandings rarely delivered British justice to Aboriginal defendants or victims.[12]

In 1995, the historical geographer Ian Clark published *Scars in the Landscape: A Register of Massacre Sites in Western Victoria, 1803–1859*. His book covered most of western Victoria (but not the Murray Valley), an area larger than Critchett's Western District, which encompasses only land south of the Grampians. Clark listed 107 fatal incidents. Like Critchett's list, Clark's is complete with all known details and sources. However, he leaves mathematical calculation to his readers. Fifty-five incidents, just over half the number, entailed one to three deaths, totalling 88 people. Another 19 incidents listed comprised between five and ten deaths, and there were a further 13 incidents encompassing 11 or more deaths. Of those counted exactly, there were 331 Aboriginal deaths. There was also the Convincing Ground tally in which 'all but two of a clan' were killed, which Critchett counts reasonably as about 60, making 391. Added to this also were six 'unknown' death tolls, and one labelled as 'dozens'. However, three of these incidents are imprecisely documented and should be discounted. Perhaps Clark's tally might approach 430. Clark's careful research does not quite match the word 'massacre' in the title, as not all the incidents can be so described, particularly the 29 single deaths and perhaps some with a tally of two or three deaths. However, one-third of the incidents were of deaths numbering more than five.[13]

In his PhD thesis on Gippsland culture contact, Bain Attwood estimated Aboriginal deaths in Gippsland at 350, but later suggested it might be lower. He noted there were only six European deaths. Don Watson's 1984 Gippsland study, *Caledonia Australis,* was published in the same year that Attwood's thesis was completed. Watson did not count the toll by incidents, but discussed some of the alleged massacres. His account was in the tradition of victimology, arguing that the destruction of Kurnai society in Gippsland was not 'inevitable' but rather 'gratuitous and grotesque'. Watson gave no overall figure but quoted settler Henry Meyrick's contemporary estimate of 450 killed and other high massacre counts without demur. Peter Gardner, a Gippsland local historian, has done assiduous archival research for his *Gippsland Massacres* (1983 and 1993) but, like Watson, gives no overall counts or estimates, and tends to victimology as well. (Responding to my statement at the National Museum of Australia's forum and the internet posting of my paper, Gardner has now carefully tallied his results and argued for 610 Aboriginal deaths in Gippsland between 1800 and 1860. This is his best mid-range guesstimate.)[14]

What then might be the overall figure of Aboriginal deaths at the hands of whites in Victoria? Michael Christie, who claimed 2000 plus, has an unsatisfactory method of working from an 1886–87 'guesstimate' percentage. The exhibition *Koorie,* by the Koorie Heritage Trust, which ran for a decade from 1988 at the Museum of Victoria, accepted Christie's base figure and added to it 'many thousands more [who] died beyond prying eyes'. In 1994, I criticised this as too high as well. While *Koorie* and Christie's estimates of more than 2000 are clearly too high, Nance's estimate of 400 Aboriginal deaths at white hands is far too low, given that this number is closely counted in western Victoria alone. (Critchett gives 350 for just the Western District and Clark perhaps 430 for a larger area, but not all of western Victoria.) The western Victorian figures, added to those of Gippsland, give a figure of about 700 (taking Attwood's lower 250 estimate to be conservative), or about 1000 (using Gardner's higher calculations). This tally excludes the Murray Valley and northeast Victoria and the fact that some deaths went unrecorded after seven settlers were hanged for the Myall Creek massacre of 1838. Thus 1000 is probably close to the reality, a figure I suggested in 1988 and again in 1995. Indeed, the lower figure of 700 black deaths, which does not include two regions of Victoria, with 59 whites killed, gives a ratio of 12 to 1 for Victoria. The higher tally of 1000 violent black deaths at white hands in Victoria gives a ratio of 17 Aboriginal dead to every European death. Both, especially the latter, are higher than the 10 to 1 ratio applied nationally by Reynolds and myself. The 1000 death tally is about 10 per cent of the Victorian Aboriginal population at settlement. Perhaps I was too sanguine when I suggested in 1995 that the Victorian frontier 'was one of the least violent of frontiers'. Nevertheless, most Victorian Aboriginal deaths were from the impact of disease, malnutrition and psychic disruption from European invasion.[15]

This analysis of the Victorian material reveals the general carefulness of historians of frontier history, who disagree, do not 'collude' and respectfully debate issues with a minimum of name-calling. It also suggests a ratio of 10 to 1 black to white deaths is not an unreasonable one to apply nation-wide. Indeed, based on a careful estimate of 1000 Aboriginal deaths, Victoria was between 12 and 17 black deaths to every one white death, with the higher ratio being more likely.

The Victorian frontier was still arguably less violent than some, for at least four reasons. Gun technology on this pre-1850 frontier comprised single shot and muzzle-loading weapons. The native police force, with some exceptions, was benign compared to the force found on northern frontiers. The Port Phillip District was unique in having a serious (albeit inadequate) protective effort, which meant that settlers were more under the eye of colonial officials, who were in turn influenced by instructions from London to apply British justice to Aboriginal people. Lastly, racial ideas hardened after the 1850s: dominant ideologies about difference shifted from environmental to racial explanations, and there was a loss of optimism because of the apparent 'fading away' of Aboriginal people on southern frontiers.

Statistics of frontier conflict deaths

Historian	Europeans	Aborigines
Australia-wide		
Reynolds (1981)	2,000–2,500	20,000
Reynolds (1987)	3,000	20,000
Broome (1982/88)	1,000–1,500	18/20,000
Victoria		
Christie (1979)	200	2,000+
Nance (1981)	59	400
Koorie Heritage Trust	–	2,000+
Western District		
Corris (1968)	20	159
Critchett (1990)	35	350
Western Victoria (excluding Murray Valley)		
Clark (1995)	–	430c
Gippsland		
Attwood (1984)	6	350/250
Gardner (1983/93)	–	610
Victoria (excluding Murray Valley and northeast)		
Broome (1988/1995)	59	700–1,000

The statistics of frontier violence are certain to be inaccurate. Thus, we need other measures of historical phenomena than the quantitative, as Alan Atkinson argues in this volume. We can only fully understand the frontier and its violent face by reading the letters of settlers, the reports of missionaries and government officials, and listening to the memories of settler and Aboriginal descendants. Settlers could be violent to each other, to the fauna and bird life, to the land they over-stocked, levelled and chopped out with little thought, and the Aboriginal people they pushed aside in the name of their God-given right to go forth, multiply and make the land fruitful. Violence towards Aboriginal people, and vice versa, while not the only human relationship that existed on the frontier, was a significant marker of the struggle to win the land.

However, we cannot ignore statistics, if only for the reason that we live in a scientifically based culture awash with statistics. Everyone and everything is measured: sporting performances, the road toll and the stock market. Some measurements, such as rainfall statistics, are exact, while others, such as those concerning the incidence of crime, are much less precise. Some, such as economic indicators, lead to estimations that shape economic policy. These are not economists' fabrications, but careful and honest attempts to judge the mood of the economy. The statistics of frontier violence share the characteristics of all the above. At times they are as precise as a rain gauge, but more often than not they mirror modern crime statistics, which depend on the level of reportage and detection, itself subject to many factors.

Historical writing demands accuracy and evidence. But in the end, our readers demand the 'big picture', a generalisation. So, if we write about the frontier, we are expected to come up with a number. This has led to 'guesstimates', but not the attempt to 'collude' and 'fabricate' that Windschuttle has asserted. In his *The Other Side of the Frontier*, Reynolds hedged his estimates of a continental death toll with phrases such as 'intelligent guess', 'it seems reasonable to suggest', and 'reasonable to suppose', all signs for his readers as to what is occurring. Similarly, I used such words as 'difficult to assess', 'there are no certainties', and 'estimates are made for such unknowns', to send clear signals that these were estimates based on case studies and transparent methodology. If Windschuttle believed these to be 'exact figures' or something like that, as he indicated during discussion at the conference, then he clearly misread these works.[16]

In the face of readers' expectations for generalisations, historians cannot stay silent but must qualify and make clear what they do. And this is generally what historians of the Australian frontier have done.

1 Norman Tindale, 'The white contact', *Australian Encyclopaedia,* Grolier Society of Australia, Sydney, 1963, vol. 1, p. 87.

2 CD Rowley, *The Destruction of Aboriginal Society* (1970), Penguin, Ringwood, 1972, p. 7; Henry Reynolds, *The Other Side of the Frontier,* History Department, James Cook University, Townsville, 1981, pp. 98–9.

3 *Ibid,* p. 99; Reynolds, *Frontier: Aborigines, Settlers and Land,* Allen & Unwin, Sydney, 1987, pp. 29–30, 53.

4 See Reynolds and Noel Loos, 'Aboriginal resistance in Queensland', *Australian Journal of Politics and History,* vol. 22, no. 2, 1976, p. 226.

5 Richard Broome, *Aboriginal Australians: Black Response to White Dominance,* Allen & Unwin, Sydney, 1982, p. 51; Broome, 'The struggle for Australia: Aboriginal–European warfare, 1770–1930', in Michael McKernan and Margaret Browne (eds), *Australia: Two Centuries of War and Peace,* Australian War Memorial/Allen & Unwin, Canberra/Sydney, 1988, pp. 116–20; Noel Loos, *Invasion and Resistance: Aboriginal–European Relations on the North Queensland Frontier 1861–1897,* Australian National University Press, Canberra, 1982, p. 190.

6 Keith Windschuttle, 'The myths of frontier massacres in Australian history. Part II: The fabrication of the Aboriginal death toll', *Quadrant,* vol. 44, no. 11, 2000, p. 21; Broome, 'The struggle for Australia', p. 118.

7 Bruce Elder, *Blood on the Wattle: Massacres and the Maltreatment of Australian Aborigines since 1788,* second edition, New Holland Publishers, Sydney, 1998, pp. vi, 256; Richard Kimber, 'The end of the bad old days: European settlement in central Australia, 1871–194', State Library of Northern Territory, *Occasional Papers,* no. 25, 1991, p. 16.

8 Windschuttle, cited in *Australian,* 11 September 2000; Windschuttle, 'The fabrication', p. 23.

9 Michael Christie, *Aborigines in Colonial Victoria, 1835–1886,* Sydney University Press, Sydney, 1979, pp. 78–80; Christie's thesis quoted in Reynolds, *The Other Side of the Frontier,* p. 99.

10 Beverley Nance, 'The level of violence: Europeans and Aborigines in Port Phillip 1835–1850', *Historical Studies,* vol. 19, no. 77, 1981, p. 533; Broome, 'Review', *Historical Studies,* vol. 19, no. 76, 1981, pp. 454–7; Broome, 'Victoria', in Ann McGrath (ed.), *Contested Ground: Australian Aborigines under the British Crown,* Allen & Unwin, Sydney, 1995, pp. 127–9.

11 Peter Corris, *Aborigines and Europeans in Western Victoria,* Australian Institute of Aboriginal Studies, Canberra, 1968, pp. 153–7; Windschuttle, 'The fabrication', p. 21.

12 Jan Critchett, *A 'Distant Field of Murder': Western District Frontiers 1834–1848,* Melbourne University Press, Melbourne, 1990, pp. 130–2, Appendices 2, 3; Windschuttle, 'The fabrication', p. 23; Suzanne Davies, 'Aborigines, murder and the criminal law in early Port Phillip, 1841–1851', *Historical Studies,* vol. 22, no. 88, 1987, pp. 313–36.

13 Ian Clark, *Scars in the Landscape: A Register of Massacre Sites in Western Victoria, 1803–1859,* Aboriginal Studies Press, Canberra, 1995.

14 Bain Attwood, Blacks and Lohans: Aboriginal–European contact in Gippsland in the nineteenth century, PhD thesis, La Trobe University, 1984, pp. 60–4; personal communication 1988; Don Watson, *Caledonia Australis: Scottish Highlanders on the Frontier of Australia,* Collins, Sydney, 1984, pp. 183, 169; Peter Gardner, *Gippsland Massacres: The Destruction of the Kurnai Tribes 1800–1860,* Warragul Education Centre, Warragul, 1983, second edition, Ngarak Press, Ensay, 1993; personal communication from Peter Gardner, 2 March 2002.

15 Koorie Heritage Trust, *Koorie,* Creative Solutions, Melbourne, no date, p. 19; Broome, 'Aboriginal victims and voyagers: Confronting frontier myths', *Journal of Australian Studies,* no. 42, 1994, pp. 70–9; Broome, 'The struggle for Australia', p. 117; Broome, 'Victoria', p. 128.

16 Reynolds, *The Other Side of the Frontier,* pp. 99–100; Broome, 'The struggle for Australia', p. 117.

Keith **Windschuttle**

Doctored evidence and invented incidents in Aboriginal historiography

Among the many cultural items produced to mark the centenary of Federation in 2001 were a number that charged Australia with having committed genocide against the Aborigines. These accusations were not simply of action by default, such as inadvertently introducing diseases that annihilated people who had no immunity to them. Australia was allegedly guilty of conscious, wilful genocide resembling the kind the Nazis perpetrated against the Jews in the 1940s. In a book written for the centenary, *Australia: A Biography of a Nation,* the expatriate journalist, Phillip Knightley, was one of those making this claim. He wrote:

> It remains one of the mysteries of history that Australia was able to get away with a racist policy that included segregation and dispossession and bordered on slavery and genocide, practices unknown in the civilised world in the first half of the twentieth century until Nazi Germany turned on the Jews in the 1930s.[1]

When the National Museum of Australia was opened in 2001, it commemorated the genocide thesis in the very design of the building itself. Architect Howard Raggatt borrowed its central structure — shaped as a lightning bolt striking the land — from the Jewish Museum in Berlin, signifying that the Aborigines suffered the equivalent of the Holocaust. The Museum's own publication, *Building History: The National Museum of Australia* (2001), acknowledged this connection: 'The most dramatic of the architectural references is in the form of the First Australians gallery, with a zigzag footprint, or outline, which closely resembles the recently completed Jewish Museum in Berlin designed by Daniel Libeskind'. The Museum's director, Dawn Casey, has described the institution as 'a birthday gift to Australia', but to symbolically accuse the nation of the most terrible crime possible is hardly the kind of present that anyone would welcome.

In 2000, when he published the passage above, Knightley was reflecting the consensus reached by the historians of Aboriginal Australia over the previous 30 years. This is not to say that the historians themselves used the Nazi analogy. Instead, they created a picture of widespread mass killings on the frontiers of the pastoral industry that not only went unpunished but had covert government support. They used terms such as 'genocide', 'extermination' and 'extirpation' so freely that non-historians such as Knightley and Raggatt readily drew the obvious connection between Australia and Nazi Germany.

When I read Knightley's book, however, I believed there was a considerable body of evidence he had not considered, which contradicted the genocide thesis. To those in authority since 1788, the idea of exterminating the Aborigines would have been appalling. In fact, colonial governors, judges and politicians saw one of their main roles as *preventing* violence towards Aborigines by the lower orders of white society, especially in the convict era.[2] The crucial ingredient of genocide — political intent — had always been lacking in Australia's history. I also knew that in the nineteenth and early twentieth centuries, many Aborigines had been employed in both the sheep and cattle industries of New South Wales and northern Australia, and that many pastoralists not only enjoyed harmonious relations with them but were dependent on their labour.[3] None of this fitted the scenario of a holocaust. So in 2000 I began a project to examine the primary sources on which the genocide thesis was based.

As a result of this work,[4] I concluded that when it is closely examined, the evidence for the claims of widespread mass killings of Aborigines turns out to be highly suspect. Much of it is very poorly founded, other parts are seriously mistaken, and some of it is outright fabrication. Even though my critique focused as far as possible on the historical evidence, most of the subsequent response to it in the media was *ad hominem*. Defenders of the orthodoxy attacked my politics, my morals and my ability to do historical research, while at the same time pretending that the academics I had criticised were reliable scholars whose opinions should be trusted.[5] Arguments of this kind, however, are irrelevant. This is a debate that will be settled not by appeals to reputation but by the presentation of evidence, and nothing else.

Despite their denials, the very fact that the orthodox school has at last been publicly subjected to some sceptical questioning has already, in this brief period, led some of its practitioners to abandon some of their more outlandish claims. These developments include:

- Whereas Lyndall Ryan was still claiming in 1996 that the Tasmanian Aborigines were 'victims of a conscious policy of genocide', Henry Reynolds now disagrees. In his latest book, *An Indelible Stain?*, he has conceded that what happened to the Aborigines in Tasmania did not amount to genocide.[6]

- Reynolds has also publicly conceded that his 1981 claim that 10,000 Aborigines were shot dead in Queensland was not based on a precise count but was only an 'educated' guess.[7]

- Reynolds has agreed that large-scale massacres of Aborigines were not typical of Australian frontier history, as the school has frequently claimed, and that most of the killings that did occur were in ones and twos.[8]

- I also think that anyone who has read with an open mind my articles in *Quadrant* in 2000 and the work of Rod Moran will concede that two of the most frequently cited sources about massacre stories, the missionaries Lancelot Threlkeld in New South Wales and Ernest Gribble in Western Australia, can no longer be treated as the reliable authorities they once routinely were.[9]

Let me take this opportunity to add a few more samples of evidence doctored and incidents invented by some of the speakers attending the National Museum's forum on frontier conflict. For several years now, Reynolds has been trying to persuade the Australian War Memorial in Canberra to mount a display honouring what he calls the Aboriginal 'guerilla fighters' of Van Diemen's Land. Reynolds has described the so-called guerilla war waged by the Tasmanian Aborigines as a struggle of momentous proportions. He claims it was 'the biggest internal threat that Australia has ever had'. The Tasmanians of the so-called Black War of 1824–1830, he says, were a superior force whose guerilla tactics outclassed the bumbling, red-coated British soldiers.[10]

The concept of 'guerilla warfare', which Reynolds claims was waged by the Aborigines in Van Diemen's Land, derived from the tactics of the Spanish forces on the Iberian Peninsula during the Napoleonic wars. Instead of large, set piece battles, small groups of Spaniards would attack French forces and then quickly withdraw. Repeated over a long period, the tactic was a way for a small force to damage and demoralise a much larger one. Reynolds states that Lieutenant Governor George Arthur, like many other officers in Van Diemen's Land, had fought in Spain and recognised he faced the same military tactic.[11] This is not true. Arthur's military career included Italy,

Sicily, Egypt and the Netherlands, but never Spain.[12] Nonetheless, there is one passage written by Arthur about conflict with the Aborigines that Reynolds interprets as confirmation of his theory. Arthur wrote:

> The species of warfare which we are carrying on with them is of the most distressing nature; they suddenly appear, commit some act of outrage and then as suddenly vanish: if pursued it seems impossible to surround and capture them.[13]

Reynolds claims that this description anticipates the anti-colonialist tactics of the twentieth century: it 'could have come from the manuals of guerilla warfare which proliferated in the 1960s'. He says it shows Arthur had grasped the military problem confronting him. It was 'a classic statement of the frustrations of a commander of conventional forces facing elusive guerilla bands'.[14] However, the full text of this statement reveals that Arthur was not talking about confrontations between conventional forces and guerillas at all. He was discussing assaults by Aborigines on isolated stockmen on the fringes of white settlement. Just before the statement Reynolds quotes, Arthur gave the context for what he said: 'Whenever they can successfully attack a remote hut, they never fail to make the attempt, and seldom spare the stockkeepers when they can surprise them'. Reynolds omits this part of the text to give the false impression that Arthur was talking about *troops* coming under surprise attack by Aboriginal warriors. He misrepresents Arthur's concerns, which were reserved entirely for isolated, unprotected civilians.

Reynolds also claims Arthur looked on the Aborigines as his warrior equivalent. 'Governor Arthur showed an old soldier's respect for his Aboriginal adversaries.'[15] But Reynolds omits to tell his readers that Arthur specifically denied that Aboriginal tactics amounted to anything that resembled real warfare. In November 1828, Arthur wrote to London:

> It is doubtless very distressing that so many murders have been committed by the Natives upon [the] stockmen, but there is no decided combined movement among the Native tribes, nor, although cunning and artful in the extreme, any such systematic warfare exhibited by any of them as need excite the least apprehension in the Government, for the blacks, however large their number, have never yet ventured to attack a party consisting of even three armed men.[16]

Arthur repeated these sentiments several times. Nothing here resembles the grudging respect of an old soldier. None of the historians who support the guerilla warfare thesis has ever shown Arthur was mistaken. The Aborigines never developed any of the forms of organisation, command, strategy, intelligence or weapons supply that have been associated with genuine guerilla warfare in other countries over the past 200 years. Even though the historians of Tasmania use the term, none of them has ever discussed its meaning in any detail to demonstrate what they are trying to prove. They have never advanced any criteria by which an action could be judged as guerilla warfare. Any kind of black hostility from 1824 onwards — even if it was nothing more than robbery with violence, as most assaults on whites were — is automatically labelled this way, with no critical analysis ever thought necessary.

The strategy of guerilla warfare was adopted by European nationalists in the early nineteenth century. In the 1950s and 1960s it was taken up by a number of anti-colonial groups in Africa, Latin America and Southeast Asia. The orthodox historians of Tasmania want us to believe that the Aborigines intuitively anticipated all this by spontaneously adopting a form of combat that was not a part of their pre-colonial cultural repertoire and whose methods and objectives they had never read about or heard explained. This is not historical analysis; it is the imposition onto Aboriginal history of an anachronistic and incongruous piece of ideology.

It is also accompanied by a great deal of fabricated and invented evidence about the scale of the violence. I will publish a long catalogue of these misrepresentations in the book I am currently preparing on the subject. Here, I will discuss a few of them. In November 1828, after 26 Tasmanian colonists had been murdered by Aborigines, Arthur declared martial law and appointed 'roving parties' to capture any Aborigines they could and to drive the rest from the settled districts. According to Ryan, they wreaked carnage throughout the colony:

> Between November 1828 and November 1830 the roving parties captured about twenty Aborigines and killed about sixty. The settlers also began to exploit their knowledge of the Aborigines' seasonal patterns of movement. When a band of the Oyster Bay tribe visited Moulting Lagoon in January 1829, they found the settlers waiting for them. Ten were shot dead and three taken prisoner. When a band of Big River people reached the Eastern Marshes in March *en route* to the east coast, Gilbert Robertson's party was waiting and killed five and captured another.[17]

Ryan backs her claim that 60 Aborigines were killed by the roving parties with a footnote that contains three references. The first is a letter from Arthur to the Colonial Secretary on 27 May 1829. Arthur did write a letter on this date and it was about the roving parties. It is in the archive location Ryan indicates: volume 1/317, file 7578, of the Colonial Secretary's Office papers, on pages 15–18. Its subject matter, however, is the number of men that should comprise Gilbert Robertson's parties, whether they should all be due for a ticket-of-leave as a result of their service, and about the rations that should be provided for them. It does not mention any Aborigines being killed, let alone 60. Her other two references are commentaries by NJB Plomley in *Friendly Mission,* his edition of the journals of the 'conciliator' of the Tasmanian Aborigines, George Augustus Robinson. One of these does discuss the reports of the roving parties, but has this to say: 'How many natives were killed in all these operations is hardly mentioned'. The other commentary does not mention any Aborigines killed by the roving parties but at one stage it does say that John Batman's party captured 11 natives in September 1829.[18] In short, none of Ryan's footnotes supports her assertion about the killing of 60 Aborigines.

Apart from Ryan, no other historian who has investigated the primary sources has ever claimed the roving parties killed 60, or anything like this number. The truth is that the roving parties were widely regarded at the time as ineffectual, either in capturing Aborigines or in removing them from the scene. The report of the Aborigines Committee of 1830 declared them 'worse than useless'.[19] My own assessment is that the roving party of John Batman killed two Aborigines and captured 13, while Robertson's party captured six but killed none. This was the sum total of their haul.

Ryan's claim that Robertson's party killed five Aborigines at the Eastern Marshes in March is another piece of invention. The diaries of the parties Robertson commanded from November 1828 until February 1830 are held by the Archives Office of Tasmania.[20] Nowhere do they mention any killings at Eastern Marshes or, indeed, anywhere else. The only Aborigine they came across was one old, unarmed man and his dog living on their own in the bush near George's River in the northeast of the island. For all of 1829 and 1830, he was their sole captive. I should point out that the roving parties had no reason to conceal their actions and every reason to publicise them. In the prevailing atmosphere of consternation among the settlers about Aboriginal atrocities, stories about white retaliations would have made the men of the roving parties popular heroes. If any of the roving party leaders had had success stories to report, they would have done so.

The incident Ryan mentions at Moulting Lagoon in January 1829, where she says settlers in the district killed ten Aborigines and took three prisoners, is yet more fiction.

She cites three newspaper reports and a letter to the Governor from James Simpson as her sources for this and related events in the same paragraph.[21] But when you check the sources you find none of them mentions any conflict with Aborigines at Moulting Lagoon, let alone any killings there. There were some newspaper reports of other incidents on the east coast at the same time, but nothing at Moulting Lagoon. In short, none of Ryan's references confirms the claims she makes in her text. She has invented these incidents.

Let me move away from Tasmania to discuss the work of Raymond Evans, whose 1999 book *Fighting Words* provides another example of what now passes for academic scholarship in Aboriginal history. *Fighting Words* recounts the now forgotten Battle of Patonga. On the Hawkesbury River, north of Sydney, Evans writes, 'the indigenous inhabitants, the Dhurag, had once waged there a war of no quarter lasting more than two decades as they were slowly obliterated. Silent Patonga hid its secrets well'.[22]

The source Evans relied on for this story was journalist John Pilger's 1986 book *Heroes*. Pilger, who used to holiday at Patonga as a child, had taken the story from David Denholm's 1979 history, *The Colonial Australians*. Denholm himself also relied on secondary sources. Evans's account is therefore four times removed from the original evidence, and it shows. For a start, despite the reverence both express for Aboriginal people, neither Evans nor Pilger took the trouble to get their name right. They were the Dharug, not the Dhurag. Secondly, David Denholm was describing a conflict in the 1790s on the Hawkesbury River near Windsor. None of this happened anywhere near Patonga, which is near the mouth of the Hawkesbury in the territory of the Guringai people, not the Dharug people.[23] A war there in the 1790s was unlikely since the first whites did not settle at Patonga until 130 years later.

In short, Evans does not have a clue what he is talking about. Patonga is a holiday village with a few dozen houses, a caravan park and a beach surrounded by a national park. It never had any settlers in the colonial period to provoke a war with the Aborigines. It was not sub-divided until the 1920s and housing has never extended more than 100 metres inland from the beach. What Evans claims as a two-decade long 'war of no quarter' is yet another piece of invention.

Since I originally made this point in July 2001, Evans has complained that I have distorted his views by taking them out of context. He was only using Pilger's story about the war at Patonga, he says, to introduce a chapter about different events in

Queensland. This is true. Patonga was not the main point of his chapter. But this kind of reply only compounds the offence. Evans has taken seriously an event that never happened and then casually dropped it into his narrative, as if a historian could take the word of the journalist Pilger without any further investigation warranted. Then, when challenged, Evans fails to acknowledge his mistake or to withdraw it. Instead, he attacks the person who has pointed out his folly, accusing him of methodological malpractice. He still refuses to admit the truth that there was never violent conflict between blacks and whites at Patonga of any kind.[24]

Unfortunately, the fictions and fabrications of our academic historians are more than matched by those created by the Aborigines themselves. Because Aborigines in the colonial period were illiterate and kept no written records, we are urged today to accept the oral history of their descendants as an authentic account of what happened in the past. My view is that Aboriginal oral history, when uncorroborated by original documents, is completely unreliable, just like the oral history of white people. Let me illustrate this with an account of the infamous Mistake Creek massacre in the Kimberley district.

There are at least four versions of Aboriginal oral history about this incident that have made their way into either print or television, and all of them are different. The former Governor-General, Sir William Deane, used his last days in office to apologise to the Kija people for this incident and for all those that Aborigines had suffered at the hands of white settlers. Deane said:

> What is clear is there was a considerable killing of Aboriginal women and children … It's essential that we hear, listen to and acknowledge the facts of what happened in the past, the facts of terrible events such as what happened here at Mistake Creek in the 1930s, which is in my lifetime.[25]

However, what actually is clear is that by relying on Aboriginal oral history, Deane got the facts of the case completely wrong. According to the Western Australian police records, the incident took place in 1915, not the 1930s. It was not a massacre of Aborigines by white settlers at all, but a killing *of* Aborigines *by* Aborigines in a dispute over a woman who had left one Aboriginal man to live with another. The jilted lover and an accomplice rode into the Aboriginal camp of his rival and shot eight of the people there. However, Aboriginal oral history later implicated the white overseer of the station concerned, a man named Mick Rhatigan. This is the same oral history that Deane relied on to say the event took place in the 1930s. However, it would have been difficult for Mick Rhatigan to have been one of the killers at this time. According to both his family and the headstone on his grave at Wyndham, he died in 1920, ten years before the date the Aborigines claim the event occurred.[26]

Another version of this same oral history was provided on ABC Television's *7.30 Report.* A woman named Peggy Patrick said her mother and father and brothers and sisters had all been massacred in this incident.[27] The program's presenter, Kerry O'Brien, said she was 70 years of age. This means she was born in 1930 or 1931. But the killings took place in 1915, which means she was born fifteen years after the death of her parents, which must be a world record for a posthumous birth.

By relying on Aboriginal oral history, and by failing to do the most elementary research into this matter, Deane made a fool of himself in what was supposed to be the final, grand reconciliatory gesture of his term of office. I would suggest that anyone else who relies on uncorroborated oral history of Aborigines — or indeed the oral history of anyone else — is likely to embarrass themselves in exactly the same way. Stories passed down orally over three or four generations are more likely than not to get some of their facts wrong, whatever the ethnic background of the storytellers. Once the facts have gone awry, so will the interpretations.

By pretending to Aborigines that their oral histories have some kind of historical authenticity, academic historians do them no favours. It is in nobody's interest, and certainly not those of Aboriginal people, for completely false stories such as the one about Mistake Creek to continue to be taken seriously, generating an unwarranted bitterness on one side and a sanctimonious sense of blame allocation on the other.

I am well aware that there is often a postmodernist spin put on oral history and ethnic legends. This claims that traditional notions of history have been undermined by recent epistemological critiques, and that all cultures are authentic in their own terms, and that all legends are therefore true for their believers. The advocates of this view often apply it to such worthy cultures as those of ethnic and indigenous minorities, as well as other fashionable political interest groups. They rarely recognise that the same argument confers authenticity on the claims of cultures of which they might *not* approve, such as those of neo-Nazis, white supremacists, Islamic jihadists and other species of political depravity. This rejection of traditional empirical history leads to cultural relativism in which the legends, myths and prejudices of *any* culture become legitimate. It is a philosophy of anything goes.

If you abandon the principles of empirical history — that evidence is independent of the observer and that truth is discovered rather than invented — you create cultural cocoons where everyone's views are legitimate. This means, however, that all these cultural groupings can do is talk past one another. No debate can ever be resolved. You are left with nothing more formidable than calling your opponents political names. Some postmodern theorists might welcome this but outside the university this position is seen for what it is — the end of rational historical debate.

In September 2001, in a general critique of the Museum's approach to social history, I also criticised its frontier conflict exhibit. I made three main points:

- The Museum made a false claim that Aborigines caught spearing cattle in Western Australia in the 1890s had been executed. No one was ever executed for such a minor offence.

- Its claim that 'numerous' men, women and children were killed by a police patrol at Forrest River in the Kimberley in 1926 omitted to mention that claims about these killings had been seriously challenged by two independent sources.

- The centrepiece of the whole section, a photographic display of the so-called Bells Falls Gorge massacre near Bathurst in the 1820s, gave credibility to a mythological event for which there was no contemporary evidence. Although it is now claimed as part of ancient Aboriginal tradition, Aboriginal activists only learnt of it from an article about local legends written by a white amateur historian in 1962.[28]

Each of these claims should have been easy for the display's curator to verify. There is a complete record available about all the executions in Western Australia, which the curator should have consulted. The study, by Brian Purdue, covers executions of both whites and blacks since the first in 1840 to the last in 1964. In this time, 154 people were executed: 136 for murder, nine for wounding with intent to murder, six for rape, two for robbery accompanied by serious assault, and one for carnal knowledge of a seven-year-old girl. None was for cattle spearing.[29]

While a magistrate at a royal commission in 1926 did find that 11 Aborigines may have been killed by a police patrol near Forrest River, when the two accused police came before a committal hearing for murder, the latter found there was no *prima facie* case that even a single person had been killed there. In his 1999 book, *Massacre Myth*, the Perth journalist Rod Moran re-examined the evidence presented at both hearings and, largely on forensic grounds, concluded the magistrate at the royal commission got it wrong while the magistrate at the committal hearing got it right. In an example such as this, where there are two clear sides to the case, the Museum is being deceptive in presenting only the conclusions from one of those sides. Significantly, for its December 2001 forum on frontier conflict, the Museum did not invite anyone to present a paper about Forrest River so that these issues could be raised.

In 1995, David Roberts published the results of his research into the Bells Falls Gorge massacre, which legends in the Bathurst district of New South Wales say took place in the 1820s. He found there was no contemporary documentary evidence for it. Roberts nonetheless argued that because there were other recorded conflicts in the region around that time and because legends about the Bells Falls Gorge event could still be found among the local white community, this should be taken as evidence that something like a massacre did take place, at least somewhere in the district at the time. He has more recently written:

> They [local residents] maintain a solemn understanding that Aborigines were once rounded up at the local landmark and were forced to jump to their deaths under fire. (Countless rural communities across Australia will recognise the story in different forms.)[30]

The problem with this argument is precisely the fact that countless rural communities do, indeed, tell similar stories about spectacular local landmarks. In fact, landmarks such as this, especially those with very high waterfalls, seem to almost irresistibly conjure up myths that have an uncanny similarity wherever they are found.

There is a comparable tale still told in the Blue Mountains, west of Sydney, where legend has it that the place called Govett's Leap was named after a bushranger named Govett who was pursued under gunfire from troopers to the edge of the waterfall there. Rather than be shot or captured, he spurred his horse over the precipice to his doom. When I was a child, my parents told me this piece of oral history in all seriousness. The local Chamber of Commerce has since erected on the main road a statue of Govett on his horse to capitalise on the location as a tourist attraction.

However, this particular legend has no connection with historic events of any kind. The real Govett was not a bushranger but the government surveyor who named the site, and 'leap' is an old Scottish term for a cataract or waterfall.

How many times do we need to learn the same lesson? Old legends and oral history, unless they are corroborated by original documents, are worthless as historical evidence, whether told by blacks or whites. Historians who go down this road leave the search for truth behind.

Let me finish with some recommendations to the National Museum's Council about the construction of the building itself. I would advise the Council to reconstruct that part of the building that provides the lightning bolt symbol. This would remove the current connection between the fate of the Aborigines and the fate of the Jews of Europe. The Aborigines did not suffer a holocaust. To compare the policies towards Aborigines of Governor Arthur Phillip or Lieutenant-Governor George Arthur, or any of their successors, with those of Adolf Hitler towards the Jews, is not only conceptually odious but wildly anachronistic.

There were no gas chambers in Australia or anything remotely equivalent. The colonial authorities wanted to civilise and modernise the Aborigines, not exterminate them. Their intentions were not to foster violence towards the Aborigines but to prevent it. They responded to violence by the Aborigines towards settlers cautiously and reluctantly, and their over-riding concern was to prevent retaliatory violence by settlers and convicts from getting out of hand. None of this is remotely comparable to what happened in Europe during World War II.

For the Australian Government to construct a permanent, national structure that advertises such a grotesque historical misinterpretation is an insult to the nation and to all its members, white and black. It is a monument to nothing more than the politically motivated allegations of one particular school of historiography whose former dominance of the field is now visibly eroding.

1 Phillip Knightley, *Australia: A Biography of a Nation*, Jonathan Cape, London, 2000, p. 107.

2 Alan Frost, *Arthur Phillip 1783–1814: His Voyaging*, Oxford University Press, Melbourne, 1987, pp. 144–5, 183–4, 187, 260–1, 309 note 18; John Ritchie, *Lachlan Macquarie: A Biography*, Melbourne University Press, Melbourne, 1986, pp. 109–10, 132, 152; Brian H Fletcher, *Ralph Darling: A Governor Maligned*, Oxford University Press, Melbourne, 1984, pp. 183–90; AGL Shaw, *Sir George Arthur, Bart, 1784–1854*, Melbourne University Press, Melbourne, 1980, pp. 123–34; Hazel King, *Richard Bourke*, Oxford University Press, Melbourne, 1971, p. 187; R Therry, *Reminiscences of Thirty Years' Residence in New South Wales and Victoria* (1863), Royal Australian Historical Society, Sydney University Press, Sydney, 1974, pp. 271–300.

3 In the 1850s, in the New England district 'the demand for labour led to the aborigines being very widely employed as shepherds, stockmen, horse breakers, and reapers at wages up to 20 pounds a year' (RB Walker, *Old New England*, Sydney University Press, Sydney, 1966, p. 172). From 1843 to 1851, Horatio Wills employed Aborigines as station hands and harvesters at his Ararat property, Lexington (TS Wills Cooke, *The Currency Lad: A Biography of Horatio Spencer Howe Wills 1811–1861*, TS Wills Cooke, Melbourne, 1997, pp. 42–54). In the late nineteenth and early twentieth centuries, the Durack family's Kimberley cattle properties were dependent on Aboriginal labour (Mary Durack, *Sons in the Saddle*, Constable, London, 1983, pp. 50, 84, 137, 192–3). See also Andrew Markus, 'Talka longa mouth: Aborigines and the labour movement 1890–1970', in Ann Curthoys and Andrew Markus (eds), *Who Are Our Enemies? Racism and the Working Class in Australia*, Hale and Iremonger, Sydney, 1978, pp. 138–57; Curthoys and Clive Moore, 'Working with the white people: An historiographical essay on Aboriginal and Torres Strait Islander labour', in Ann McGrath and Kay Saunders (eds), *Aboriginal Workers, Labour History*, no. 69, 1995, pp. 1–29.

4 See Keith Windschuttle, 'The myths of frontier massacres in Australian history, Parts I, II and III', *Quadrant*, vol. 44, nos 10–12, 2000, pp. 8–21, 17–24, 6–20.

5 See, for example, Robert Manne, 'When historical truths come in dreams', *Sydney Morning Herald*, 18 September 2000; Bain Attwood, 'Attack on Reynolds scholarship lacks bite', *Australian*, 20 September 2000; Raymond Evans et al., 'Attack on historian well timed for global media', *Australian*, 15 September 2000. All of these authors went into print on the basis of press reports of a conference paper of mine and before any of the articles in my series for *Quadrant* had actually been published.

6 Lyndall Ryan, *The Aboriginal Tasmanians*, revised edition, Allen & Unwin, Sydney, 1996, p. 255; Henry Reynolds, *An Indelible Stain?: The Question of*

Genocide in Australia's History, Viking, Ringwood, 2001, Chapters 4, 5.

7 Bruce Montgomery, 'Historian defends his best guess', *Australian*, 12 September 2000.

8 Reynolds, 'The perils of political reinterpretation', *Sydney Morning Herald*, 25 September 2000.

9 Windschuttle, 'The myths of massacres', Parts I and III, 2001, *passim*; Rod Moran, *Massacre Myth*, Access Press, Bassendean, 1999.

10 Montgomery, 'The first patriots', *Australian*, 3 April 1995; Reynolds, 'A war to remember', *Australian*, 1–2 April 1995.

11 Reynolds, *Fate of a Free People*, Penguin, Ringwood, 1995, p. 66.

12 Shaw, pp. 5–16.

13 Reynolds cites this passage (*Fate of a Free People*, p. 223, endnote 59) from Arthur to Murray, 12 September 1829, *Historical Records of Australia*, series I, vol. XIV, p. 446. This is the wrong volume; it is in vol. XV, same page.

14 Reynolds, 'The Black War: A new look at an old story', Tasmanian Historical Research Association, *Papers and Proceedings*, vol. 31, no. 4, 1984, p. 2; Reynolds, *Fate of a Free People*, p. 66.

15 *Ibid*, p. 36.

16 Arthur to Murray, 4 November 1828, *British Parliamentary Papers*, Colonies, Australia, vol. 4, p. 181.

17 Ryan, p. 102.

18 NJB Plomley, *Friendly Mission: The Tasmanian Journals and Papers of George Augustus Robinson, 1829–1834*, Tasmanian Historical Research Association, Hobart, 1966, pp. 30, 472–4.

19 Report of the Aborigines Committee 1830, *British Parliamentary Papers*, Colonies, Australia, vol. 4, p. 217.

20 Journal of the proceedings of a party employed under the direction of Gilbert Robertson, 1 January 1829 – 13 March 1829, pp. 114–31; Journal of a party under the immediate orders of Gilbert Robertson, 2 February 1829–27, February 1829, pp. 132–44; Memorandum for a journal of the proceedings of a party under my charge in pursuit of the Aborigines, 27 February 1829 – 13 February 1830, pp. 79–92, CSO 1/331/7578.

21 Ryan, pp. 104, 113 (endnote 4).

22 Raymond Evans, *Fighting Words: Writing about Race*, University of Queensland Press, St Lucia, 1999, p. 111.

23 Jocelyn Powell and Lorraine Banks (eds), *Hawkesbury River History: Governor Phillip, Exploration and Early Settlement*, Dharug and Lower Hawkesbury Historical Society, Wiseman's Ferry, 1990.

24 Windschuttle, 'When history falls victim to politics', *Age*, 14 July 2001; Evans, 'Open letter to Keith Windschuttle', National Museum of Australia, Canberra, December 2001.

25 David Burke, *Dreaming of the Resurrection: A Reconciliation Story*, Sisters of St Joseph, Mary MacKillop Foundation, North Sydney, 1998, pp. 33–5; William Deane, A few instances of reconciliation, address to Southern Queensland Theology Library, Toowoomba, 5 November 1999; Charlene Carrington, 'Mistake Creek massacre', heritage statement on 1999 painting; 'A look at Sir William Deane's term as Governor-General', *7.30 Report*, ABC Television, 11 June 2001, transcript.

26 Report of Constable Flinders and statements of witnesses, 4 June 1915, Western Australian Police, Colonial Secretary's Department, CO 1854/15; Moran, 'Mistaken identity', *West Australian*, 17 November 2001.

27 *7.30 Report*, 11 June 2001.

28 Windschuttle, 'How not to run a museum', *Quadrant*, vol. 45, no. 9, 2001, pp. 11–19.

29 Brian Purdue, *Legal Executions in Western Australia*, Foundation Press, Victoria Park, 1993.

30 David Roberts, 'Bells Falls massacre and Bathurst's history of violence: Local tradition and Australian historiography', *Australian Historical Studies*, vol. 26, no. 105, 1995, pp. 615–33; Roberts, 'Site unproved: "War" certain', *Australian*, 18 March 2001.

Alan **Atkinson**

Historians and moral disgust

The three articles by Keith Windschuttle published in *Quadrant* late in 2000 aim to revise, in a fundamental way, our understanding of frontier conflict in Australia. This revisionist approach is partly shaped by a distinctive view of the discipline of history as a whole and it seems to involve the indiscriminate rejection of methodological advances over the last 30 years. In a period when we have been struggling to make historical method stretch to comprehend the real diversity of human faith and understanding and the spiritual depth of human experience, and at the same time to communicate those issues to the world at large, the revisionist approach seems to lead in the opposite direction. This amounts to a failure of genuine, energetic curiosity and a failure of imagination, both of which are fundamental to good scholarship. Most of what revisionist critics such as Windschuttle have argued so far in their account of frontier violence is informed by these failures.

Any attempt to understand conflict between Aborigines and Europeans on the frontier raises a variety of questions about physical violence in the past. For instance, we can ask how much violence there might have been at different times — how many deaths, for instance (as Richard Broome does in this volume) — and this is a vast and complex question; and we can ask about the causes and effects of violence. But we can also ask about the way in which violence works, and worked, as an aspect of culture and thought, varying as it always does within particular periods and among particular people. Good answers to the first two questions really depend on good answers to the last.

To take another set of alternatives, problems of violence can be considered as matters of blame, as they must be to some extent for many narrative historians. They can also be tackled in terms of 'social pathology', as a sociologist might do. And they can be treated from an ethnographic point of view or in terms of *mentalité*, with the emphasis on violence as an aspect of culture. All these scholarly approaches are more or less available to the historian. To complicate the matter, none seems to me to pre-empt moral judgement and moral disgust, neither of which can really be avoided in dealing with the combined issues of nation and frontier. In fact they are central to any such exercise.

How is moral disgust to be managed side by side with scholarly method? In his book, *The Warrior's Honor,* Michael Ignatieff tells the story of the making of the first Geneva Convention in 1864. This convention established not only the International Red Cross but also certain minimal standards for the medical treatment of the dead and wounded in war. The principal instigator was a Swiss merchant and philanthropist, Jean-Henri Dunant, who was moved by the sight of the Battle of Solferino — one of the bloodiest battles of the nineteenth century — and especially by the sight of the dead and wounded who lay afterwards, neglected, on the battlefield.

As Ignatieff tells this story several points emerge. His book is about the maintenance of moral standards amid violence, worldwide, in the late 1990s. It is subtitled *Ethnic War and the Modern Conscience.* In this way it makes a point central to what I want to argue. The establishment of the Red Cross involved very finely articulated — and it could be said contradictory — forms of moral judgement. It involved a complete detachment from the causes of war and a complete involvement in the immediate effects of war. Something like this kind of balance, or contradiction, seems necessary in dealing with violence in history. Historians have to take it for granted that moral standards change from one period to another, but contrariwise they also have to work with the belief that moral standards, at least in matters of life and death — let alone genocide — are absolute and fixed. They march in step with the first but they stand with the second. The contradiction is a problem but, as with the Red Cross, it is essential to the job. It may not seem logical, but it is right.[1]

Ignatieff's account of the making of the Geneva Convention also points to the way in which not only moral but also cultural and intellectual attitudes to violence might shift, such that one paradigm of understanding gives way to another. This is material for an ethnographic approach to violence. Presumably something such as the Geneva Convention would not have been possible, say, 50 years earlier, during the Napoleonic wars. The historian has to ask why.

Dunant's reaction to the battlefield at Solferino has specific significance for Australia. The battle took place in 1859, and the 1850s mark the end of what might be called the first period of racial violence in this country. During the 1820s, 1830s and 1840s the colonial governments had tried hard to come to grips with frontier conflict and with what they understood to be their competing responsibilities: first, to protect the business of white settlement; and second, to prevent the unlawful injury and slaughter of indigenous people. By the 1850s, any hope that these two duties might be kept in balance had ended. From this time, the colonial governments were prepared largely to turn a blind eye to the destruction of people who were, in principle, British subjects.

This might seem strange, given the movements abroad that led to achievements such as the Geneva Convention. The convention did not aim to prevent war. But it did aim to treat all casualties, fighting in whatever cause, as human beings who deserved the best medical treatment available. It established a kind of egalitarianism in warfare, a principle completely at odds with evolving practice in Australia. The contrast can be explained partly by the fact that idealists such as Dunant were moved by brutality among Europeans. Their likely response to a murder site on the Australian frontier we cannot know.

The Geneva Convention was not due to any hatred of violence, pure and simple. It was designed for the better ordering of violence, according to the humanitarian sense of mid-nineteenth-century Europe. This is where I want to stress the peculiarities of cultural understanding about the place of violence in society. The unfolding of humanitarian ideas during the 1820s, 1830s and 1840s was extremely complicated, and the complexities are as obvious in the Australian experience as they were in Europe. There is nothing here that looks much like a simple, clear and unpolluted stream of idealism, a noble river which might be seen as bearing humanity straight towards the high standards of the present day (whatever they may be). Those complexities were a direct result of complex thinking and feeling about violence itself. In other words, the adventures of humanitarianism — or opposition to violence — at that time were deeply entangled with the various *uses* of violence, and I would argue that that is true of any period and place.

In order to draw out some of the complexities, I want to examine a small publication which first appeared in Sydney in 1841. This is Charlotte Barton's book, *A Mother's Offering to Her Children*. In spite of being written as a children's book —

Title page from Charlotte
Barton's 1841 edition of
*A Mother's Offering to
Her Children.*

indeed a book for small children — it is mostly about violence, including frontier
conflict. That fact itself suggests a world of understanding different from ours.

To some extent, this is a children's textbook on the proper place of violence in
society. The author seems to be struggling in her own mind with the changing
ideas of her day, and maybe with the fact that in Australia grotesque forms of
violence were strangely close to nurseries and schoolrooms. The stories in the
book are set up as a series of conversations between a mother and her children,
which gives the subject matter a peculiar kind of immediacy. It also makes some
passages seem not only grotesque but also ludicrous. Mrs Barton worked with
moral premises that are now more easily laughed at than understood. She aimed
to give children a hatred of violence in everyday life. In a passage about insects, for
instance, readers are told how wrong it is to destroy life, however ephemeral.
'Some people', the mother says, 'have a sad cruel habit of throwing insects into the
fire! I always consider it not only a sure proof of want of feeling; but of having had
a neglected education also'.[2]

And yet Charlotte Barton herself brings frontier violence to the evening fireside.
The East Indies, to the near north, was her frontier of choice and she dwells at length
on conflict between islanders and the crews and passengers of British ships. In one
massacre by islanders a European boy was spared and brought to a campfire on the
beach, where, so the mother explains, 'The heads of the murdered people [including
those of his parents] were arranged in a row'. Wide-eyed children listening to the story
were gently — if implicitly — invited to imagine themselves in such an adventure,
eyeing off at bedtime the severed heads of Mamma and Papa.[3]

What lessons about frontier conflict did the book teach its readers in the 1840s?
Most of all, it draws a dramatic contrast between the 'unrestrained passions' of
'savages' and the habits of properly educated Europeans. After one bloody episode —
it is the story of Eliza Fraser and her murdered husband — one of the little girls sitting
at the mother's feet makes her feelings known. 'Such wanton barbarities', says little
Clara (who seems to be about six years old), 'fill one with horror and indignation; and
a wish to exterminate the perpetrators'.[4]

Clara had learned her lessons well. She was horrified and indignant, as she was
supposed to be. But in spite of her horror and indignation, or really because of it, she
called for extermination. Here there is an obvious link with Henry Reynolds's argument

about extermination, as idea and as fact, in his recent book, *An Indelible Stain?,* Reynolds shows pretty well that the words 'exterminate' and 'extirpate' had become familiar in colonial conversation, with reference to indigenous people, during the 1820s and 1830s.[5] Little Clara was only echoing a word in common use among her elders. She was also echoing a common and contradictory set of ideas. This was a set of ideas in which a refined moral sensibility and an apparently perfectly natural desire to exterminate worked side by side.

If Charlotte Barton could put the word 'exterminate' into the mouth of a child in 1841 then surely this says a good deal about the way in which the idea of extermination had taken on a type of moral weight during the previous two decades. It had become one of those political terms that somehow, within themselves, seem to carry the proper solution to a great practical problem. It was one of those extremely useful words that might be taken as typical of a period of emerging popular media and popular politics. In the process of being popularised, it is easy to imagine that the meaning of the word began to harden. Originally meaning nothing more than 'banish' or 'excommunicate', it is likely that even by the beginning of the nineteenth century it did not have quite the pristine and clinical connotations it has now. Lingering ambiguity might have added to its political uses. But it was also a word easily harnessed to the expression of popular horror and indignation.

The word 'exterminate' appeared in influential speeches by popular leaders. In the Supreme Court in Sydney in May 1827, the young barrister William Charles Wentworth and his partner Robert Wardell defended the white murderer of a black man named Jackey Jackey by arguing that the indigenous people had no existence in law. The colonists must deal with them as they found them, they said, within in a Hobbesian state of nature, and, given their evil propensities as a people, 'an exterminating war' against them might be perfectly justified.[6] This was little Clara's logic precisely. These were speakers perfectly capable of moral disgust themselves, of a civilised sensibility, and they were ready to prove it with violence wholesale.

There is a mystery here, which the historian needs sophisticated tools to unravel. Such an apparently tangled knot of language and ideas belongs to the essential context of race relations, and, if we are to understand what happened on the frontier, it needs to be examined just as carefully as, say, the daily habits of Aborigines and stockmen and the capability of contemporary weapons.

Wentworth and Wardell were in the process of becoming leaders of public opinion in New South Wales. One of the achievements of Wentworth in particular was to give a legitimacy and an intellectual refinement to ideas hitherto expressed only in idle, angry and furtive conversation, in bark huts and public houses. In this way he became a champion of popular rights. Words such as 'exterminate' and 'extirpate' are not likely to have been part of popular talk in previous years. They are Latinate words, better used to express high policy. They also proceed from a type of broad geographical understanding and a sense of control beyond most colonists. Such transformations in word use are important markers of cultural change. Marie Fels has explored the extent of racial conflict during the first seven years of white settlement in Van Diemen's Land. She describes the way in which three or four convict men, known by name, gained a reputation for their brutal treatment of Aborigines. One of them was said to have 'exercised his barbarous disposition in murdering or torturing any who unfortunately came within his reach'. Writers before Fels had guessed that these men were typical of their kind. She concludes, to the contrary, that they were not typical, that we know about them because they were remarked upon as unusual. In other words, for a time wholesale violence was the work of individuals. Only in the 1820s did men of superior skill and education, such as Wentworth in New South Wales, build a bridge between this kind of 'barbarous disposition' and government policy.[7]

The same kind of point can be read into a proclamation issued by Governor Lachlan Macquarie in 1816 in which he ordered the indigenous people themselves to stop fighting each other, 'not only at and near the British Settlements but also in their own wild and remote Places of Resort', wherever they might be. Such an order, whimsical as it might seem, has to be understood as symptomatic of the serene authority which government could still use in its dealings with black and white. Here we see the result of a pre-1820s moral consensus, dictated by government. Within it the word 'extermination' could have had no force at all. During the 1820s, on the other hand, educated men and women, outside government, began to make an impact on government business. Now, in both colonies officials had to speak of 'extermination' themselves, whatever they thought of it.[8]

The 1820s, then, saw a marked shift in the way violence was talked about in New South Wales and Van Diemen's Land. Here is one of those periods in Australian history — and there have been several since — when it is possible to see how moral leadership, or a failure of moral leadership, can suddenly make a dramatic mark on common opinion. Such changes are a real problem for the historian of life and ideas, and they are a problem to be tackled with the best methodology available. Among the great mass of Australians who read history without writing it there are a good number who believe it is an easy discipline to master, that academics who use complex methodology are inventing problems to justify their existence. As we can see from this small example, this involves a dramatic failure of intellectual and moral imagination, a refusal to believe in fundamental human difference.

The varied uses of violence are an aspect of that difference. In 1985 Michael Sturma published an article called 'Myall Creek and the psychology of mass murder', which, in a mere eight pages, demonstrates a better sense of the difficulty of such issues than do Windschuttle's three long articles in *Quadrant*. Sturma was mainly interested in comparing the killings at Myall Creek with the My Lai massacre in Vietnam in 1968. Among other things, he offers some enlightening statements by soldiers who had fought in Vietnam. 'Here in Vietnam', one said, 'they're actually shooting people for no reason ... Any other time you think, it's such an extreme. Here you can go and shoot them for nothing ... As a matter of fact it's even smiled upon, you know. Good for you ... That is part of the unreality of the thing'.[9]

There are several immediate responses we can make to this kind of unreality. We can ignore it, as the revisionist critics seem to do. We can turn away bewildered. We can laugh, as we might laugh on reading Charlotte Barton's book. And we can feel, and wrestle with, a type of moral disgust. Only the last is really productive. More than any of the others, perhaps, the last proves we are human and that we can think.

Australian history is full of deep shifts in an ocean of feeling about race, shifts of feeling which have been matched, in complicated ways, by shifts in behaviour. The description and explanation of those shifts is a task of enormous difficulty. It seems perverse to try to tackle it by using only the tools of an earlier generation.

[1] Michael Ignatieff, *The Warrior's Honor: Ethnic War and the Modern Conscience*, Viking, London, 1999, p. 100.

[2] [Charlotte Barton], *A Mother's Offering to Her Children*, Gazette Office, Sydney, 1841, p. 100. For the authorship of this book, see Marcie Muir, *Charlotte Barton: Australia's First Children's Author*, Wentworth Books, Sydney, 1980.

[3] Barton, p. 31.

[4] *Ibid*, p. 177.

[5] Henry Reynolds, *An Indelible Stain?: The Question of Genocide in Australia's History*, Viking, Ringwood, 2001,

pp. 52–66.

[6] *Sydney Gazette*, 21 May 1827.

[7] Cited in Marie Fels, 'Culture contact in the county of Buckinghamshire, Van Diemen's Land, 1803–11', Tasmanian Historical Research Association, *Papers and Proceedings*, vol. 29, 1982, p. 60.

[8] Proclamation, 4 May 1816, *Historical Records of Australia*, series 1, vol. IX, pp. 142–3.

[9] Cited in Michael Sturma, 'Myall Creek and the psychology of mass murder', *Journal of Australian Studies*, no. 16, 1985, p. 66.

Deborah Bird **Rose**

Oral histories and knowledge

The question 'how do we know' what we know of the past presupposes another question: 'who is the we who wants to know?'. The perspective of the historian is central to any historical inquiry and is especially relevant to oral history. My perspective is that of a member of two settler societies — the United States and Australia. The 'we' I wish to consider first are those who are the descendants of global expansion that brought us as refugees, outcasts and migrants and, most particularly, as colonisers, to the continents which have become our homes. There is, I believe, no controversy around the fact that to enter someone else's country in order to possess it on your own behalf is an act of aggression. The 'we' who want to know are the inheritors of our forebears' invasion, and we are here as victors. Only because our ancestors were successful is there now a 'we' to ask probing questions about how we came to be here.[1]

It is said that to the victor belong the spoils, and one of the spoils of war is narrative. And if victors choose to eradicate stories other than their own, they often have the power to do so. History, however, is a scholarly practice that can oppose this power to erase memory. The social and political theorist Hannah Arendt credited Homer with writing the first impartial histories in the West. Today, our purposes in writing history differ in many respects but we still hold to this value. Arendt called this impartiality 'the highest type of objectivity we know'. However, she also accorded Thucydides the honour of expressing another aspect of objectivity: Thucydides spoke of the multiplicity of viewpoints surrounding public events, and contended that the task is to look upon the world from the standpoint of others, and to articulate these varied, and often opposing, viewpoints. In sum, I wish to argue that these values, which developed in the West in antiquity, should continue to inform our practice today.[2]

I now turn more specifically to the subject of oral histories and focus the question 'how do we know' on the issue of how we know. Investigations into oral history presume at least two parties: one who knows already and one who asks. For the scholar whose life and culture is outside this community, the interpersonal encounter takes place in a cross-cultural context, with many possibilities for communication failure. Often it is a daunting prospect to try to understand what it is that one's fellow human beings are actually trying to communicate, and often it is daunting to consider what one might intelligently say in response.

My research into oral histories has been carried out primarily among people in the community of Yarralin in the Victoria River District of the Northern Territory. Here in the savanna regions of the monsoonal north, white settlers established large cattle stations just over 100 years ago. When Darrell Lewis and I started in 1980 documenting Aboriginal people's oral histories in this region, we worked with a few people who had lived through a large portion of this period and whose parents had witnessed the invasion and lived to talk about it. The people with whom we spoke described the early massacres and other forms of violence and spoke of their dispossession under European law. They described the harsh conditions under which they worked, comparing themselves to prisoners, and told how their own labour, and that of their parents and grandparents, had been forcibly extracted from them. People recounted with pride how they had gone on strike and how through their own actions they managed to achieve a few local victories, as well as the broader one, which was the recognition of land rights. These accounts were published in *Hidden Histories*.[3]

The settler-descended anthropologist or historian who desires to learn enters a field loaded with power relations and histories of violence. Our desire for knowledge raises the question of why Aboriginal people would want to share their knowledge with us. And of course it needs to be said that not everybody does and, further, that nobody has to do so. We are privileged to receive what we receive; there is no natural right to be told history. I spent a lot of time sitting on the ground with Aboriginal people, often with a cassette recorder on the calico between us, listening to stories of extreme violence and cruelty. Often I wondered why we were doing this: why were they speaking and why was I listening?

Late in 1980, the Yarralin mob and I travelled to a small community not too far to the north of Yarralin, called Gilwi. We were called for ceremony, and the whole

Hobbles Danaiyarri, 1981
Photograph Deborah Bird Rose

community decided to go. At that time, Gilwi was just a little outstation with no houses at all and only a few humpies made of corrugated iron and tarpaulin. It was raining when we got there and so people were really packed in, kinship was pressed to the limit, and nobody, it seemed, wanted to shelter an American anthropologist. I was feeling quite desperate when Hobbles Danaiyarri came to the rescue. He took up a big fighting stick and stamped up and down the central area of the camp haranguing people for not being kinder to me. As a result they opened up a broken-down car they were using as a storehouse for their wet season supplies, cleared a place on the back seat, and told me that I could sleep there and eat some of the Weetbix if I got hungry. Danaiyarri was a gentleman and offered to sleep in the trunk but they had lost the key, so he organised himself in the front seat and told me stories all night long.

One of these stories was about Ned Kelly. Danaiyarri said Kelly had come out to the Victoria River District long before there were any other whitefellows. He had gone to the Wave Hill area and had met up with the Gurindji people and taught them how to cook damper and how to boil tea. And although there was only one little damper and one billy of tea, all the Gurindji people were fed.

People respond differently to this story, but most non-Aboriginal Australians come hard up against their certain knowledge that Kelly never went anywhere near this district. Whether or not he ought to be equated with Jesus of Nazareth seems a matter of divided opinion. But here is a story that is obviously saying something very significant. I will develop a set of propositions that lead to the conclusion that when Ned Kelly fed the Gurindji multitudes he was establishing a basis whereby indigenous people and colonisers could actually share a moral history and thus speak to each other and be understood. In the story, Kelly was here before all the other whitefellows; therefore, he is to be considered along the lines of a foundation figure who brought law. He is also equated with Jesus, another founding figure. For both these reasons his law is to be understood as morally binding. Kelly was a white man; therefore white people are capable of understanding law that is morally binding. This point is not necessarily self-evident to Aboriginal people. For about a century, there was very little in cattle-station society in the Victoria River District (and other parts of Australia for greater or lesser periods of time) which would have led Aboriginal people to conclude that white people had these capabilities. In this story Danaiyarri makes the claim that white people are human beings who can be communicated with, have law to respect, and can live up to it.

I offer this story as an account that gives a foundation for the question of 'how we know'. If we know anything orally, we know because someone chose to tell us. When we ask why they might tell us, one answer is this account: they believe we are people who are capable of understanding and responding.

I now turn to the 'know' part of the question: what are the criteria for accepting an oral history as a faithful account of what happened? In order to address this question, I need to distinguish between two aspects of oral histories: their content and their analysis of intention. One is a question of facts, the details of what happened. The other deals with the intention of the participants who propelled those events, the question of why these things happened.

Western historians are heirs to the proposition that historical truthfulness is a matter of reconstructing, as best we can, an event or series of events that happened in the past. The achievement of this — a correspondence between an event and an account — is by no means irrelevant, but it does not exhaust the task of history. Equally significant in Aboriginal oral histories is what we might call a faithfulness to the *moral* content of events.

In such stories a range of people are likely to coalesce into one or two people, and events that may have been relatively disconnected from the perspective of the participants are organised into connections based on a presumption about their intention. Danaiyarri's long narratives faithfully recount Victoria River history through the personages of Captain James Cook and a few other key figures.[4] Similarly, numerous killings in different places by different people are now often held to be the work of one man, Jack Beasley, sometimes said to have been working with a gang of killers who travelled through the district killing people.[5]

Stories that start to coalesce detail around the participants' intention tend to be placed further back in the past; that is, as events recede, those who tell the stories focus on the intention of the participants rather than on an event. The truthfulness, or what I prefer to call the faithfulness, of these stories is directed towards understanding and recounting the *meaning* of what happened (as well as the relationships between present and past). What stands out is the moral content of the process of colonisation. Details of specific content are coalesced or telescoped. From the perspective of historians wishing to represent a specific event, the results are disappointing. However, from another perspective (which is, I argued in my introductory remarks, just as consistent with the traditional concerns of historians), such stories are deeply significant. Like the Ned Kelly story that distils whitefellow lawfulness into the person of Ned Kelly, stories of Captain Cook distil the violence of conquest into the person of that founding figure. These stories reveal understandings otherwise unavailable to non-Aboriginal people. They are told for some of the same reasons that scholars like myself have sought to listen: to ensure that silence does not swallow up memory, and thus to enable a faithful account of the past, which can guide us in imagining a different future.

For Aboriginal people, the achievement of some correspondence between an event and an account of it depends on criteria for discerning faithfulness. The main criteria are:

- place — criteria of faithfulness are *located*: knowledge of where an event occurred lays out one set of criteria as to who can tell the stories and also constitutes a form of proof;

- presence — being an eyewitness to an event is taken to be a significant criterion of reliability, coupled with the general reliability of the person;

- genealogy — if the speaker had not been there, their account is accompanied by a statement of who told the story and whether or not that person had been there as an eyewitness.

Aboriginal criteria for faithfulness are not, therefore, inconsistent with the kinds of criteria Western historians bring to bear on historical sources. In both there is a strong desire to separate faithful accounts from what is colloquially termed 'bullshit'. Where both written and oral accounts of an event exist, they can be compared. The results are often, but not necessarily, constructive. Before discussing a few examples, I will return briefly to my earlier comments on perspective.

Many of the written accounts of frontier encounters are first-hand statements from white people who were involved in the events they recorded. They were in the process of wresting the country from Aboriginal people, and subsequently wresting labour from the survivors. Their representations of themselves are thus often limited, as I will discuss below. Other written sources include court records, in which one can fairly presume an effort towards impartiality although one cannot assume achievement of it. Almost all of these people, whether bushmen or judges, were influenced by the implicit racial knowledge of the day, which held, in Constable WH Willshire's pithy phrase, that Aboriginal people were 'destined to extinction with the progress of civilisation'. Many of the people whose words we now read thought this was a good thing, and some of them hastened the process.[6]

I offer four examples of contrast between oral and written accounts. The first is one in which oral and written accounts tell much the same story but do not add much depth to each other. The early large-scale killings in the Victoria River District are now related in oral histories as significant events but they provide us with little detailed information. Settler accounts also lean towards extreme brevity, although for different reasons. Bilinara people say that the first policeman, whose station was in their country, shot a big mob of people in their country. That policeman, Constable Willshire, wrote up several incidents. The statement that 'It's no use mincing matters — the Martini-Henry carbines at this critical moment were talking English' is just one of his. The oral accounts state plainly what Willshire chose to say indirectly but neither adds much to the other. The description that a Yarralin man, Daly Pulkara, provides, recreates a sense of people's terror and is more vivid than Willshire's, but both agree on the horror of it all.[7]

Alternatively, oral histories can augment written accounts. In 1895, when Constable Willshire was stationed on Victoria River Downs, two Aboriginal men from the station ran away to the bush with guns. Willshire feared a general uprising. His accounts of the event in the police journals show a man in the grip of terror. To his great relief, the men were killed by bush blacks. There was no uprising. Willshire does not offer an account of why the men were killed. If we had to rely wholly on the written record, we could form no view whatsoever, for there is no evidence on which to form a view. However, one of the oldest of my Aboriginal teachers, the late Big Mick Kankinang, filled out the story. We told him the policemen had written about this event and asked if he knew the story. Big Mick explained that the two Aboriginal men were from far away and had been involved with the whites in shooting blacks and stealing women. When the men made good their escape and joined the bush mob, the bushies flattered them by appealing to their superior knowledge of guns and then asked them to dismantle the guns in order to show how they worked. Once the men were disarmed, the bush mob killed them in payback.[8]

A third example shows how the written record can augment oral history. We were told by a number of teachers that a man named Carl Linderoth had murdered an Aboriginal man and were shown the approximate place where this happened. Details were scanty. Court reports, however, offer a vivid and grisly first-hand account of the horrific beatings Lindroth inflicted on his Aboriginal worker in 1913. I quote from a letter written by WG Stretton, the Chief Protector of Aborigines:

> Paddy an Aboriginal stated that he had seen Dick chained by the neck and roped by the legs. That while he was so secured, Carl Lindroth ... had beaten Dick on the head with a large stone which Lindroth held in both hands; that Lindroth had also kicked Dick repeatedly about the body; that Lindroth had left Dick chained up for hours and finally after loosing him had thrown him violently to the ground. Lindroth had then forced Dick to mount a horse and that he [witness Paddy] had held him on but that Dick was too ill to ride and that he had crawled away into the shade where he died ... In this case the Jury were absent from the box just three minutes when they returned a verdict of 'not guilty'.

Anyone who cares to read the court records can make up their own mind whether on balance Linderoth was implicated in the man's death. It is worth noting, however, that the reason for Stretton's letter to the Northern Territory Administrator was to provoke thought about alternatives to current trial practices 'in order that the bias of racial prejudice might be eliminated'.[9]

A fourth example is brief. According to one of my best teachers, an Aboriginal man was shot and his body dumped into a limestone chasm around the time of World War II. There is no written evidence to confirm this report. The event took place in the speaker's country (he knows the place), and he was told the story by others who had been there. This event is consistent with other accounts in which whites killed people and subsequently attempted to conceal evidence. A white man who spent time in this area just before World War I reported:

> a drastic practice in urgent cases was to induce the offending nigger to accompany a party of whites to a suitable place well out on the run where he was clandestinely 'accidentally' shot dead. The whites of course never 'talked' officially of these matters.

If the purpose of such killings is to destroy people, it stands to reason the written records will be silent and that only the memories of the family or countrymen of the deceased will seek to perpetuate the knowledge of what happened.[10]

Aboriginal oral histories are replete with accounts of silence. One kind of silence has its origins in trauma. An example of this was told by Danaiyarri: in the 1920s some women were killed when they refused to submit to gang rape. Danaiyarri said he had known some of the survivors and that 'they were broken hearted inside and always crying'. They could not tell this story; others told it for them. There are no written documents. There are many such instances — Aboriginal accounts of single killings as well as mass killings, whether brief or detailed — that have no counterpart in the written record. In *Hidden Histories,* I documented many of the whitefellow accounts of the construction of silence. I drew on pioneer accounts, such as Mary Durack's brief discussion of 'a conspiracy of silence'. I also drew on other witnesses to the imposition of silence and on court records that indicate efforts to conceal evidence. Oral histories include many stories in which bodies were burnt or otherwise disposed of in ways that Aboriginal people understood to have been intended to erase the evidence of the event.[11]

I have mentioned the practice of dumping a body in a remote place. Another practice was the use of fire to destroy the remains of killings. An example is that of two white men, William Henry Nolan and Sydney Maxwell Turner, who were on their way to Hodgson Downs with a small group of people in July 1906. During the night, at their camp near Pine Creek, they allegedly shot two Aboriginal men and burned the bodies. Staying up all night to stoke the fire, rake the ashes and break up bones, they broke camp the next morning and headed down the track. Authorities in Pine Creek were alerted to the incident in the morning, and Nolan and Turner were arrested before the day was out. The case went to trial in August 1906 and the two men were acquitted because of the apparent absence of motive. It took the jury 20 minutes to reach this conclusion. The author of a newspaper account expressed surprise: 'the general impression being that there would probably be a disagreement. The case for the crown [sic] was a strong one, consisting of three native eyewitnesses ... supported by a powerful chain of circumstantial evidence'. This evidence derived from the scene of the event and included official eyewitness accounts of the huge pile of ashes, the bloodstains, and the items removed from the ashes while they were still warm, among them fragments of burnt bones, charred beads, pieces of buttons, a spent bullet, some burnt pieces of cloth and a pipe. Other evidence included reports from white men who had heard the shots on the night of the event. This case is typical of those that ended up in court in that the evidence was not found to be conclusive. Although nobody was convicted, it is clear people were shot and their bodies were burnt. Somebody did it.[12]

If we had only written records, our knowledge of the past would often be both extremely partial and extremely shallow. We can say this with certainty because of the few but significant white people's accounts of self-censorship, and we can say this with even greater certainty because of the oral histories. Once we know that people regularly conspired to conceal public knowledge of their actions, the importance of oral histories is clear.

As we probe the silence of the Australian frontier, we discern the cumulative effects of many local erasures. Whether as individuals or as members of groups, white people in the Northern Territory were ambiguously situated: on the one hand they were achieving what society wanted to accomplish, but on the other, they were using means that society did not officially condone. They could be arrested and punished for doing that which their own society would prefer to avoid knowing. It is clear that settlers actively constructed silences through a variety of practices. With time, however, silences have come to tell an ambiguous story: does silence cover and conceal the knowledge of deeds, or does it mean that nothing happened? Perhaps it is not always possible to know. The intention of concealment was to obliterate knowledge; it must have had successes about which we will never know anything. This is our heritage: a history riddled with unnamed death.

Arguably silence still matters and it provokes this question: do we build our national stories out of partial accounts told by people who needed to forget more than they wanted to remember? From our settler perspective, shall we assert belonging to this country through partial knowledge, silences and our long tradition of erasure? Are we confined to a belonging that through its attachment to its own silences refuses to honour the blood which has been shed here? To put it more positively, can we imagine a more paradoxical fidelity whereby we would learn our history in order to be able to unmake violence and work towards some form of peaceful presence?

These questions bring me to my final point, which concerns what we know from Aboriginal oral histories. One thing we know is that our knowledge is fragmentary in many respects, and will forever remain so. Along with the many extinctions our forebears caused in the world, they also extinguished possibilities for knowledge. Yet, we can recognise the limits to Western history-making or historicising. Dipesh Chakrabarty has contended that minority histories such as Aboriginal oral histories have the potential to 'make visible what historicising does and what it cannot do'. His analysis focuses on the 'supernatural' as a historical agent and on history's inability to accommodate such thinking within its rationality. Aboriginal oral histories make visible another aspect of Western history. Until I started listening to Aboriginal oral histories, I had not thought about the degree to which history is constructed around the relatively abstract temporal categories of 'past' and 'present', the relationship between the two, and their links to possible futures. These categories form limits to history, much as Chakrabarty describes. We know of many contemporary efforts to enrich these categories by asking: whose past, whose present, whose stories and whose remembrance? Such questions underlie much of my own contribution here, as well as some of the other essays in this volume. Aboriginal oral histories, however, offer something more. Rather than proceeding in terms of abstract temporal categories such as 'the past', they offer accounts founded in relations between the living and the dead.[13]

One of my teachers, Old Johnson Bididu, told me that he stayed at Lingara, a little outstation with marginal land and uncertain tenure, because there they camped on the blood and bones of their people who had been murdered. He often spoke in an oratorical manner but he was not being allegorical. The evidence that white people sought to disperse through fires or drownings, or unmarked graves, or through silence, has for Old Johnson and others become part of the place. Memory, place, dead bodies and genealogies hold the stories that tell the histories that are not erased and which refuse erasure. Painful as they are, they also constitute relationships of belonging, binding people into the country and the generations of their lives. Daly Pulkara likewise told me stories of 'blackfellow wars' as well as massacres by whites, including one of how he himself had killed a man. These stories identify people on the basis of their descendants, and on whether they are living or dead. As such, they offer a commentary on many of the deaths. The stories locate people: living and dead bodies are situated in country, in specific places as well as in the more generalised pervasion of bones and blood. In any given place, the presence of the dead among the living is cause for the living to remain in country, as Old Johnson explained so eloquently. Historians, I hope, will spend many years exploring the consequences of thinking history through bodies and places rather than simply through time.

One of the finest achievements of academic scholarship in the last few decades has been to enter this field of history, remembrance and opposition to silence, and to find some common ground of shared purposes directed towards life. Danaiyarri tells us of this possibility, and it is implicit in every story that Aboriginal people share with outsiders. At its best, this common ground, where the participants are historians on all sides of the many frontiers, is deeply ethical. Here we all have the potential to turn stories into action, and to generate new possibilities for life in our place on earth.

1 Dipesh Chakrabarty draws our attention to the exclusions that the settler–indigenous binary may promote in a multicultural migrant society. I do not wish to exclude, but I do follow my Aboriginal teachers who, in the 1980s and 1990s, asserted that there is an axis of power and violence that draws indigenous and non-indigenous (often labelled 'white') people into an ongoing confrontation over our history, our future and our possibilities for peace ('Reconciliation and its historiography: Some preliminary thoughts', *UTS Review*, vol. 7, no. 1, 2001, pp. 6–16).

2 Hannah Arendt, *Between Past and Future: Six Exercises in Political Thought* (1954), Faber and Faber, London, 1961, pp. 51–2.

3 Deborah Bird Rose, *Hidden Histories: Black Stories from Victoria River Downs, Humbert River, and Wave Hill Stations, North Australia*, Aboriginal Studies Press, Canberra, 1991.

4 See my 'The saga of Captain Cook: Remembrance and morality', in Bain Attwood and Fiona Magowan (eds), *Telling Stories: Indigenous History and Memory in Australia and New Zealand*, Allen & Unwin, Sydney, 2001, pp. 61–79.

5 Rose, *Hidden Histories*, pp. 39–40.

6 WH Willshire, *Land of the Dawning: Being Facts Gleaned from Cannibals in the Australian Stone Age*, WK Thomas, Adelaide, 1896, p. 56.

7 *Ibid*, pp. 40–1, 61; Daly Pulkara, in Rose, *Hidden Histories*, p. 39.

8 Gordon Creek Police Journal, March 1895, Northern Territory Archives Service, F302. Rose, *Hidden Histories*, p. 51.

9 WG Stretton, in Trials for Murder, Northern Territory, National Archives of Australia, CRS A1640, item 1914/426.

10 T Lavender, Young Bill's happy days: Reminiscences of rural Australia, 1910–1915, introduced, edited and annotated by Peter Woodley, unpublished manuscript, p. 311.

11 Mary Durack, *Kings in Grass Castles* (1959), Corgi Books/ Transworld Publishers, Condell Park, 1986, p. 301; Rose, *Hidden Histories*, pp. 20–4, 34–5, 167.

12 *Northern Territory Times*, 6 July 1906, 3 August 1906.

13 Dipesh Chakrabarty, 'Minority histories, subaltern pasts', *Humanities Research*, Winter 1997, p. 27.

Part Three

How do we remember?

Tom **Griffiths**

The language of conflict

A war of words about Australia's frontier has been declared. Historians are exhuming bodies from the archives and counting them. What was the nature of the violence between Aborigines and settlers? How many Aboriginal people were shot or poisoned during the European occupation of the continent? Keith Windschuttle has accused a generation of historians, in particular Henry Reynolds, of grossly exaggerating the number of Aborigines killed by Europeans in the occupation of the continent. He has been especially critical of the historiography of massacres and of Reynolds's estimate that 20,000 Aboriginal people died in frontier conflict.[1]

I believe Reynolds's estimate is conservative, and a reasonable and intelligent quantification that will continue to be revised and can never be definitive. Windschuttle's challenge to count the dead with scepticism has elicited detailed responses from other scholars, including Reynolds.[2] I am interested here in the politics, psychology and language of his scepticism. Debates about the number of dead, I shall argue, continually founder on fundamental disagreements about the nature of history and memory, and also the language and idea of 'war'.

The killing of history

Windschuttle's 1994 book, *The Killing of History: How a Discipline is Being Murdered by Literary Critics and Social Theorists*, expressed his anxiety and anger over the impact of postmodernism, deconstructionism and other forms of 'critical theory' on the discipline of history. His concern — a common one since the 1980s — was that the distinctions between history and fiction were being dissolved and the past had been deemed unknowable. More fundamentally, Windschuttle's book was a defence of the idea of history as an objective science and a privileged product of Western society. A number of those scholars he chose to attack — Greg Dening, Inga Clendinnen, Paul Carter and Anne Salmond — were among those who have tried to step outside the imperial, European view of the past in order to embrace a cross-cultural history. Windschuttle was unsettled by the relativism that discarded the notion of unilinear, directional time and placed indigenous perspectives on equal terms with Western ones. He affirmed his belief that there is such a thing as *History* and not a multiplicity of histories. History was not just written by the winners; it helped put Western culture at the top of the social evolutionary ladder; it was one of the gifts of civilisation and one of the tools of colonisation. The substitution of history for myth was one of the triumphs of European civilisation, and it spiritually paved the way for the occupation of the New World. Europeans had a history and were continually *making* it, whereas 'primitive' people were the timeless subjects of a different form of analysis, anthropology. In the nineteenth century, history became scientific by being accurate and factual, by revering the official documents of the new nation states, and by championing a discriminating concern with 'the primary source'. Such a view of history — as the triumph of the West, the end and the means — makes one contemptuous of history from 'the other side of the frontier'.[3]

Windschuttle's argument that much frontier violence has been fabricated is, therefore, partly a campaign for a simpler empiricism, one that privileges counting, figures of authority and legal conventions, and one in which a 'reliable figure' of clandestine violence is achievable. This amounts to a rejection of the insights of histories that are cross-cultural in both subject and method. He resents the fact that indigenous memory and forms of history have been given serious attention by the Western tradition. Much of the oral evidence among Aboriginal people of violence on the frontier, he argues, is 'mistaken', mistaken because their knowledge is less scientific, and emotive and parochial.[4]

When, as historians, we get close to the 'frontier', we often find it evaporating either into intimacy or distance. Early European collectors of Aboriginal artefacts, for example, might be thought to be 'primary sources' on Aboriginal culture because they dealt in the raw material of cross-cultural exchange. In a recent study of ethnographic collectors in South Australia, Philip Jones has portrayed the frontier as 'less a line which separated than a zone which unified' and as a source of 'new and potent forms of culture'. But collecting could also be an act of distancing, a way of keeping the frontier

No 26

Oscar

Dispersing usual way

Oscar's sketchbook, late 1890s

National Museum of Australia

Oscar, an Aboriginal youth from the Palmer River in far north Queensland, sketched aspects of Aboriginal life and contact with Europeans. His illustrations were captioned at the time by the local station manager, Augustus Glissan, who accurately expressed Oscar's intentions. 'Dispersal' was one of the most familiar euphemisms of the frontier, especially when applied to the activities of the native police.

at bay, a means of denying the vitality and continuity of the other culture. In other words, the frontier messes mischievously with that conventional division between primary and secondary sources, between contemporary and reminiscent ones, between eyewitnesses and hearsay, between presence and absence. The frontier is a phenomenon supremely designed to undermine the rule of law and the legal method. Thus, a historical method that applies these distinctions too slavishly is prey to comic error and serious oversight.[5]

The construction of silence

In his 1980 Boyer Lectures entitled *The Spectre of Truganini,* Bernard Smith suggested Australian culture is haunted by the dispossession and violence done to Aborigines. It is 'a nightmare to be thrust out of mind', he wrote. 'Yet like the traumatic experiences of childhood it continues to haunt our dreams.' Bernard Smith and WEH Stanner (in his earlier series of Boyer Lectures) urged their fellow Australians to interrogate 'the great Australian silence' about Aborigines, not only to reveal suppressed facts about the frontier but also as part of an essential exploration of the white Australian psyche. For the great Australian silence was often 'white noise': it sometimes consisted of an obscuring and overlaying din of history-making. But the denial was often unconscious, or only half-conscious, for it was embedded in metaphor and language and in habits of commemoration. Silences are not just absences, although they can be manifested in that way. Silences are often discernible and palpable; they shape conversation and writing; they are enacted and constructed. We need to pay them as much attention as we pay official white noise. And analysing the uneasy language of conflict helps us discern the emotional and political slippage — the distinctive dissonance — at the heart of the Australian frontier experience.[6]

The euphemisms of the frontier, laconic and sharp, entered the Australian language. Aborigines were 'civilised' or 'dispersed' or 'pacified', white settlers went on a 'spree' and boasted of the 'black crows' they had shot. The land itself received new names — such as Murdering Creek and the Convincing Ground — that mapped the unofficial violence. The word play was conscious and mischievous. 'A quiet tongue' was said to be a qualification for a frontier policeman, and the infamous WH Willshire boasted that it was his carbines that 'were talking English'. These forms of language and description slip in and out of recognising the violence of the frontier. They reveal that many colonists accepted murder in their midst; but they reveal, too, their awareness that it could not be openly discussed. There were good reasons to be silent, especially after Myall Creek. Describing the organised shooting of Aborigines in Gippsland in the 1840s, FJ Meyrick noted: 'these things are kept very secret as the penalty would certainly be hanging'. Even those who were appalled by what was happening found themselves forced into impotence and silence. Meyrick commented in 1846: 'If I could remedy these things I would speak loudly though it cost me all I am worth in the world, but as I cannot I will keep aloof and know nothing and say nothing'.[7]

As an example of the construction of silence, let me introduce you briefly to Alfred Kenyon, the leading writer of Victorian pastoral history in the first half of the twentieth century. The 'greatest romance' in Australian history, reflected Kenyon, 'is the rise of the sheep breeder or pastoralist ... [T]he finest example of man's mastery over the opposing forces of nature, of his justification of his position at the head of the organic world, is ... the breeding of fine wool'. Through an account of the pastoralist, Kenyon told the story of what he called 'the peopling of the continental spaces' or 'the filling up of Victoria's vacant corners'. He and RV Billis produced a much used map of squatting runs in Victoria which represented pastoral holdings as discrete, bounded territories (rather like Aboriginal tribal areas) that pieced together into a jigsaw claiming the whole of the colony. Kenyon disparaged the possibility of Aboriginal antiquity and yet was a keen collector of Aboriginal artefacts. He removed thousands of stone tools from the landscape of southeastern Australia, and in their place he erected stone cairns marking the paths of European explorers. Australia's occupation by Europeans was simple, he claimed, because of 'the absence of any coloured race worthy of consideration'. He described it as '[a]n occupation where the dispossessors and the possessors lay down in amity side by side like the lion and the lamb, with the usual result to the lamb'.[8]

Kenyon went out of his way to excuse the squatter of any violence towards Aborigines. 'The old-time mission station has more to answer for than the squatter's station', he explained. His was a class history, of wealth versus labour. Any frontier violence, said Kenyon, hedging his bets, was perpetrated by the lower classes and was unsanctioned and regrettable. He repeatedly scoffed at the tales of massacres and poisoned flour, while admitting that the rumours were widespread. In fact his continual slapping down of these stories reveals that a strong current of oral testimony about frontier violence did exist, and that Kenyon and others sought to control and suppress it. Kenyon was not inhabiting a silence, he was creating it. He was confronting a cacophony of undisciplined voices. Noise there was, and he sought to overwhelm it. Kenyon's carefully constructed 'white noise' was in response to an unruly babble of whispers.[9]

In the language of conflict, there is a constant conflict over language. In 1998 in the Kimberley, I discovered someone had carefully scratched out three words on a recently erected government interpretation sign about Aboriginal–settler relations. One of the words removed was a local Aboriginal name, *malngarri*, implying the existence of a distinct language and people; another was the word 'religious', implying an alternative belief system; and the final word scratched out was 'invasion', invoking the possibility of war and land rights. Recognition of Aboriginal culture, religion and country constituted the offensive language of this sign. The great Australian silence continues to work in quiet ways.

The sinews of settler memory

For over five years in the 1980s, I officially ministered to popular anxieties about the changing boundaries between public and private in Australian history. I was employed as Field Officer for the State Library of Victoria, a job that involved the acquisition of historic manuscripts and pictures for the Library's Australiana research collections. It was known as the 'cup of tea' job, for it took one into the lounge rooms of Victoria to discuss the future of family papers and the likely public uses of quite personal pasts. That work exposed me to the politics of the past, to the dilemmas of collection, possession and preservation.

It was a time when the political and scholarly revolution in Aboriginal studies was making its mark on the history and commemoration of the Australian frontier. Victoria's sesquicentenary in 1984–85 prompted the controversial memorialisation of conflict between Aborigines and settlers, even on official plaques. Descendants of pioneering settlers were unsettled, and wondered what historians might find in family papers donated to libraries. The transformation of family history into national heritage could seem, in these circumstances, a dangerous honour.

Libraries attract unusual popular faith and esteem. It is, I believe, because they have a recognised role as the generators and custodians of stories. From the experience of my 'cup of tea' job, I can tell you an immensely heartening thing: people generally give private papers to libraries not to make money or to become famous, but to connect with — and to discover — stories in their culture. They believe, rightly, that once family things pass over to a public institution, they enter a world of popular and scholarly conversation that draws out unexpected meanings and understandings. In other words, people give to a library to learn — to learn about themselves as well as their society. Libraries and museums link people and things to the world of storytelling and scholarship. Donors of archives therefore warily monitor the fashions of research. There is a tense, symbiotic relationship between what they choose to make public and how history is told.

Of course, historical records are constantly lost and destroyed, randomly and carelessly, without purpose or import. But what is kept is kept with purpose, and what is made public has import. And therefore the gaps and silences in the public record might also signify. A fascinating graph might be sketched of the cycles of preservation and destruction and their relationship to the fashions and politics of scholarship.

In the 1970s and 1980s, there might have been an increase in the burning of early pastoral diaries and letters. As an official collector of such records, I heard stories that this was so. The reasons for such culling could be defensive or constructive. One descendant of both settlers and Aborigines (and a supporter of native title) told me that he had once destroyed a station's records 'to protect people from an explosive political situation' and 'in the hope that it might clear the air for a fairer future'. He described how and where he set the evidence of massacre to flame. He regrets doing it now. 'I thought I was doing the right thing at the time. I hope I don't burn in Hell for it.' It is possible that the sense of alarm created by conservative pressure groups in the wake of the High Court's 1996 Wik decision has led to the suppression of evidence of another kind, this time evidence not so much of conflict as of sharing and negotiation.

When records are officially preserved, they often leave the locality of their origin, go to the city, become institutionalised and thereby become subject to local suspicion. For anyone schooled in the professional discipline of history, it is a shock to encounter the proud oral culture of rural Australia. In a small community, oral sources of history are often regarded as the pre-eminent means of access to the local past.

Academic historical tradition, founded as it was on the craft of documentary scholarship, has often viewed oral history with distrust. But on the local scene, the tables are turned. There, history is a possession of the town's elders, the approved custodians of the past, sometimes 'the oldest resident'. They are people who have earned the right to pass on and interpret their town's inherited wisdom. Knowledge gains authority from its genealogy. Residents view with scepticism any alternative, outside avenues of access to that past, especially if they are literary, official or urban.

Because of their attention to particular places, local and colonial historians were always more alert to the Aboriginal past than were academic historians, who were overwhelmingly concerned with establishing their discipline through the writing of national history. Even as Aboriginal people were excluded by national histories, they found a place in local histories. The recent rediscovery of the Aboriginal past has as much to do with a new academic valuing of the local and the oral as it does with cross-cultural insights.

In the year following the High Court's 1992 Mabo decision, David Roberts explored 'the knowledge' of the New South Wales country town of Sofala and found a resilient oral tradition of a local massacre (at Bells Falls Gorge), telling of a large number of Aboriginal people who were shot or pushed off a cliff. Most residents, reported Roberts, maintained 'that the story is not just a yarn or a myth but a "local knowledge", not requiring the details and tangible proofs that historians use as the foundation of their work'. Although surviving documents tell of the declaration of martial law in late 1824, of reprisal parties sent out against the Aborigines, and of several incidents of multiple murder, no contemporary written evidence precisely confirms the oral tradition. Pages of letters are missing and official reports were not filed or have not survived. The discrepancies and uncertainties surrounding the massacre story prompted Roberts to reflect on the politics, past and present, that lead people to suppress or exaggerate violence. The community Roberts visited and questioned in 1993 clung to the oral tradition of violence but also seemed averse to discussing Aboriginal association with the area in any detail. Residents declined to recognise registered Aboriginal sites in the region at the same time as they memorialised the place of a remembered massacre. There were stories that, because of fear of land claims, farmers may have destroyed large collections of bones, presumed to be Aboriginal, which they uncovered on their properties. People kept quiet about local discoveries of Aboriginal relics. The proprietor of Sofala's museum declared: 'you tend not to want to find Aboriginal stuff for obvious reasons. You're asking for trouble'. The local massacre may well have happened, and written evidence suggests its likelihood; but the story may also have focused the memory of widespread violence onto one dramatic feature of local topography, concentrating diffuse conflict into a conclusive parable. 'What of the local Aborigines?', asked Roberts at Sofala's Royal Hotel. 'They're all killed mate', replied the bush storyteller. And so the story of the massacre could have served a similar purpose to the 'last of the tribe' monuments erected across Australia in the late nineteenth and early twentieth centuries. Such forms of commemoration, even where they were sympathetic to Aboriginal people or angry about their suffering, served mostly to reinforce a sense of inevitability about what happened, and gave a misleading sharpness to the notion of frontier.[10]

In the 1970s and 1980s, there emerged a new scholarly and popular interest in stories of frontier conflict, and Roberts explains how the Bells Falls massacre became enshrined in regional and national histories, 'the nation now believing what many small rural communities have long known'. The politics of reconciliation, suggests Roberts, sometimes means that 'plausible speculation has given way to sensationalism', and the oral tradition has been elaborated in print and given wider prominence, blurring the boundaries between the local and national, oral and written, popular and scholarly.

The importance of this study is that, unlike Windschuttle's work, it considers the motivations for both the suppression and exaggeration of violence and assesses oral culture with seriousness as well as scepticism. The sinews of settler memory are palpable and strong, and historians have to wrestle with them. The Australian frontier reveals its character through memory and history-making as well as through recorded contemporary experience. We need history because some things cannot be recognised as they happen.

The history of killing

At the heart of the frontier conflict debate — and of the concern with the number of dead — is the language and idea of 'war'. It was a frustration to many colonists that the constant domestic tension and sporadic conflict of the Australian frontier did not fit their image of a war, although they often used that term. In 1913, Western Australians even inscribed the phrase 'Lest we forget' on a monument to explorers killed by Aborigines.[11] But the experience of settlers was generally not of public violence against a respected foe, but more frequently a private drama of betrayal, fear, suspicion and disdain. 'Deep down', wrote poet Les Murray in 1975, 'we scorn the Aborigines for not having provided us with the romantic vision of a remembered war'. A proper war would have dignified the settlers' violence, brought it out in the open and allowed them the romance of heroes and campaigns. But 'war' — much as it might have offered psychological relief — was legally and politically unacceptable.[12]

'War' was also culturally imagined as occurring elsewhere. In nineteenth and early twentieth-century Australia, there was a curious conflation of a vision of pastoral peace and a keen anticipation of war. Colonists yearned for the sort of blooding on an international stage that would prove their racial vigour and exorcise their convict inheritance. At the same time as they celebrated the peaceful occupation of their new land and projected sunny images of patrician pastures and woolly flocks, they hungered for war — a real war — that would baptise their nationhood. So denial of war on the Australian frontier underpinned nationalist yearnings. And a powerful silence was cemented at the core of an emerging Australian identity.

'War' is a word that Windschuttle is keen to avoid. It is because he is bending over backwards to hang on to that word 'murder'. Concerned above all to demonstrate that colonists embraced British law and justice, he finds it easier to recognise 'murder' than 'war'. Constant, sporadic and personal violence is less disturbing to the state than slaughter. 'Massacre' is an ambiguous word because it uncomfortably slips between the categories: it describes organised mass killing that is nevertheless unequal and illegal. The Myall Creek massacre of 1838 is Windschuttle's favourite example because it is one of the few massacres officially described as murder. And so Windschuttle concludes, as if it were a new insight, that most Aborigines were not killed in massacres, but in ones or twos. He appears to find civic relief in this.

Reynolds sees settlers defending newly won land. Windschuttle sees 'legitimate police operations'. Police were 'doing their duty' he tells us again and again, clinging innocently to that word. But what was their 'duty'? Was it civil or military or something uncomfortably in between? Did the violence take place within the civic frontier, that is, within the effective embrace of British law and justice, or did it take place on 'the other side of the frontier', in a war zone? Or was it neither completely one nor the other?

La Grange Memorial,
Fremantle, Western
Australia
Photograph by Photocall

Erected in 1913, this monument was intended to preserve the
memory of three explorers who died in conflict with Aborigines
in 1864 in the northwest of Western Australia. The memorial
was silent about the Aboriginal people who died during a
punitive exhibition the following year. In 1994, the Karajarri
people of the region added a plaque 'In memory of the
Aboriginal people killed at La Grange'. Both the original
monument and the plaque included the words 'Lest we forget'.

Windschuttle turns away from the most interesting dimensions of frontier history —
the gaps between expectation and reality, and between experience and language. It
is in these dissonances that we find the distinctive character of the Australian frontier
— and the origins of the unease at its heart.

Henry Reynolds is the historian most identified with the rediscovery of frontier
conflict. Reynolds is a strange target for Windschuttle because his work embodies
empiricism and empire in some of the ways that Windschuttle wants. As Peter
Cochrane has noted in a perceptive critique of Reynolds's work, he piles up his
evidence, indulges in 'relentless documentation' and writes with 'a morally charged
positivism'. Reynolds casts imperial restraint on colonists in the most positive terms,
downplays home-grown humanitarianism, and resists the Australian nationalist
narrative that equates 'self-government' with democracy and fairness. His history
gives the high moral ground to the common law — which was ignored, defied or
misunderstood by settlers — with a consequence that he writes, as one commentator
put it, 'the kind of history that the law can take notice of'.[13] Reynolds is therefore
particularly infuriating to his conservative critics, argues Cochrane, because he has
defeated them on their own ground.

Windschuttle and other critics have branded Reynolds a 'separatist', arguing that
the invention of widespread frontier violence, now and in the past, has been in the
service of a politics of 'separatism' that aims to isolate Aboriginal people from white
society. Separatists of every era, argues Windschuttle — from the missionaries of the
nineteenth century to the likes of Reynolds today — exaggerate frontier violence to
justify protective reserves, land rights or a separate Aboriginal state. The language of
war certainly makes conflict political and links violence to land and nation. There is
a clear political lineage, and one pursued in Reynolds's work, that moves from frontier
conflict to war to land rights to sovereignty. But labelling Reynolds a separatist
completely misunderstands his work.

Reynolds's *oeuvre* is daring for the very reason that it attempts nothing less than
the integration of Aboriginal history into one of the great themes of Australian settler
nationhood. He has explicitly contrasted the forgotten Aboriginal dead with the
revered fallen warriors of Australia's overseas wars. 'All over the continent', he argued:

> Aborigines bled as profusely and died as bravely as white soldiers in Australia's
> twentieth-century wars ... [But] do we make room for the Aboriginal dead on our

> memorials, cenotaphs, boards of honour and even in the pantheon of national heroes? If they did not die for Australia as such they fell defending their homelands, their sacred sites, their way of life.

'Fell' is an immensely powerful and symbolic word here, as Ken Inglis has noted in his book, *Sacred Places*. It is an impressive appropriation of the imperial language of war. And putting a number on the dead enables Reynolds to bring this whole arena of Australian history and memory into the conventions of military commemoration.[14]

Reynolds began his research by enumerating the whites killed by blacks with the aim of demonstrating that 'settlement' was not peaceful but contested and at times uncertain. The numbers of fallen whites became a measure of the challenge of occupation and also established Aborigines as agents and not just victims, as enemies and not just subjects. Then Reynolds took seriously the far more difficult task of estimating black deaths. A conservative estimate of the casualties (20,000) enabled him to compare its significant size with the numbers of Australia's overseas sacrifices. Another reason to count — or at least to try — was to recognise, as our culture does in war, that each individual life lost in such a cause was heroic, a death to be honoured in its uniqueness, another sacrifice without a genuine grave.

Reynolds's work might be placed in that great twentieth-century tradition of historiography about the Anzac legend, a lineage that includes CEW Bean, Geoffrey Serle, Bill Gammage and Ken Inglis. Many historians have acknowledged frontier conflict and have now travelled to the other side of the frontier, but no one other than Reynolds has so tenaciously championed Aborigines as Anzacs.

We know just how controversial this strategy is from the response to Ken Inglis's suggestion in 1998, at the launch of *Sacred Places,* that the Australian War Memorial should represent warlike encounters between black and white.[15] Inglis's proposal came out of his lifelong study of the settlers' culture of commemoration and in a book steeped in intelligent sympathy for the rituals of war. It wasn't a war, wrote his critics. And even if it was a war, then it wasn't an officially declared war and both sides didn't wear uniforms. And even if it still rated somehow as a real war, then Aborigines were the other side, and they were the losers, and victors don't put up monuments to the losers. Aborigines are not Us. Here speaks the real politics of separatism in Australia today.

In focusing on frontier violence, Windschuttle takes us back to the beginnings of the modern historiographical revolution that was unfolding as Henry Reynolds commenced his work. The renewed revelation of frontier violence soon led to more serious treatment of other aspects of cross-cultural relations in Australia, and many scholars, including Reynolds, went on to develop more subtle and varied analyses of the frontier. They argued that the frontier was more intimate and personal than previously allowed, that there was as much sharing and accommodation between black and white cultures as there was confrontation and violence. Historians became critical of the limitations of what was called 'massacre history'. It was white history, they said, and it diverted attention from personal and institutional forms of violence.

It is interesting to remind ourselves of the critical reception of Roger Milliss's book, *Waterloo Creek,* published in 1992, a book Windschuttle describes as having been 'reviewed with universal favour when it appeared'. Although there was widespread admiration for Milliss's archival tenacity, and the book won several literary prizes, historians found aspects of it disappointing. By the early 1990s, there was a strong feeling among people researching Aboriginal history that a narrow obsession with violence and white guilt ignored more subtle and complex understandings of the frontier. Historians criticised Milliss for contributing to a simplified and uncomplicated morality, for perpetuating a fixation with overt violence, for returning to a concept of a purely oppositional frontier, for overlooking the Aboriginal experience and for failing to interrogate the silences.[16] Peter Read summed up the situation with these words: 'Waterloo Creek would have been state-of-the-art in 1970, it would have been in the mainstream in 1980. In 1992 it is dated in conception and analysis'.[17]

Windschuttle's critique of frontier history, by affirming the effectiveness of the rule of law, might be seen as part of the recent academic willingness to explore the range of non-violent interactions on the frontier. The problem is that he has not yet demonstrated a commitment to that exploration himself. Furthermore, by denying a whole dimension of violent interactions and the complexity of their evidentiary legacy, he has provoked a revival of 'massacre history', ignored more vital and subtle analyses of cross-cultural relations, and returned us to an old language of conflict.

The author is grateful to Bain Attwood and Tim Rowse for their comments on an earlier draft of this chapter.

1 Keith Windschuttle, 'The break-up of Australia', *Quadrant,* vol. 44, no. 9, 2000, pp. 8–18; Windschuttle, 'The myths of frontier massacres in Australian history', *Quadrant,* vol. 44, nos 10–12, 2000, pp. 8–21, 17–24, 6–20.

2 For example, Henry Reynolds, 'From armband to blindfold', *Australian Review of Books,* vol. 6, no. 2, 2001, pp. 8–9, 26; Lyndall Ryan, 'The Aboriginal history wars', *Australian Historical Association Bulletin,* no. 92, 2001, pp. 31–7; Raymond Evans and Bill Thorpe, 'Indigenocide and the massacre of Aboriginal history', *Overland,* no. 163, 2001, pp. 21–39; Richard Hall, 'Windschuttle's myths', in Peter Craven (ed.), *The Best Australian Essays 2001,* Black Inc., Melbourne, 2001, pp. 117–30.

3 Windschuttle, *The Killing of History* (1994), Encounter Books, San Francisco, 1996, pp. 304–13.

4 Windschuttle, 'How not to run a museum', *Quadrant,* vol. 45, no. 9, 2001, p. 16.

5 Philip G Jones, 'A box of native things': Ethnographic collectors and the South Australian Museum, 1830s–1930s, PhD thesis, University of Adelaide, 1996.

6 WEH Stanner, *The 1968 Boyer Lectures: After the Dreaming,* ABC, Sydney, 1969; Bernard Smith, *The Spectre of Truganini,* ABC, Sydney, 1980, p. 17.

7 Evans and Thorpe, p. 31; DJ Mulvaney, *Encounters in Place: Outsiders and Aboriginal Australians 1606–1985,* University of Queensland Press, St Lucia, 1989, p. 129; FJ Meyrick, *Life in the Bush (1840–1847): A Memoir of Henry Howard Meyrick,* Nelson, Melbourne, 1939, pp. 136–7.

8 AS Kenyon, The pastoral pioneers of Port Phillip, Address to the Dickens Fellowship, 6 November 1930, Kenyon Papers, State Library of Victoria, Box 3/1 (vii) (b).

9 Kenyon, 'Treatment of the Aboriginals', Draft letter to the editor of the *Age,* 25 March 1930, Kenyon Papers, Box 13/1 (i).

10 David Roberts, 'Bells Falls massacre and Bathurst's history of violence: Local tradition and Australian historiography', *Australian Historical Studies,* vol. 26, no. 105, 1995, pp. 615–33.

11 See Raelene Frances and Bruce Scates, 'Honouring the Aboriginal dead', *Arena,* no. 86, 1989, pp. 32–51.

12 Les Murray, *Sydney Morning Herald,* 25 January 1975, quoted in Ken Inglis, *Sacred Places: War Memorials in the Australian Landscape,* Melbourne University Press, Melbourne, 1998, pp. 447–8.

13 Peter Cochrane, 'Hunting not travelling', *Eureka Street,* vol. 8, no. 8, 1998, pp. 32–40. The unnamed commentator is quoted by Cochrane, p. 35.

14 Reynolds, *The Other Side of the Frontier,* Penguin, Ringwood, 1982, p. 201; Inglis, p. 448.

15 The Governor-General, Sir William Deane, launched *Sacred Places* and was attributed with Inglis's views in some reports of the book launch. See, for example, Helen McCabe, 'Governor-General pushes memorials for Aborigines', *Courier-Mail,* 18 November 1998; Glen St J Barclay, 'The politics of war ... and a memorial', *Courier-Mail,* 20 November 1998.

16 See Peter Read, 'Unearthing the past is not enough', *Island,* no. 52, 1992, pp. 49–53; Marian Aveling, 'The Waterloo of white guilt', *Australian Book Review,* no. 139, 1992, pp. 6–7; Gillian Cowlishaw, 'Review article', *Australian Journal of Anthropology,* vol. 4, no. 1, 1993, pp. 62–7; Adam Shoemaker, 'Exorcising old ghosts', *Australian,* 14–15 March 1992; Stuart Macintyre, 'Founding moments', *London Review of Books,* 11 March 1993, pp. 12–13; Lyndall Ryan, 'Review', *Australian Historical Studies,* vol. 25, no. 99, 1992, pp. 330–1; Bain Attwood, 'Massacre: Our absence from our past', *Overland,* no. 128, 1992, pp. 83–5.

17 Windschuttle, 'The myths of massacres', Part I, p. 16; Read, pp. 49–53.

David Andrew **Roberts**

The Bells Falls massacre and oral tradition

In August 2001 Keith Windschuttle commented on ABC Radio National:

> Oral history of events that happened 150–180 years ago can't possibly be accurate ... It's obviously healthy to get the facts right because, you know, schoolchildren go through these things. People who don't know how historical evidence should be judged look at these things and presume they're true when in fact, the slightest bit of degree of investigation can show that they're false.[1]

The particular example of oral history that Windschuttle was referring to has circulated for many years among the residents of a small, ex-mining village north of Bathurst, named Sofala, in the central west of New South Wales. There, a local oral tradition maintains that Aborigines were once massacred at a prominent landmark named Bells Falls Gorge, a dramatic site in the hills above the town where, according to the account, Aborigines had been rounded up at the top of the precipitous cliffs and either shot or forced to jump to their death under fire.

In 1993, I researched the so-called Bells Falls massacre for an honours thesis in history at the University of Newcastle, a shortened version of which appeared in *Australian Historical Studies* in 1995.[2] That research has lately resurfaced amid controversy surrounding the National Museum of Australia's Contested Frontiers exhibit, which includes an evocation of Aboriginal–settler hostilities at Bathurst that focuses on the alleged massacre of Aborigines at Bells Falls Gorge. In criticism of the Museum that appeared in *Quadrant* in September 2001 (and on ABC Radio National's *PM* program and in the *Australian* of 7 August 2001), Windschuttle used my work to suggest that the massacre was 'a complete fabrication' and, by extension, to underline the proposition that such atrocities rarely occurred.[3] This is a rather coarse misrepresentation of my findings and I welcome this opportunity for comment and clarification.

The problem with the Bells Falls massacre is that our knowledge of it rests solely on the oral testimony of local residents, who have apparently inherited a solemn understanding that Aborigines were killed there in some haunting atrocity. Exactly *when* this was supposed to have occurred is not known (except that it was safely in the distant past), nor does anyone offer any pertinent detail to flesh out the story. There is no apparent explanation of why it occurred, who the perpetrators were or how many were killed. It is simply something that happened, related plainly and matter-of-factly by the residents of this small village. The story has evidently been preserved through generations by word of mouth and is specifically regarded as a local tradition, unique and particular to that area. In the words of one old cocky, it was 'only talked about in these parts'.

Although it is not specifically stated by those who hold the tradition, it might be assumed that it emanates from the early 1820s, a period of violent conflict on the colonial pastoral frontier around Bathurst. This violence was a pivotal and formative phase of frontier conflict, being one of the earliest outbreaks of Aboriginal–settler confrontation in colonial New South Wales, and one that set the pattern for the cycles of violence that emerged elsewhere across the continent during the nineteenth century. The conflict produced several notable incidents and aggressions, including numerous Aboriginal assaults on stock stations. In one series of attacks in late May 1824, seven stockmen were bludgeoned, speared and burnt to death. This occurred in the immediate vicinity of Bells Falls Gorge, and the actual site, at least until recent times, was still known by residents under the sombre title of Murdering Hut. It is plausible that a massacre at Bells Falls was one of the repercussions of this 'outrage'.

The period was made infamous when Governor Sir Thomas Brisbane was coaxed by the Bathurst stock-owners to take the extraordinary measure of placing the entire western district under martial law on 14 August 1824, one of only two occasions in which martial law was proclaimed in the Australian colonies to deal with frontier conflict. The detachment of the 40th Regiment at Bathurst was augmented to number 75 troops. The convict stockmen were armed and the stock-owner magistrates crossed the mountains to organise and legitimise the 'summary justice'. The campaign lasted for about four months until martial law was repealed on 11 December 1824.[4]

The Bathurst conflict was also instructive and typical in its documentary legacy. We cannot be certain about what happened around Bathurst in 1824, and although more written evidence might be discovered,[5] it is likely that we will never know. The specific incidents were too distant from the seat of central authority to ever receive proper reportage. Whatever reports were filed by the local authorities seem not to have survived, and the colonial government appears to have whitewashed its account by claiming that 'not one outrage was committed ... neither was a life sacrificed or even blood spilt' during the period. This is at odds with the circumstantial evidence available. We have a large number of ambiguous hints and rumours, mostly penned by informants who were not directly involved, and numerous descriptions that emerged decades later in the form of family reminiscences and local traditions. They convey an almost unanimous opinion that the troops were engaged in fierce action, obliging us to imagine this was a time in which some extremely dark deeds were committed.[6]

This, then, is the apparent historical background to the Bells Falls massacre: a climate of hostility that could well have resulted in the atrocity related 170 years later by the townsfolk of Sofala. Nevertheless, today we are confined to reconstructing the circumstances under which the massacre *might* have occurred, for the fact was not documented in contemporary records. There is no explicit written contemporary evidence to verify the belief that Aborigines were murdered at Bells Falls Gorge.

In light of this, I set about examining the character and lineage of the oral tradition in order to determine its authenticity and assess its reliability as a source of evidence. It quickly became apparent that it was a very problematic form of evidence. As noted, there was not a great deal that could be added to the basic tenet of the story. There was simply a belief or understanding that some great atrocity had occurred at this famous local landmark: Aborigines had been rounded up at the top of the gorge, and they had been shot at or forced to jump to their deaths under fire. Few people to whom I spoke furnished their story with any further details.

It was, nonetheless, a story that was widely and sincerely accepted as being true. Locals objected to my using the terms 'legend' or 'myth' to describe the tradition. They regarded it as a 'local knowledge', and were untroubled by a lack of documentary evidence and were indifferent to the standards of proof required of scholarly history. Moreover, it was a knowledge that was respected as being intrinsically local, something contained and preserved only in the Sofala area. Locals imbued it with a strong sense of ownership, belonging to them as part of the singular and distinctive shared wisdom that defines this community, binding them to the soil and distinguishing the local from the outsider or newcomer. Certainly, at least until recent times, it was a story that was only likely to be considered relevant to those who had the attachment to place and the knowledge of local geography necessary to associate a massacre with that particular landmark.

With regard to the lineage and antiquity of the story, I was told by a number of sources that it had been in circulation since at least the beginning of the twentieth century. Several old-timers assured me they had grown up with the knowledge of a massacre at Bells Falls, having heard the story as children from their parents and grandparents. As some were descended from families who had lived in the area since the 1850s, they knew this was a knowledge that had been around for well over a century. While maintaining the appropriate air of scepticism, I found no reason to doubt the antiquity and authority of this tradition. These sorts of legends are commonplace in rural Australia, and there are numerous comparable cases in the central west of New South Wales around Bathurst. Nor are they by any means a recent invention. Similar traditions were recorded in the reminiscences of local settler families dating from the late nineteenth century. One of the earliest was given by William Henry Suttor Jnr in 1887. Based on stories told by his father and grandfather, who were prominent landowners in the region, Suttor related an incident in which Aborigines were enticed to approach a group of soldiers and 'were shot down by a brutal volley, without regard to age or sex'. Another related by Henry H Neary in 1940 pertained to a site near Bells Falls where armed settlers were said to have mercilessly slaughtered a group of Aborigines and buried their bodies in a shallow grave. The story was used to explain an eerie patch of barren earth in the back paddock of Neary's father's property.[7] These sorts of stories, apart from being widespread, seem to have a long history.

Without documentary evidence that records when someone has heard a story first hand, however, we cannot be certain of the antiquity of an oral tradition. In the case of the Bells Falls story, the first published recognition appeared in the *Bathurst Times* in 1962. In a serialised history of the Bathurst Aborigines, written by a local anthropologist and historian, Percy Gresser, reference was made to a local tradition maintaining that hundreds of Aborigines were killed at Bells Falls Gorge. Gresser, who discovered the story, much as I did, by hearing it from an old-timer who grew up in the Sofala–Wattle Flat district, was prepared to believe that this was 'a tradition with a solid basis in fact', although he remarked that the estimate of numbers killed was likely an exaggeration.[8]

By writing for a general public audience, Gresser removed the story from its traditional local oral context. Since then, the Bells Falls massacre story has undergone considerable change. It first received a much wider exposure after Gresser's death in 1969 when his research was republished in a well-known and highly regarded work, *Windradyne of the Wiradjuri* (1971), a book which has since been the staple source of every history of the Bathurst conflict written in the last 30 years. More recently, in the late 1980s, Gresser's work was resurrected and recrafted in populist works by Al Grassby and Marji Hill, Bruce Elder, and Mary Coe. In these, Gresser's casual and cautious remark on a local tradition was ignored as detailed highly dramatised accounts of naked atrocity were produced, replete with descriptions of soldiers advancing in a pincer movement around an Aboriginal camp, of Aboriginal women grabbing their children and leaping over the cliffs, of broken bodies piling up on the rocks below and the water running red with the blood of murdered Wiradjuri. These highly sensational accounts, which have no provenance in historical sources, disguised or completely disregarded the fact that there is no contemporary historical evidence for a massacre at Bells Falls Gorge.[9]

This is the basis of criticism of the inclusion of the so-called Bells Falls display in the National Museum of Australia's frontier conflict exhibit: it does not meet the stringent standards of proof required to establish beyond doubt that it actually occurred. While the standards of proof demanded by some are preposterous and plainly betray an unfamiliarity with both the documentary legacy of the Australian frontier and the nature of the historian's trade, we must nevertheless be circumspect about the credibility of oral tradition. One has to conclude, at least in the case of the Bells Falls massacre story, that it is hard to accept as sound historical evidence. It is essentially a vague, slender testimony that has left no trace of its origins: there is no record of the circumstances in which the story was conceived and whether it originated with a perpetrator, an onlooker or survivor; and from the evidence to hand we cannot trace the history of the story through the generations. Such is the nature of a purely oral tradition that we cannot ascertain whether any pertinent details have been changed or lost over time, and we cannot test the suspicion that this tradition may have derived from another quite different event, or series of events, which may have been

The British declared Martial law on Wiradjuri land in 1824. This, from our point of view, was an excuse for the soldiers and armed settlers to go out and kill hundreds of Wiradjuri men...

Windradyne was a great Wiradjuri warrior. In 1823 and 1824 he led our people in a campaign of resistance against the settlers. He was driven to fight after his family were killed in a dispute over a few potatoes.

Bill Allen, Wiradjuri Mayingu 2000

1823–1827 Wiradjuri War

conflated, distorted or expanded over the years. In short, there is no possibility of determining whether or not the story is based on an actual event.

Yet, this is an especially interesting historical narrative and possibly a very instructive one. What we might have here is a faint but tangible echo of our history of violence, a particular wisdom that has survived in a local tradition, albeit in a very diminished form, to remind us of something that was, until very recently, lost to the popular historical consciousness. While frontier violence was removed from the textbooks of national history, knowledge of it survived in the secluded and serene corners of rural Australia, and it was preserved there without reference to, or reliance on, historical documents.

As far as the National Museum's exhibit is concerned, criticisms of the reference to the Bells Falls massacre are not entirely unfounded. Recounting the massacre as a proven reality without reference to the nature of the evidence is problematic. Yet,

Part of the Contested Frontiers exhibit in the National Museum of Australia.
Photograph by George Serras

Following the Frontier Conflict forum in 2001, a text panel was added to address the question 'How do we know?'.

the display cautiously avoids the term 'Bells Falls massacre', as if to intimate that its factuality is questionable. Moreover, the curators have refrained from embellishing the display with the type of lurid, unsubstantiated details that characterised the journalistic accounts of Elder, Coe and others. Those authors can be said to have invented their accounts of a massacre at Bells Falls Gorge. Yet, this does not mean that the massacre itself is a 'complete fabrication'.

There are numerous problems with the exhibit, as Graeme Davison notes in his chapter in this volume. One misrepresentation is the implication that the Bells Falls tradition is derived from Aboriginal sources. My research, at least, suggests it is not — although research conducted by Brad Manera for the Museum does support the existence of a separate Wiradjuri tradition concerning a massacre at Bells Falls.[10] In 1993 the story I studied was unequivocally a settler tradition. This is not to deny or denigrate the importance of the site to the Wiradjuri community, or to dispute the words of Wiradjuri elder, Bill Allen, imprinted on the glass display cabinet, that Bells Falls is 'a place of great sadness' where 'our people still hear echoes of the women and children who died'. The intention here is to express an Aboriginal perspective. However, in light of the problematic nature of the evidence in this case, some clarification is required.

Although the oral tradition of a massacre at Bells Falls cannot be either verified or dated, it is wrong to claim, as Windschuttle does, that it 'can't possibly be accurate', or that 'the slightest bit of degree of investigation' proves it to be 'false'. Continuing research is yielding additional contemporary evidence on the nature and extent of the conflict in the region, furthering our comprehension of the historical context of the alleged Bells Falls massacre in such a way as to make the tradition seem more credible. Moreover, the tradition is suggestive of the ways in which knowledge of violent colonisation has been preserved in settler communities in Australia. It denotes an understanding that encapsulates the reality of the frontier experience.

1 *PM*, ABC Radio National, 13 August 2001.

2 David Roberts, 'Bells Falls massacre and Bathurst's history of violence: Local tradition and Australian historiography', *Australian Historical Studies*, vol. 26, no. 105, 1995, pp. 615–33.

3 Keith Windschuttle, 'How not to run a museum', *Quadrant*, vol. 45, no. 9, 2001, p. 19.

4 Sir Thomas Brisbane to Lord Bathurst, 3 November 1824, *Historical Records of Australia*, series I, vol. XI, pp. 410–11.

5 Among recently discovered evidence is an editorial in the *Monitor*, 7 July 1826, relating the slaughter of Aborigines 'in the late war' at Bathurst and the exportation to England of around 40 Aboriginal skulls for phrenological study. This would seem to provide some support for an account given 30 years later by Rev. Lancelot Threlkeld in his reminiscences in the *Christian Herald*, 5 August 1854, which Windschuttle rashly dismisses as an example of the missionary's supposedly dishonest and self-serving agenda ('The myths of frontier massacres in Australian history', Part III, *Quadrant*, vol. 44, no. 12, 2000, pp. 7–8). Additionally, my recent research on the Wellington Valley agricultural station has yielded more information on the clashes between convicts and Aborigines that precipitated the Bathurst crisis, including one report of the suspected involvement of Wellington Valley convicts in the murder of three Aborigines at a cattle station on the Bathurst road in March 1824 ('Binjang or the Second Vale of Tempe': The frontier at Wellington Valley, 1817–1851, PhD thesis, University of Newcastle, 2001, p. 215).

6 Brisbane to Bathurst, 31 December 1824, *Historical Records of Australia*, series I, vol. XI, p. 431. *Sydney Gazette*, 14 October 1824.

7 WH Suttor, *Australian Stories Retold*, Glyndwr Whalan, Bathurst, 1887, p. 45. Henry H Neary, *Ghosts of the Goldfields: Pioneer Diggers and Settlers on the Turon*, Merritt, Sydney, 1940, pp. 90–3.

8 Percy J Gresser, 'The Aborigines of the Bathurst district', *Bathurst Times*, 20 August 1962.

9 T Salisbury and Percy J Gresser, *Windradyne of the Wiradjuri: Martial Law at Bathurst in 1824*, Wentworth Books, Sydney, 1971. Al Grassby and Marji Hill, *Six Australian Battlefields: The Black Resistance to Invasion and the White Struggle against Colonial Oppression*, Angus and Robertson, Sydney, 1988, pp. 160–1; Bruce Elder, *Blood on the Wattle: Massacres and Maltreatment of Australian Aboriginals since 1788*, Child & Associates, French's Forest, 1988, pp. 51–2; Mary Coe, *Windradyne: A Wiradjuri Koorie*, Aboriginal Studies Press, Canberra, 1989, pp. 57–8.

10 See Brad Manera, Fighting for the land exhibition: Bunuba and Wiradjuri modules, unpublished manuscript, 2001.

Part Four

How do we tell?

Geoffrey **Bolton**

Reflections on comparative frontier history

During the 2001 Federal election campaign, Prime Minister John Howard stated that the inhabitants and government of Australia had the right to determine who entered the country and under what circumstances they should be admitted. Consciously or otherwise he was evoking a theme central to Australian history and indeed to the history of all settler societies. Immigration and the construction of a White Australia provided a major ingredient in the movement towards Federation and in the agenda of the first Commonwealth parliament 100 years ago. Probably similar ideas occurred to the Eora of Sydney Harbour in 1788 or the Nyoongar at the establishment of the Swan River colony in 1829. The conflicts and compromises that occur when newcomers seek to enter a territory already occupied have provided a major and significant theme for many historians. It is, however, often a misfortune in Australian historiography, and it has been in the recent controversy over conflict history, just as it is in so many aspects of Australian public life, that we often tend to address these issues as if they were unique to Australia; as if no other societies had undergone experiences that might provide benchmarks, examples, even processes of learning and accommodation from which Australian practice might benefit. The purpose of this chapter is to suggest some parallels and contexts from other English-speaking societies that might be of use in discussing the relationship between Aboriginal Australians and more recently indigenous Australians.

We should not exclude the British Isles from these comparisons. The dominant interpretation of British history usually begins about 2000 years ago with an indigenous population who were believed to paint themselves blue with woad and to roast their enemies in wicker cages.[1] These primitives were successively invaded by the Romans, the Angles, the Saxons, the Vikings and the Normans, all of whom eventually inter-married with their predecessors. The modern British took pride in their origins as a mongrel race. The heroes whose names survived in popular recollection from these centuries of invasion and assimilation tended to be the heroes of the resistance: Boadecia, King Arthur, Alfred the Great.

Yet the modern British also identified themselves with the Roman invaders, whose civilising mission set a prototype for the British Empire: in Virgil's phrase *parcere subjectis et debellare superbos,* to bring mercy to the oppressed and to subdue the troublemakers. It is probable that many British administrators and policy-makers believed that, like the Romans in Britain, they would have 300 to 400 years in which to advance their colonies to a state of cultural equality with themselves. Critics of imperialism tended to depict the colonised people as victims of capitalist greed, unable to resist the superior technology and resources of the colonising powers. Thus the colonising powers and their critics both denied a sense of agency to the colonised people and under-estimated their capacity to choose to resist, cooperate with, or manipulate their overlords.[2]

Challenges were bound to emerge after the process of decolonisation began at the end of World War II. The recognition of Indian independence in 1947 was shortly followed by revisionist histories in which events such as the 'Indian Mutiny' of 1857 were portrayed as abortive liberation movements. KM Panikkar in *Asia and Western Dominance: A Survey of the Vasco da Gama Epoch of Asian History 1498–1945* (1953) offered a polite but convincing questioning of Eurocentric traditions of historiography. By the later 1950s and the 1960s, seminars in British Commonwealth history at the major British universities — Oxford, Cambridge and London — were coming to recognise that the history of colonialism was multifaceted, and might as aptly be studied from the viewpoint of the colonised as of the British colonisers. In turn, this recognition led to a readiness to extend the range of methodological tools that could be used in exploring colonial history. Historians borrowed from other social sciences, notably sociology and social anthropology. Young British historians of eastern and southern Africa, such as Anthony Low, Terence Ranger and John Iliffe, came to acknowledge that in dealing with pre-literate societies where the archival record was silent it was sometimes possible to trust the testimony of oral history.

A list of the rulers of the Pedi people of the northern Transvaal purporting to cover a period of 400 years gained in validity when scholars checked the statement that a certain individual ruled for four years and eight months. During his reign, nothing happened of importance save that in his second year the sun was darkened at midday for half an hour; an entirely accurate dating of a total eclipse visible in May 1680 in southern Africa. Anthony Low, researching from official and missionary records the dynastic wars of the Ankole people of Uganda, was impressed with the restraint of an elder statesman who, although the son, brother and uncle of Ankole chiefs, made no attempt to grab the leadership for himself. It took oral tradition to establish that the man in question had only one eye and, being physically imperfect, was debarred by the traditions of his people from aspiring to leadership. So oral history gained credibility as a useful auxiliary to the more conventional tools of scholarship, although it was never seen as replacing them.[3]

During the 1960s, the study of Native American history was also coming to the fore in the United States. It should have surprised nobody that in tandem with the struggle for civil rights of Black Americans, the indigenous groups formerly lumped together under the name of Red Indians should have turned to their history, not only for its intrinsic value and interest but also as a reinforcement of political claims. Regional studies such as RK Andrews's *The Long Death: The Last Days of the Plains Indians* (1964) were eclipsed in 1970 by the immediate popular success of Dee Brown's *Bury My Heart at Wounded Knee.* Several non-Native American historians produced general histories, among them M Underhill's *Red Man's America: A History of the Indians of the United States* (1971) and WE Washburn's two works, *Red Man's Land, White Man's Law* (1971) and *The Indian in America* (1975). Washburn went on to become for many years the head of American studies at the Smithsonian Institute, whose trustees were presumably aware of his stance on indigenous responses to North American colonisation. At the same time Native American historians were assuming a more sharply polemical tone, as in the works of Vine Deloria Jnr, *Custer Died for Your Sins: An Indian Manifesto* (1969) and *Behind the Trail of Broken Treaties: An Indian Declaration of Independence* (1974), and the Mohawk Press anthology, *I'm Not Your Indian Any More* (1973).

The theme of broken treaties persisted during the 1970s and 1980s as Native American groups appealed to the historical record to support litigation over land rights. An example of the genre is Edward Lazarus's widely acclaimed *Black Hills, White Justice: The Sioux Nation versus the United States, 1775 to the Present* (1991), with its strongly phrased dustjacket:

> For all its triumphs, white America has yet to live down — or face up to — the
> primal sins of its birth: the mass importation of slavery to the New World and the
> mass destruction, spiritual if not physical, of its native people.

Such formulations of the American past did not go unchallenged. The curious thing
from an Australian perspective is that although several Australian universities had
been teaching American history at least since the 1960s, and although Australian
historians were researching the contacts between indigenous Australians and later
settlers, no echo of these American controversies seems to have informed the
Australian debate. It was only in the 1990s that an undergraduate course on Native
American history was taught at Murdoch University.[4]

Nor does there appear to have been much awareness of the work of British
scholars such as Terence Ranger who, in the late 1960s, began publishing a series of
articles on indigenous reactions to colonisation in Rhodesia and Nyasaland (now
Zimbabwe, Zambia and Malawi). Ranger charted a whole series of responses, covering
the gamut from armed resistance to manipulative collaboration. He paid particular
attention to the adaptation of the teachings of Christian missionaries to African
chiliastic and at times proto-nationalist movements, and he was also alert to the ways
in which Africans entering a European-dominated workforce could blend indigenous
traditions of negotiation with the methods of Western-style trade unionism.[5] Yet
Australian historians seemed slow to learn from such examples that indigenous
responses to colonisation could be varied and versatile.

Probably one of the least excusable failings of Australian historiography is our
sustained neglect of New Zealand history, and yet the debates between Maori and
Pakeha afford many suggestive insights for Australians. Of course the Maori were never
marginalised in New Zealand society to the same extent as Australia's Aborigines. Amid
all the disputes over the Treaty of Waitangi the cardinal facts remain that there was
a treaty, that the subsequent Maori wars were seen as full-scale conflicts entitling
British soldiers to the award of a Victoria Cross, that disputes over land were appealed
to legal process and that the Maori had representation in the New Zealand parliament.
As early as 1910 the Polynesian Society was publishing substantial works, if of a
somewhat antiquarian character, such as S Percy Smith's *Maori History of the Taranaki
Coast,* based largely on pre-annexation sources. The first modern accounts of
Maori–settler relations were produced by scholars returning from the Oxford and

Cambridge seminars of the 1950s such as Keith Sinclair and Brian Dalton. Dalton was to become a significant figure in the evolution of Australian historiography.[6]

Studies in Maori–Pakeha relations continued during the 1970s, and as they did scholars began to address the problems of reconciling the Maori use of oral history with the printed and written archives that formed the mainstay of conventional history. Michael King, author of a biography of the Maori leader, *Te Puea* (1977), which drew on both oral and written sources, addressed the problem in an important article in 1978. He cited the case of the famous pact of 1883 in which Maori leaders opened the King Country of North Island for farming selection, among other conditions stipulating that no liquor should be sold in some of the country opened for settlement. As the years passed, this stipulation was inevitably eroded until in 1953 the Parliamentary Librarian was requested to research the treaty. He reported that he could find no record of any agreement to ban liquor. Of course not, replied the Maori, the condition had been so widely known and understood that there was no need to write it down.[7]

King, having himself employed oral history, nevertheless concluded that it was a resource to be used with caution, and not to be regarded as a short cut to factual accuracy in the absence of other evidence. As Alan Ward summarised King's warning, users of oral history should take heed of 'the warping effects of recounting over time and the cultural purposes of the recounting — namely to support important values and myths rather than to strive for objectivity'. This did not mean that historians should cease to use oral sources. On the contrary, in the ensuing 20 years much New Zealand research has been enriched by such material, a good deal of it collected through the tribunal hearings arising from the Treaty of Waitangi. New Zealand historians worked in a favourable environment for the development of a sophisticated critical sense in their handling of oral sources.[8]

It is usually acknowledged that the first blast of the trumpet towards the recognition of the Aboriginal place in Australian historical discourse was sounded by WEH Stanner in his ABC Boyer Lectures of 1968. However, even before these, regional historians were beginning to pay greater attention to the indigenous contribution.

In 1961, Melbourne University Press published posthumously Margaret Kiddle's study of the Western District of Victoria in the nineteenth century, *Men of Yesterday*, the first and still in many respects the finest of Australia's modern regional histories.

Her account included some early chapters on the Aboriginal presence in the Western District that went well beyond the usual perfunctory acknowledgement of their presence. In particular, she included some especially perceptive comments on their environmental impact, something that would not be thought unusual now but was innovative pioneering 40 years ago. The appearance of this book made a considerable impression on younger regional historians in Sir Keith Hancock's department at the Australian National University such as Gordon Buxton, Duncan Waterson and myself.

In my own case, Kiddle's example reinforced earlier exposure to the British Commonwealth seminar at Oxford when I was writing a history of north Queensland. I wanted to acknowledge the Aboriginal factor in north Queensland history and I was acutely aware, and made some mention, of the hostilities of the 1860s and 1870s on a rapidly encroaching frontier of settlement. However, it was only in 1959 that the Queensland Government appointed its first full-time government archivist, Robert Sharman. He was energetic and capable, and performed prodigies in rescuing archives and newspaper files from the white ants, so that by the end of the 1960s it was possible for a recently arrived historian, such as Henry Reynolds, to embark on his path-breaking re-interpretation of frontier history. Ten years earlier, it would have been far more difficult.

I mention this issue of archives because it goes some way towards answering Reynolds's question 'Why weren't we told?'. Archival practice varied a good deal from state to state. Although some material was destroyed deliberately and much more through accident, a great deal remained in most states, provided researchers could gain access to it. In Western Australia, the nineteenth-century files of the colonial secretary's office provided the raw material for Paul Hasluck's pioneering study *Black Australians* (1942). By 1960, these were augmented by the files between 1897 and 1954 of the Aborigines Department and its successors. These were used by Peter Biskup for *Not Slaves, Not Citizens* (1973) and were freely available to researchers until 1980, when the state government placed restrictions on access. This was ostensibly because the files were held to contain material that might be embarrassing to individuals or families. It was also the time of the Noonkanbah controversy and a growing agitation over land rights, and some of us harboured the unworthy suspicion that the restrictions were politically inspired. Access was improved to some extent after a change of government in 1983. Western Australians were still better off than their colleagues in

Queensland, where restrictions lasted until the 1990s. There now appears to be a wealth of Queensland material awaiting research. My point is that it has sometimes been impossible to provide complete and objective histories of the Aboriginal presence in Australian history because researchers have not been able to get at the materials.

Henry Reynolds has already described the genesis of frontier history at James Cook University,[9] and it only remains to reinforce his tribute to the founder of the Department of History at that university, Brian Dalton. Dalton not only had the imagination to see that a remote regional university might best contribute to national historiography by making its regional focus a strength, but he also brought to the study of settler–indigenous relations the perspectives of his New Zealand experience, against which the findings of north Queensland researchers could be tested. This enabled Henry Reynolds, Noel Loos and others to go forward with their seminal re-interpretation of Australian frontier history.

Nevertheless, it remains problematic that Australian frontier history has been, to all appearances, largely autonomous in its development, without drawing on the comparative perspectives available from other settler societies, as Reynolds himself acknowledges, although in his own work he has shown awareness of Canadian and New Zealand parallels.[10] Others might follow his example. We are not the first society to confront the problem of reconciling indigenous oral traditions of frontier conflict with the printed and written versions provided by officials and settlers. Australian landowners and Australian indigenes are not the first who have to balance the economic development needed for civilised living standards and the just recognition of indigenous land rights. Australians are not the first to allow contemporary political issues to colour interpretations of the past. Australian museums are not the first to grapple with the challenge of providing the public with accounts of past events about which there are contested and conflicting histories. If, in the decade since Mabo, Australian debate on these issues has generated more heat than light this is partly because historians have not done enough to place Australian experience in an international context. It is an assignment that should not be delayed further.

1 I owe this observation to the late Professor Oskar Spate.

2 *Aeneid,* Book vi, line 853.

3 Personal communication from Anthony Low.

4 Edward Lazarus, *Black Hills, White Justice: The Sioux Nation versus the United States, 1775 to the Present,* HarperCollins, New York, 1991.

5 See, for example, Terence Ranger, 'Missionary adaptation of African religious institutions: The Masasi case', in Ranger and IN Kimambo (eds), *The Historical Study of African Religion,* Heinemann, London, 1972, pp. 221–51; Ranger, 'The Mwsana Lesa movement of 1925', in Ranger and John Weller (eds), *Themes in the Christian History of Central Africa,* University of California Press, Berkeley, 1975, pp. 45–75.

6 Keith Sinclair, *The Origins of the Maori Wars,* New Zealand University Press, Wellington, 1957; Brian Dalton, *War and Politics in New Zealand, 1855–1870,* Sydney University Press, Sydney, 1967.

7 Michael King, 'New Zealand oral history: Some cultural and methodological considerations', *New Zealand Journal of History,* vol. 12, no. 2, 1978, pp. 104–23.

8 Alan Ward, 'Documenting Maori history', *New Zealand Journal of History,* vol. 14, no. 1, 1980, p. 27.

9 Henry Reynolds, *Why Weren't We Told?: A Personal Search for the Truth about Our History,* Viking Books, Ringwood, 1999, Chapters 6, 7.

10 See the papers in Reynolds and Richard Nile (eds), *Indigenous Rights in the Pacific and North America,* Sir Robert Menzies Centre for Australian Studies, London, 1992; Reynolds, *Aboriginal Sovereignty,* Allen & Unwin, Sydney, 1996, *passim.*

Bain **Attwood**

Historiography on the Australian frontier

In recent years, conservative commentators have lambasted what they have called 'black armband history' and in particular the historical accounts of the relationship between settlers and Aborigines that have been published since the early 1970s. To academic historians familiar with this new Australian history, it has been apparent that critics such as Keith Windschuttle have little understanding of the nature of the colonial frontier. In this chapter I will first seek to demonstrate that Windschuttle has a similarly slender understanding of the historiography of the frontier; and, second and more briefly, I will endeavour to explain his interpretation of the frontier and suggest why it has struck a chord in some quarters in Australia today.

Windschuttle's historiography

Keith Windschuttle's account of the historiography of the Australian frontier goes like this: 1 Over the past 20 years a field of historical research has developed that has been 'defined' by the work of one historian, Henry Reynolds; his thesis that frontier warfare spread across Australia from 1788 to the 1920s 'has provided an intellectual framework, or "paradigm", that has determined how research is done and how evidence is interpreted'. Consequently, the history of the Australian frontier we now have does not rest on a body of historical evidence but is merely a fiction that reflects the dominance of a particular historian and his 'followers'; 2 These historians have not questioned this paradigm but have merely worked 'with the same assumptions'; indeed, there has been an 'almost complete lack of criticism' among the historians who have worked in the field over the last two decades as they have 'colluded' with one another; 3 Reynolds and his followers are bad scholars: some are postmodernists, others have forgotten good historical method since they make 'little critical evaluation of the reliability of evidence' and use '[i]nformation from any source ... as long as it fits the dominant thesis'; 4 This is so because these radicals of the 1960s or 1970s have sought to produce 'a version of Australian history designed to serve highly politicised ends'. In short, 'most of [their scholarship] is very poorly founded, other parts are seriously mistaken, and a good deal of it is outright fabrication' and amounts to 'academic deception'. As such, Windschuttle concludes, the picture academic historians have painted of Australia's colonial frontiers has 'little basis in reality'.[1]

This account bears little relationship to the body of work it purports to describe. Windschuttle misrepresents the historiography in various ways. In a highly selective reading of the historiography, he incorrectly implies that historical scholarship in the field only emerged in the early 1980s, marked by the publication in 1981 of Henry Reynolds's *The Other Side of the Frontier.* This mis-dating supports the fiction that Reynolds has defined the historiography since it overlooks several major historical studies undertaken in the previous decade or so, in particular Charles Rowley's seminal 1970 study, *The Destruction of Aboriginal Society,* which told the story of a widespread conflict on the Australian frontier — of European violence and Aboriginal resistance — and influenced a generation of younger scholars, Reynolds included. As RHW Reece observed in a review essay published in 1979, Rowley (and the anthropologist WEH Stanner) heralded a 'revolution in historiography' in the early 1970s and his work 'had a very substantial influence' on the major studies undertaken during that decade — Reynolds's documentary compilation *Aborigines and Settlers* (1972), Raymond Evans's contribution to *Exclusion, Exploitation and Extermination: Race Relations in Colonial Queensland* (1975), and three doctoral dissertations: Lyndall Ryan's The Aborigines in Tasmania (1975), Noel Loos's Aboriginal–European relations in north Queensland (1976), and Michael Christie's Aborigines in colonial Victoria (1978). (Another major study, Reece's own *Aborigines and Colonists: Aborigines and Colonial Society in New South Wales in the 1830s and 1840s* [1974], based on his 1969 thesis, predated Rowley's study.) In his attacks on the historiography, Windschuttle not only fails to mention these studies;[2] he obscures what he previously recognised to be the case. In his 1994 *The Killing of History,* in which he lavishly praised *The Destruction of Aboriginal Society* (a point to which we will return), Windschuttle observed that these historians — Evans, Reynolds, Ryan and so forth — only 'added [to] or reshaped some of Rowley's themes'.[3]

Windschuttle, it should be noted, now claims Reynolds's interpretation (in *The Other Side of the Frontier*) departed from the earlier work on the frontier and persuaded other historians that the conflict had actually been much more widespread and bloody than anybody had previously imagined. This is also incorrect. Reynolds's path-breaking study was warmly welcomed and greatly influenced many scholars but *not* because of its interpretation of frontier conflict. Rather, as several reviewers noted, it had enormous impact because, above all else, it was the first major work to try and interpret the frontier from an Aboriginal point of view (as well as to cast Aborigines as historical subjects or agents); for example, Andrew Markus noted that *The Other Side of the Frontier* marked 'a conceptual breakthrough to the realisation that there [was] sufficient evidence ... to provide an understanding of the Aboriginal perspective'. Similarly, Reynolds in *The Other Side of the Frontier* and, more especially, his 1987 *Frontier: Aborigines, Settlers and Land,* did articulate a frontier paradigm for interactions between Aborigines and Europeans, emphasising the ubiquity of racial violence and stressing its longevity and its continuing influence on later relations. His approach, however, was regarded by historians in the field as one that simply extended Rowley's analysis rather than radically broke with it. Ann Curthoys described *The Other Side of the Frontier* as 'an advance' in many ways on Rowley's work, while Donald Denoon noted of *Frontier* that it and Rowley's work were 'largely compatible'.[4]

There can, however, be no gainsaying the influence of a frontier paradigm that was and is associated with Reynolds's name among the readers of Australia's frontier history. As one historian observed in 1987 'the dispossession–resistance "model" or interpretation of Aboriginal–European interaction' had become 'a powerful academic orthodoxy'. However, at the same time this was noted, authors of historiographical surveys observed that several scholars were severely critical of it, questioning whether it was an accurate portrayal of relations on the Australian frontier. I pointed out in 1989–90 that 'another school of interpretation ha[d] become more evident in academic historiography, one which challenges the emphasis on conflict and resistance', while in 1991 Peter Read remarked that 'the previously tight homogeneity between non-Aboriginal writers of Aboriginal history has widened, and is likely to widen further'.[5]

Among the studies Read might have had in mind was DJ Mulvaney's *Encounters in Place: Outsiders and Aboriginal Australians 1606–1985*. A frequent critic of work that casts frontier relations merely in terms of 'goodies' and 'baddies', Mulvaney described a range of contacts between Aborigines and Europeans, which encompassed the intimacy of cross-cultural friendships, the ravages of introduced diseases and the savagery of violence. In so doing he remained true to the criticisms he had previously made of work in the field: 'It is fashionable', he wrote in 1989, 'for some historians ... to emphasise the thread of [Aboriginal] resistance [but] ... they also should acknowledge that there were communities ... which chose a very different response', while a few years earlier he had wholeheartedly endorsed Diane Barwick's criticism of 'revisionist accounts of Aboriginal history ... [that] seem to commemorate examples of confrontation with more eagerness than they describe the process of accommodation'. In her *'Born in the Cattle': Aborigines in Cattle Country* (1987) Ann McGrath similarly questioned Reynolds's assertion that 'violent conflict' was of 'overwhelming importance' in determining the course of relations between the colonisers and the colonised. Significantly, she also challenged the concept of the frontier implicit in his work: it should not be seen as a line or boundary but a place where Aborigines and Europeans met, and where Aboriginal people moved backwards and forwards so they 'lived on *both* sides of the frontier'.[6]

Another historian was even more explicit in his criticism of the frontier paradigm. In 1987 Reece, one of the most senior and respected scholars in the field, unambiguously took the likes of Reynolds to task in an article entitled 'Inventing Aborigines', in the sub-discipline's flagship journal, *Aboriginal History*. The concept of Aboriginal resistance, he argued, had 'served a useful purpose' in bringing into question the hoary old myth that Aborigines had simply 'faded away', but there was now a misleading impression that indigenous people could be regarded as 'a national political entity' (as signified by the term 'the Aborigines') rather than as hundreds of 'identifiable groups or peoples' and that resistance was 'the typical Aboriginal response to the European presence from one end of the continent to the other'. Likewise, he claimed that Reynolds and other historians had been so eager to uncover 'the bloodiness of the process of colonisation' that they had not been 'so interested in documenting and highlighting that other major characteristic of Aboriginal–European interaction: accommodation'. To advance this latter contention, Reece presented a case study of contact between Aborigines and Europeans in Perth in the 1840s, at the end of which he concluded:

> The picture that emerges from the Swan River situation during the first decade of European occupation is of a number of local Aboriginal groups who were not essentially inimical to the European presence, sometimes seeing it as a form of sanctuary or protection against traditional enemies. They were willing to share their resources, principally land, with the newcomers and when this proved impossible they attempted to make compensatory arrangements which would supply them with food and other items ... If there is anything that can be helpfully described as 'resistance', it is a series of Aboriginal attempts by means of force to share the food resources which the Europeans had derived from land they never ceased to think of as theirs. The whole process of interaction was characterised by a series of accommodations or adjustments made by people who did not appear to have had an essentially hostile reaction to the European presence.

Here, Reece was questioning the paradigm with regard to 'resistance'. A decade earlier, though, he had also been highly critical of what he once called 'the whole genre of "massacre history"'. Referring to recent studies that had revealed the bloody nature of Australia's frontier, Reece cautioned that there was 'a danger that recitation of this inglorious side of our history may become fashionable and self-serving. If there has been a "cult of forgetfulness" towards Aborigines in the past', he added, 'then surely there has been a "cult of anti-racism" among Australian intellectuals'. This 'anti-racism and its "conscience history"', he warned, 'has serious limitations. Recitation of iniquity upon iniquity comes closer to polemics than to history and there is a danger of over-simplification'.[7]

    Academic historians took these criticisms to heart. Consider Richard Broome's work: his measured 1982 general history, *Aboriginal Australians: Black Response to White Dominance* (which has been purchased and presumably read by more Australians than any single title by Reynolds);[8] his 1994 article, 'Aboriginal voyagers and victims', subtitled 'Confronting frontier myths' (in which he set himself the task of challenging 'a popular [but not universal] conception that Australian frontiers were violent places where whites slaughtered Aborigines indiscriminately' and argued that there 'should be an honest and sober recognition ... of both white and black violence ... [and] not an exaggerated, emotive recognition which claims all fighting and all Aboriginal fatalities as massacres'); his subtle commentary on 'massacres' in the

1998 *Oxford Companion to Australian History.* This reference volume was dismissed by the editor of *Quadrant,* PP McGuinness, as 'a kind of compendium of every wild allegation advanced for political or other purposes against earlier generations of white Australians' but the following passages from the entry contradict this:

> Aboriginal people have emphasised massacres ... in oral evidence. Some of these accounts play loose with the numbers killed in massacre ... So, too, do popularisers such as Bruce Elder ... [This] threatens to dominate our understanding of the frontier, obscuring other themes ... [Those] like Michael Christie and Elder, out of shame and their enthusiasm to detect white barbarism, have accepted colonial gossip that Aborigines were shot in their 'hundreds' in some episodes ... Politicised views of massacres have obscured instances of *black massacres of whites* and all-Aboriginal (*inter se*) killings.

'[M]assacres', Broome concluded, need 'to be discussed critically'. (In the light of the passage italicised above, it is difficult to account for Windschuttle's assertion that 'the *Oxford Companion's* entry on *massacres* ... completely omits any mention of the mass killing of Europeans by Aborigines'.)[9]

As we have seen from the preceding discussion, Windschuttle's claim that historians have merely accepted a paradigm of frontier relations advanced by Reynolds and that there has been no major critical debate in this field cannot be sustained. Instead, his characterisation of the academic historiography is, at best, a very partial account of work published in the 1970s. What should also be evident is that one of Windschuttle's central contentions — that '[r]ather than nationalist hostility, the Aboriginal response to the arrival of the British was quite different. In some places, Aborigines were fascinated by, and strongly drawn towards, white society' — is hardly original. Instead, it simply repeats an argument first advanced by Reece and other historians — indeed by Reynolds himself — some 15 years ago.[10]

Having noted a body of historical work that argues for accommodation between settlers and Aborigines on the Australian frontier, it is important to make two points here, lest we conclude that the frontier is better characterised as a place of accommodation rather than conflict. Historians such as Reece have rightly argued 'there is no point merely substituting "accommodation" for "resistance" as the key to an understanding of Aboriginal–European relations in Australian history' and have contended that '[r]esistance and accommodation can be seen [instead] as forming part of the spectrum of Aboriginal–European relations'. Second, some historians — and they include Reece — fail to consider the typicality of relationships of accommodation. Most scholars in the field have recognised that relationships of the kind Reece described at Swan River were, unfortunately, quite rare. It thus still seems reasonable to argue that in most areas frontier relations were determined by European force.[11]

Windschuttle's claim that most, or even all, the historians in the field have abandoned good historical method has been presented in a number of ways but here we will just consider an example relating to historiography: his treatment of fellow journalist Roger Milliss's *Waterloo Creek* and the response of academic historians to this book. Windschuttle attacks Milliss's historical method, in particular what he sees as his undue reliance on second-hand reports of clashes at Waterloo Creek between Major James Nunn and his troopers, and the Kamilaroi; 'what will strike the sceptical reader who bothers to wade through the whole book', he writes, 'is the sheer paucity of evidence Milliss offers for any of this'. Largely on these grounds, Windschuttle dismisses this mammoth study of the frontier in northern New South Wales in the 1830s: 'this sort of stuff should not be flattered with the title of history, or indeed, scholarship of any variety'. At the same time, he claims this book 'is now cited as the definitive work on the subject [of Waterloo Creek] by several ... historians' and was 'reviewed with universal favour when it appeared'. '[W]hat this reception amounts to', Windschuttle asserts, 'is that traditional scholarly standards are no longer applied to works of Aboriginal history in this country. As long as it takes the correct line, any big book on the subject, no matter what fantastic claims it makes, will be praised to the skies'.[12]

Windschuttle adduces no evidence for his claim regarding the book's status beyond a reference to the entry on Waterloo Creek in *The Oxford Companion to Australian History,* while reviews of the book by academic historians (as Tom Griffiths has also noted) do not suggest it is regarded as a definitive study. In fact, Windschuttle's claim regarding academic negligence rests on a selective reading of these reviews. He tells us, for example, that Lyndall Ryan described *Waterloo Creek* as a 'mighty book'. And so she did, but a reader less determined to tell a particular story might have noted the serious reservations Ryan expressed in her review. The paragraph preceding her observation of the book's 'might' reads:

> At this point the reader realises that apart from the determination to 'nail' Major
> Nunn for the Waterloo Creek massacre ... Milliss has no clearly defined purpose

in writing this book. With no introduction to guide the reader and with his obsession with detail, Milliss leaves the reader floundering in many parts of the text. The larger points that are crucial to making 1838 relate to the present become obscured. He is not interested in explaining how the structures of colonialism condone wilful behaviour on the frontier by soldiers, squatters and their servants.

Windschuttle, moreover, is not alone in being troubled by the lack of reliable evidence Milliss adduces for his claim that a massacre occurred at Waterloo Creek. In a review I wrote I argued:

> Through exhaustive research of the archival record, Milliss amasses a wealth of historical detail, hoping to create the illusion that this *is* the past, to persuade the doubters that this is what really happened ... This results in extreme prolixity ... I wonder whether anyone but reviewers and literary judges will persevere to the end of the 750 pages of text and 150 pages of notes. Apart from the tedium this occasions in the reader though, Milliss' diligence proves to be of no avail in the end since his case fails for lack of evidence.[13]

Windschuttle's assertion that the historians in the field are radicals of the 1960s and 1970s who have written history for political design can also be questioned. Many historians who have worked in the field *are* baby boomers but several were, or are, not and they include three of the most influential scholars in the field — Charles Rowley, WEH Stanner and DJ Mulvaney, born 1906, 1905 and 1925, respectively. More importantly, Windschuttle misconstrues the complex relationship between historians' political opinions and their historical work. For example, in trying to substantiate his claim that Reynolds's work has been governed by political purposes, he has stated: '[Reynolds] says in *The Other Side of the Frontier* ... "This book is written for political purposes"'. But this is a misrepresentation of Reynolds's introductory remarks to this book, in which he commented:

> It is based on extensive research among a vast array of historical records. Yet the book was not conceived, researched or written in a mood of detached scholarship. It is inescapably political, dealing as it must with issues that have aroused deep passions since 1788 and will continue to do so into the foreseeable future.

Historians' work has, of course, been influenced by subjective factors, but this does not mean that it has been *determined* by a particular political *agenda*.[14]

Since Reynolds has been the major target of Windschuttle and earlier revisionist attacks on the historiography of the frontier, some further discussion of his place in the field is warranted. Reynolds has been cast as a demon by conservatives mostly because of his prominence in the public realm and the considerable influence his historical scholarship has had in Australian political and cultural life.[15] This has obscured the fact that even though Reynolds has commanded respect in the academy, his increasingly popular work has also been consistently criticised by other academic historians. Much of this has taken place 'in house', in lecture theatres and tutorial rooms and at conferences and seminars, as well as in book reviews and review articles in specialist journals, perhaps because academics have been fearful that more public criticism might be used by 'white blindfold historians' to discredit their most important lines of interpretation.[16] Consequently, it is not surprising that Windschuttle is unaware of this discourse.

Yet, in recent times, the reservations of academic historians have been expressed in more public forums, most notably by Peter Cochrane in an incisive critique of Reynolds's *oeuvre* as a historian, published in the magazine *Eureka Street* in 1998, in which he drew on the criticisms his fellow historians had already made. He discussed, for example, Reynolds's emphasis on an 'oppositional' model of frontier relations and his downplaying of other patterns of contact; his method of drawing thinly described historical examples from all over the country; his failure to situate his work in relation to other historical scholarship, both here and overseas; his penchant for conventional moral and political frameworks; his indifference to theory and the subsequent lack of conceptual frameworks; and his morally charged empiricism. Yet, noting that the claim that 'Reynolds "overdoes the violence theme" is now a throwaway line in Australian history circles', Cochrane also remarked that 'tall poppies [like Reynolds] are easily caricatured'. Indeed, these days it can be argued that criticism of Reynolds's work in the academy has almost become *de rigueur,* so much so that some historians have complained about 'Reynolds bashing'.[17] Some of this criticism no doubt springs from the jealousy of some of Reynolds's academic brothers and sisters as well as the envy of his professional sons and daughters.[18]

Governor Arthur's proclamation to the Aborigines, 1828
National Library of Australia

Contrasting images of Aborigines and British justice: Arthur's proclamation, distributed on bark panels in 1828, aimed to communicate the principle of equality under the law. Frome's watercolour recorded the aftermath of an event in South Australia in 1840, when two Aborigines were brought to 'summary justice' for murdering the survivors of a shipwreck. The execution, conducted under instructions from Governor Gawler and witnessed by other members of the 'tribe', went badly wrong. When Frome came across the scene seven weeks after the event, the corpses were still hanging. (See Geoffrey Dutton, *White on Black,* Macmillan, Melbourne, 1974, pp. 124–5.)

EC Frome
Pilgaru — Two natives hung for murder, September 1840
watercolour, 10.1 x 18.5
Art Gallery of South Australia

Windschuttle's history

Windschuttle has not only attacked the historical consensus on the broad features of the Australian frontier that has emerged as the result of scholarly historical research; he has also advanced his own interpretation. Here, we will consider the first, and presumably the most important, of his 'three principal arguments':

> rather than genocide and frontier warfare, British colonisation of Australia brought civilised society and the rule of law ... The penalty for the unlawful killing of an Aborigine was death, the same as for killing a white man. This was enshrined in one celebrated incident, the Myall Creek Massacre [*sic*, that is, the trial] of 1838 ... Modern historians try to argue this event away by saying it was the exception rather than the rule. The fact remains, however, that it was a highly publicised case of the rule of law being upheld and justice being done in a way that could not fail to impress even the most crudely racist member of the then penal colony. There is a considerable body of other evidence from the pastoral frontier that shows the colonial police did their duty and the authorities scrutinised their activities closely.

Claiming that the rule of law characterised the frontier in the Australian colonies is, as Reynolds has remarked, 'truly extraordinary'. (Why, one might ask, does the author of *The Killing of History* invest so much in an ideal that the law worked strongly enough to prevent the killing of large numbers of Aboriginal people?)[19] Detailed historical research by the likes of AGL Shaw has shown that, however much colonial governors and others tried to implement this ideal, they were either foiled on the ground by settler opposition, the tyranny of distance, legal constraints and so forth, or they failed in their resolve. This lack of control was all the greater when government authority shifted from the imperial centre to most of the colonies in the 1850s, most notably in the case of Queensland (since this occurred at the very time that the invasion of Aboriginal lands began in earnest).[20]

Myall Creek, moreover, *was* exceptional. As Andrew Markus has noted, the Myall Creek trial 'was a landmark event' but 'its full significance is often misunderstood' by historians. Although it can be seen as an example of 'the impartial administration of the law', it also reveals many colonists were unwilling 'to treat the murder of Aborigines as a crime'. More importantly, there is no evidence that the case set a precedent. On the contrary, there are only four known cases in which Europeans were executed for the murder of Aborigines during the period of frontier conflict, and only ten Europeans are known to have been executed for killing Aborigines in the nineteenth century, and seven of these were for the same deed at Myall Creek. Markus acknowledges that executions could have taken place unbeknown to historians but regards this as unlikely given that 'such unusual events as the hanging of white men for the murder of Aborigines were long remembered'. Despite Windschuttle's penchant for historical arithmetic or accountancy, he has not taken any note of Markus's statistical report.[21]

Historians have questioned why Windschuttle has constructed such an interpretation of the frontier. Some have contended that he has a political purpose: Lyndall Ryan, for example, has argued that he has contributed to 'a well orchestrated campaign' by the conservative magazine *Quadrant,* which has been 'designed to cast doubts in the mind of ordinary Australians about the significance of frontier conflict in the past and how it has shaped relations between Indigenous and non-Indigenous Australians in the present'. Certainly, Windschuttle has a history of political allegiances: 'In the '70s I was a Marxist, in the '80s I was a social democrat and in the '90s I'm a conservative. It's called growing up', he has commented. Other historians have suggested that Windschuttle's work is better understood more broadly as a defence of Western civilisation. This seems to accord with the way in which Windschuttle himself describes his project: 'the West', he remarked recently, 'is the only game in town'. Whether his work is politically motivated or not, it readily lends itself to political purposes, as the American historian Dominick LaCapra observed in a review of *The Killing of History* in 1998: 'Windschuttle argues for rationality, detachment, objectivity, and being open to evidence, but he does so in a vitriolic style that attests to a closed mind and is suited to the narrowest form of party-political agitation, if not to a bloody crusade'. In particular, Windschuttle's bellicose writings seem to have struck a chord among those whom he has called 'dead white males' — Anglo-Australians who, in the age of uncertainty, see themselves under siege, threatened by multiculturalism, Aboriginality and the like.[22]

The more Windschuttle's work has been subject to critical scrutiny in the course of this controversy, the more extreme his interpretation has become. Having begun by questioning massacres and the number of those killed, he now questions whether Australia was a violent frontier at all. In the light of this, it is instructive to consider what Windschuttle wrote several years ago in *The Killing of History*:

> Probably the greatest claim to artistry that research and evidence can make occurs when they allow us to see things from a new, unexpected and illuminating perspective. For my money, the outstanding example of this in Australian historiography is Charles Rowley's 1970 publication *The Destruction of Aboriginal Society* ... [It] ... threw the history of European settlement since 1788 into a vivid new relief that has since been impossible not to recognise.

Even as recently as October 2000 Windschuttle still seemed to have been of this mind, given the following passage in the first of his three-part series for *Quadrant:*

> The broad historical framework about these matters was established in 1970 by Charles Rowley in his book *The Destruction of Aboriginal Society*. Rowley was the first historian to demonstrate that the Aborigines had endured a long, unbroken arch, stretching from the eighteenth century to the twentieth, of violence, dispossession and incarceration. Nothing I have read for this essay has persuaded me that his overall assessment is fundamentally wrong.

Here at least Windschuttle was still able to recognise the basic reality of Australia's colonial history. Now, he has lost sight of this.[23]

Windschuttle's work has provoked strong critical responses from historians in the field of Aboriginal history, but his intervention is essentially irrelevant in scholarly terms. This does not mean there are no serious weaknesses in the academic historiography. Most significantly, academic historians have not done enough to demonstrate the most important processes of colonisation in Australia, those that relate to land (or other forms of capital) *and* labour. In focusing on frontier conflict we can too readily lose track of the keen insights of those such as Charles Rowley who realised the plight of Aboriginal people has been the outcome of their being dispossessed of the means of production, time and time and time again. Too few of our histories show satisfactorily how the colonial past has, on the one hand, led to the present and, on the other, is still present. Instead, they tend to have what Patrick Wolfe has called 'an insulating effect', inserting 'a screen into Australian historical consciousness' and thereby rendering colonisation as 'a past event' rather than as a process that has continued and continues, and has had, and still has, devastating effects. In today's political climate, answering ill-informed conservative criticisms of the work of academic historians has, sadly, been necessary. But now it is time to move on. We have work to do.[24]

[1] Keith Windschuttle, 'Exposing academic deception of past wrongs', *Sydney Morning Herald*, 19 September 2000; Windschuttle, 'The myths of frontier massacres in Australian history', Part II, *Quadrant*, vol. 44, no. 11, 2000, p. 22; Windschuttle, 'Selected readings', *Australian Review of Books*, vol. 6, no. 3, 2001, p. 5; Windschuttle, 'The fabrication of Aboriginal history', *New Criterion*, vol. 20, no. 1, 2001, <www.newcriterion.com>, pp. 3, 6.

[2] Windschuttle refers to Ryan's and Christie's later books but not to the theses on which they are based.

[3] RHW Reece, 'The Aborigines in Australian historiography', in John A Moses (ed.), *Historical Disciplines and Cultures in Australasia*, University of Queensland Press, St Lucia, 1979, pp. 266–8; Windschuttle, *The Killing of History: How a Discipline is Being Murdered by Literary Critics and Social Theorists*, Macleay Press, Sydney, 1994, p. 117.

[4] Andrew Markus, 'Review of *The Other Side of the Frontier*', *Journal of Australian Studies*, no. 10, 1982, p. 69; Ann Curthoys, 'Rewriting Australian history: Including Aboriginal resistance', *Arena*, no. 62, 1983, p. 103; Donald Denoon, 'Review of Frontier', *Australian Historical Studies*, vol. 23, no. 90, 1988, p. 130.

[5] Reece, 'Inventing Aborigines', *Aboriginal History*, vol. 11, no. 1, 1987, p. 16; Peter Read, 'Review of *A Picnic with the Natives* [*et al.*]', *Australian Historical Studies*, vol. 24, no. 97, 1991, p. 483; Bain Attwood, 'Aboriginal history', *Australian Journal of Politics and History*, vol. 41, 1995, p. 140.

[6] Diane Barwick, cited in DJ Mulvaney, '"A sense of making history": Australian Aboriginal studies 1961–1986', *Australian Aboriginal Studies*, no. 2, 1986, p. 55; Mulvaney, *Encounters in Place: Outsiders and Aboriginal Australians 1606–1985*, University of Queensland Press, St Lucia, 1989, p. 54; Henry Reynolds, *The Other Side of the Frontier: An Interpretation of the Aboriginal Response to the Invasion and Settlement of Australia*, History Department, James Cook University, Townsville, 1981, p. 49; Ann McGrath, *'Born in the Cattle': Aborigines in Cattle Country*, Allen & Unwin, Sydney, 1987, p. 21, her emphasis.

[7] Reece, 'Aborigines in Australian historiography', pp. 262–4; Reece, Aboriginal community history: A cautionary tale, Paper delivered to the Australian Historical Association Conference, Sydney, 1982, p. 6; Reece, 'Inventing Aborigines', pp. 14–17, 22.

[8] This title (and its revised edition of 1994) has sold over 35,000 copies, whereas Reynolds's *The Other Side of the Frontier* has sold fewer than 30,000 copies (personal communications, Richard Broome, Henry Reynolds and Clare Forster, 3, 8 and 10 December 2001).

[9] Richard Broome, 'Aboriginal victims and voyagers: Confronting frontier myths', *Journal of Australian Studies*, no. 42, 1994, pp. 71–2, 74; Broome, 'Massacres', in Graeme Davison, John Hirst and Stuart Macintyre (eds), *The Oxford Companion to Australian History*, Oxford University Press, Melbourne, 1998, p. 415; PP McGuinness, 'Truth, sentiment and genocide as a fashion statement', *Sydney Morning Herald*, 14 September 2000; Windschuttle, 'The myths of frontier massacres in Australian history', Part I, *Quadrant*, vol. 44, no. 10, 2000, p. 21.

[10] Windschuttle, 'The fabrication', p. 8. In his criticisms of Reynolds's work, Windschuttle has also overlooked an important part of his *oeuvre*, *With the White People*.

[11] Reece, 'Inventing Aborigines', p. 22.

[12] Windschuttle, 'The myths of massacres', Part I, pp. 14–16.

[13] Ryan, 'Review of Waterloo Creek', *Australian Historical Studies*, vol. 25, no. 99, 1992, p. 330; Attwood, 'Massacre: Our absence from our past', *Overland*, no. 128, 1992, p. 84.

[14] Windschuttle, quoted in Andrew Stevenson, 'A voice from the frontier', *Sydney Morning Herald*, 22–23 September 2001.

[15] The nature of this influence is commonly misunderstood. For example, it is often claimed that Reynolds's book *The Law of the Land* (1987) swayed the majority of the High Court judges in the Mabo decision. As Reynolds and others have argued, historians undoubtedly 'played a major role in the fundamental re-interpretation of Australia's past which found expression in the Mabo decision'. However, this was so because their work helped to deepen 'a crisis of legitimacy for the rule of law' in Australia, which had emerged in the late 1960s and early 1970s in the context of demands for Aboriginal land rights, such that the highest court in the land was eventually forced 'to bring [the] law into line with the now-acknowledged "facts" of history in order to restore the law's legitimacy' (see Reynolds, 'Introduction', in Reynolds (ed.), *Race Relations in North Queensland*, second edition, History Department, James Cook University, Townsville, 1993, p. 3; Rosemary Hunter, 'Aboriginal histories, Australian histories, and the law', and Richard Broome, 'Historians, Aborigines and Australia: Writing the national past', in Attwood (ed.), *In the Age of Mabo: History, Aborigines and Australia*, Allen & Unwin, St Leonards, 1996, pp. 1–16, 54–72; David Ritter, 'The "rejection of terra nullius" in Mabo: A critical analysis', *Sydney Law Review*, vol. 18, no. 1, 1996, pp. 5–33).

[16] See especially Curthoys, pp. 100–10, but also, for example, Markus, *passim*; Richard Broome, 'Review of *The Other Side of the Frontier*', *Historical Studies*, vol. 20, no. 78, 1982, pp. 125–7; Denoon, *passim*; Heather Goodall, 'Review of *The Law of the Land*', *Labour History*, no. 55, 1988, pp. 88–90; DJ Mulvaney, 'Review of *The Law of the Land*', *Overland*, no. 111, 1988, pp. 94–5; Attwood, 'Aborigines and academic historians: Some

recent encounters', *Australian Historical Studies*, vol. 24, no. 94, 1990, pp. 130–1, 'Review of *Dispossession*', *Aboriginal History*, vol. 15, part 2, 1991, pp. 169–70, 'Review of *With the White People*', *Overland*, no. 122, 1991, pp. 73–5.

17   Peter Cochrane, 'Hunting not travelling', *Eureka Street*, vol. 8, no. 8, 1998, pp. 32–40; Tom Griffiths, personal communication, July 1999.

18   See, for example, Beverley Kingston, 'A letter from Sydney', *Australian Historical Studies*, vol. 32, no. 111, 2001, pp. 141–5.

19   See my 'The historian's sigh', *Australian Financial Review*, 22 February 2002, for a consideration of this question.

20   Reynolds, 'From armband to blindfold', *Australian Review of Books*, vol. 6, no. 2, 2001, p. 8; Windschuttle, 'The fabrication', p. 7.

21   Markus, *Australian Race Relations, 1788–1993*, Allen & Unwin, Sydney, 1994, pp. 46–9.

22   Ryan, 'The Aboriginal history wars', *AHA Bulletin*, no. 92, 2001, p. 32; Dominick LaCapra, 'Review of *The Killing of History*', *American Historical Review*, vol. 103, no. 1, 1998, p. 149; Stevenson; David Myton, 'Windschuttle's way', *Campus Review*, vol. 12, no. 2, 2002, pp. 10–11; Windschuttle, 'How not to run a museum', *Quadrant*, vol. 45, no. 9, 2001, p. 12.

23   Windschuttle, *The Killing of History*, p. 246; Windschuttle, 'The myths of massacres', Part I, p. 21.

24   Patrick Wolfe, 'Nation and MiscegeNation: Discursive continuity in the post-Mabo era', *Social Analysis*, no. 36, 1994, p. 96.

Ann **Curthoys**

Constructing national histories

Throughout the 1990s and now in the early years of the twenty-first century, Australia's past has been hotly contested territory. Such contests are not peculiar to Australians, but are important in many other countries, including Japan, Germany, the United States and Britain. As a former colonial and settler society, however, Australia has some particularly difficult issues to confront. How brutal and destructive was our own colonial past, and what, if anything, ought non-indigenous Australians now think and do about it? Are apologies, reparations and conciliation in order? Public debates over the meaning of the past for the present have focused on a number of fronts: land rights and native title; the child-removal policies of the past; and the nature and degree of violence and death on the frontiers of settlement between 1788 and the 1930s. The forum at the National Museum of Australia confronted the last of these issues. In this chapter I do not consider the details of the debate about frontier conflict but rather the broader political and historiographical context in which the debate has occurred.[1]

In the last two decades of the twentieth century, Aboriginal people challenged existing Australian understandings of the colonial past by emphasising their prior occupation, direct experience of invasion and racism, and their ongoing struggles for survival. This counter-history was told especially through written life stories and oral testimony, and had a significant impact on historians, the law and public life. Aboriginal voices successfully converted the bicentennial commemoration of 1988 from a celebration to a reconsideration of the meaning of white settlement itself. Several years later, the view of history embedded in two legal decisions concerning native title — the Mabo decision of 1992 and the Wik decision of 1996 — challenged the deeply held beliefs of Australians. Aboriginal prior ownership and occupancy of the land was for the first time legally recognised, and the moral and legal basis of white Australian society further brought into question.

Aboriginal testimonial reached its maximum public impact and apotheosis in *Bringing Them Home,* the report of a government inquiry into the 'stolen generations' — those indigenous people taken away as children from their parents through most of the twentieth century. This 1997 report shocked many in describing Australian child-removal policies as genocidal, and as motivated by the desire to destroy Aboriginal identity and distinctiveness altogether. The question of 'genocide' was then debated in relation to both child-removal policies and the motives and actions of settlers on the frontier. The magazine *Quadrant* became the flag-bearer of angry rejections of any suggestion that 'genocide' might be an applicable term in the Australian context, whether as a description of child-removal policies or of conflict on the frontier.

Thus the specific debate over how many people were killed, and why, has a larger context. It is a debate about the moral basis of Australian society. Where an older tradition of Australian historiography saw British colonisation of the Australian continent as a worthy enterprise, leading to the transplantation of European civilisation and people, and to political, social, cultural and especially economic development where there had been little before, more recent historical work — dubbed by its opponents as 'black armband' history — tells a profoundly discomforting story of invasion, colonisation, dispossession, exploitation, institutionalisation and genocide. Aboriginal people, who appear in the earlier accounts either as savages who had to be fought if settlement were to proceed or as harmless people offering little resistance and tending simply to fade away in the face of British civilisation, appear in current historical accounts clearly and unambiguously as victims of white aggression and racism. In the last 20 years or more, a recognition that white settlement occurred at the expense of the indigenous occupiers of the land has influenced much Australian historical representation, from widely read books such as those by Richard Broome and Henry Reynolds, through to school textbooks and popular cultural forms such as television series, film, poetry, novel, song and drama.

At the same time as this kind of history has been growing in prominence and acceptance, so also has its widespread rejection. Conservative politicians detest it, for it tends to locate them, as critics of current indigenous demands, in a rejected past.

So do many other non-Aboriginal Australians, who, facing significant economic problems of their own, are in no mood to consider themselves as 'invaders' or the beneficiaries of colonisation. Many do not wish to be told their whole society was built on a process of invasion and child theft; they want, instead, to re-assert pride in their history, institutions and culture. In public debate on radio and newspapers, many non-Aboriginal Australians openly express a preference for returning to a 'positive' understanding of Australian history, which assumed or argued explicitly for the rightfulness of colonisation, and emphasised colonists' struggles and difficulties, processes of 'pioneering' and settlement, and the hard-won achievement of economic development, political freedoms and social harmony.

The angry rejection of the idea that Australia has a racist or violent past, I argue in this chapter, has its basis in some deeply held beliefs about white Australian historical experience. Many non-indigenous Australians have difficulty in seeing themselves as the beneficiaries of the colonisation process because they, like so many others, from the United States to Israel and elsewhere, see themselves as *victims,* not oppressors. The idea of settler innocence remains powerful in Australian popular culture, just as it does in the United States. Australian popular historical mythology stresses struggle, courage and survival, amidst pain, tragedy and loss. There is a special charge associated with the status of victim in Australian historical consciousness, and it is notable how good non-Aboriginal Australians are at memorialising their own sufferings. Looked at more closely, the contest over the past is perhaps not between positive and negative versions, but between those that place white Australians as victims, struggling heroically against adversity, and those that place them as aggressors, forcing adversity onto others.

Several commentators have already noted this attraction to a self-image of suffering, sacrifice and defiance in defeat. Andrew Lattas, for example, has examined how Australian nationalist discourses emphasise a struggle in which the pioneer, the explorer and the artist all suffer as they seek to possess the land: 'Their suffering takes on the epic proportions of a pilgrimage that redeems and heals the nation'. White settler suffering, he suggests, becomes a means for conferring right of ownership to the land. Ross Gibson also points to the salience of stories of heroic failure in Australian popular culture, although he sees this tradition as having waned in the 1980s, replaced by new themes of success. Gibson seems to me too hasty here; new themes did emerge in the 1980s, but they did not replace or efface the old. Indeed, the revitalisation of the film industry, and the consequent flood of representations of older stories in new film and mini-series modes, did a great deal to give the long-standing themes of heroic defeat new life and vitality. In *Sacred Places,* Ken Inglis has explored in great detail the ways in which Australians remember their own suffering from World War I and other conflicts, and indeed many commentators have noted that the Anzac story provides one of the most important and enduring of white Australian myths of grief, loss and sacrifice.[2]

I want to build on this insight regarding the attraction to failure and defeat as a powerful part of Australian national identity, and apply it more specifically to Australian historical consciousness. I will consider a number of ways in which Australians see themselves as victims in their own history, especially in their popular understandings of the taking of the lands of indigenous peoples. My focus throughout is on foundational white narrative and mythology as created by, and associated with, those who came from Britain and Ireland, making up the majority of immigrants before World War II, and still the forebears of the majority of the population.[3] My argument is that the emphasis in white Australian popular historical mythology on the settler as victim works against substantial acknowledgment and understanding of a colonial past, and informs and inflames white racial discourse.

Exodus

Australian popular historical narratives embody major themes of Judeo-Christian history — expulsion, betrayal, suffering, revenge, persistence, guilt and love. For such a secular society, the influence of biblical stories is profound, but this is not really so odd. As Benedict Anderson has suggested, nationalist thought rests on older religious dreams and ideals, while Regina Schwartz has noted that 'sacred categories of thought have not just disappeared. They have lingered into the modern world where they are transformed into secular ones'.[4] Stimulated by Edward Said's re-interpretation of the Exodus story from a Canaanite perspective,[5] Schwartz draws attention to the continuing resonances of the story. The Israelites who had gone to Egypt to escape famine, grew to a great multitude, to the alarm of the Egyptians, who enslaved them. Under the leadership of Moses, the Israelites fled from their oppressors in Egypt, wandered through the desert, and came to the Promised Land — the land of Canaan — that they then conquered and occupied. The original Exodus, fleeing bondage under the Pharaoh, becomes the moral justification for the later conquest of the Canaanites. The earlier victimhood warrants the later aggression.[6]

The biblical narrative of Exodus rests on a rhetoric of victimisation. A persecuted past is invoked to legitimate present policy. Conquest is justified by the injustices of the past, and a new society and people are created through the displacement and destruction of another people, the Canaanites. Several scholars have noted the way the story of Exodus is reworked to provide the foundations for both American and Israeli national historical narratives. The pilgrims left Britain for America, a new Promised Land reserved by God for his new chosen people, liberating themselves from the tyranny of the British Pharaoh. Sacvan Bercovitch argues that the Puritans, identifying New England as the New Canaan, saw the worldly enterprise of colonisation as a mission to restore mankind. Where Christian thinking traditionally saw the material and the spiritual as unrelated, the Puritans thought that in New England alone salvation and riches went together. These ideas became the foundation of an enduring national dream of a distinctive American mission.[7]

Deborah Bird Rose has taken up Bercovitch's idea: Americans feel they have freed themselves from a 'hardened, sullen-tempered pharaoh' in order to inhabit a New Promised Land and secure a New Covenant with God. She argues that in contrast to this American foundational mythology, Australian historical consciousness has a somewhat different narrative of exile and expulsion:

> Australia, in contrast, was from the first conceived as hell on earth, and its foundation owes more to the myth of Expulsion than to any myth or dream of liberation. In the first decades the majority of the people who settled here did so not to escape Pharaoh, but at the precise will and directive of Pharaoh ... The Expulsion myth situates Home as Eden, the monarch as God, and the convicts as sinful fallen people doomed to a life of toil and sweat amidst thorns and thistles.

It seems to me, and this is hinted at by Rose, that in the Australian case both stories sit together, the story of the fall and expulsion from Eden, and the story of the exodus from Egypt for the Promised Land.[8]

The pioneers

The victimological narrative, protean, durable and endlessly resurrected, involves first of all the convicts, expelled from their own country and condemned to suffer in another. While public discourse during much of the nineteenth century was harsh on convict discipline and morality, by the twentieth century convicts were often seen as innocent victims of a harsh British penal and economic system. Even more innocent were the free immigrants drawn mainly from Britain and Ireland who had to fight for New World freedoms against the class rigidities and hierarchies of the Old. If the convict era called up a strange fascination with a past almost too horrible to contemplate, it was much easier to remember the 'pioneers', a loose general category of early settlers admired for their difficult victory in the task of settlement. Australia is not alone, of course, in memorialising these pioneers: they are common to all settler societies. Australian pioneers have their own particular features, though. They are thought to have endured the harshest continent on earth, with its endless drought, fire and flood, their struggle most poignantly signified by the near starvation in the first years of settlement, or in the story of the selectors later in the century who attempted to carve out a living from an often unforgiving land.

Originally denoting simply those who came early, before self-government, John Hirst points out that 'pioneer' came to acquire its particular associations with land in the 1890s and the early years of the new century, when a newly forming nation created a nationalistic golden age from the recent past. The pioneer legend was developed in poem, painting, novel and history book, and continues still in these forms, as well as in reconstructed villages, re-enactments and anniversary celebrations. It is popular because it is so inclusive of Anglo-Celtic Australia, crossing the serious social divides of class and gender, celebrating small and large farmers, and men and women alike. Indeed the presence of women pioneers was particularly admired, since the bush and the outback were originally thought of as no place for a white woman at all. Women were the symbol of the arrival of domesticity and civilisation where none had existed before.[9]

Far less inclusive in terms of class and gender, the radical nationalist legend celebrated the itinerant male workers of the bush and the outback. Building on the work of earlier writers and intellectuals such as Vance Palmer, Russel Ward's popular history *The Australian Legend* (1958) argued that the characteristics that Australians like to think of as typically Australian — 'a fiercely independent person who hates officiousness and authority, especially when these qualities are embodied in military officers and policemen' — derived from the itinerant workers of the pastoral industry. These men of the lower classes bequeathed a distinctive Australian type, with profoundly egalitarian values: self-deprecating laconic humour, irreverence, anti-authoritarianism, informality and anti-pomposity. This Australian masculine type lives on, especially in film, from Chips Rafferty in *The Overlanders* (1946), to Jack Thompson in *Sunday Too Far Away* (1975), Bryan Brown in *A Town Like Alice* (1981), and most notably Paul Hogan in *Crocodile Dundee* (1986).

Yet these two enduring national myths — the pioneer legend and the 'Australian' legend — are not so opposed. Although one is inclusive of class and gender, forming as Hirst suggests 'a national rural myth, democratic in its social bearing, conservative in its political implications', and the other is a more class-conscious celebration of the male worker, both are silent on race and ethnicity. Both refer only infrequently to non-British immigrants, and both obscure the dispossession of indigenous peoples almost entirely. In both, the hardships endured by white people, especially British and Irish white people, are at the heart of the narrative.[10]

The quarrel with nature

In the pioneer legend, the obstacles the settler-hero must fight are mainly the land itself. The desert and the bush become powerful adversaries. In this sense of the land as antagonist, Australian popular narratives are again not alone. Margaret Atwood says of the Canadian North, for example, that 'popular lore, and popular literature, established early that the North was uncanny, awe-inspiring in an almost religious way, hostile to white men, but alluring; that it would lead you on and do you in; that it would drive you crazy, and, finally, would claim you for its own'. Where Canadian sense of danger centred on snow, ice and water, Australian fears were, not surprisingly, located in heat, fire and thirst.[11]

The land as relentlessly hostile is only one strand, and over time a declining one, in settler perceptions of the Australian landscape. Not everyone saw it in this way, and there were some, perhaps many, who loved the countryside from the beginning. The desert was, and remains, a source of ambivalence, explored at some length in JW Gregory's *The Dead Heart of Australia,* describing a journey around Lake Eyre in 1901–02. For Gregory, the desert was fascinating, casting a spell, as deserts do everywhere: 'I feel a longing to see the great bare desert again — to enjoy once more its soothing solitude, and the exhilaration of its buoyant sense of freedom'. Yet the desert can also be 'an enemy that must be fought'. Its 'distances are vast, and they have to be wearily traversed; its heat is intense, and it has to be patiently endured'. There is the horror of being hopelessly lost, and the agony of death by thirst, the fear of going mad. Experience in the desert enables us to 'understand how Nature can rival the malignant tortures of the Inquisition'.[12]

Such fears are expressed most profoundly in the Burke and Wills story, with its tragic coincidences and bitter defeats in the struggle with nature. Alan Moorehead perceptively pointed out that the Burke and Wills story quickly acquired the status of an Australian myth because it 'perfectly expresses the early settlers' deeply-felt idea that life was not so much a struggle against other men as against the wilderness — that wilderness that made all men equal anyway. The quarrel, basically, was with nature'.[13]

The quarrel with indigenous peoples

So far, this chapter has alluded to those forms of settler historical narratives in which indigenous people barely appear. Indeed, indigenous invisibility is part of their power. Peter Otto suggests that the popular narrative of horror in the desert, of the land and landscape as the malignant Unknown, is neither innocent nor transparent. Rather, it offers a colonial society a way of displacing the conflict between settlers and indigenous people onto a more acceptable narrative of a direct conflict between the settler and the land itself. The land and the indigenous peoples become merged, the former foregrounded, the latter denied a place in history at all.[14]

Frantz Fanon wrote eloquently of the way the settler regards himself as the original inhabitant: 'He is the absolute beginning: "This land was created by us"'. To which we might add: 'We discovered it'. And so it happened in Australian historiography, although this erasure of the Aboriginal presence was more a twentieth than a nineteenth-century understanding of the colonial past. Nineteenth-century histories varied widely in their attitude to Aboriginal people and cultures, sometimes sympathetic, more often crudely racist, regarding them as 'savages' and 'low on the scale of humanity'. But they usually did exhibit an awareness of a history of frontier conflict, and worried over its moral implications. Nineteenth-century observers were generally aware of the rapid population decline among indigenous people that seemed to follow Europeans everywhere, and spent their time not denying its existence but rather trying to work out why it happened and how it might accord with God's will.[15]

In common with other colonial and settler societies, the colonising societies developed narratives of reversal, placing indigenous people as the invaders and settlers as the defenders of their land. Captivity narratives were one form of fictional representation of colonisation, in which the white woman, especially, is at the mercy of her Aboriginal captors. A particularly long-standing form of narrative reversal has been the idea that it is white settlers who belong, who own the land, who are at home, in contrast to the indigenous people, perceived as nomads, whose hold on it is tenuous and undeserved. A contemporary indigenous leader, Galarrwuy Yunupingu, has pointed to the irony of a situation in which Aboriginal people who stay on their own land as far as they are permitted, to protect it, become in white Australian mythology the wanderers, the nomads, on 'walkabout', while those inveterate wanderers, the European immigrants who have crossed oceans and strayed far from their homelands, and who continue restlessly to roam and wander within the continent, are named the settlers, those who stay at home.[16]

Such concerns and debates, however, gradually faded from public consciousness, written histories and school texts in the twentieth century. Sometimes the nineteenth-century interest in Aboriginal habits and customs survived in a section (rarely a whole chapter) on Aboriginal life, but more often such information vanished completely. Walter Murdoch's school history, *The Making of Australia: An Introductory History* (1917), was explicit on the exclusion of indigenous people from white Australian histories:

> When people talk about 'the history of Australia' they mean the history of the white people who have lived in Australia ... We should not stretch the term to make it include the history of the dark-skinned wandering tribes who hurled boomerangs and ate snakes in their native land for long ages before the arrival of the first intruders from Europe ... for they have nothing that can be called a history.

Sean Leahy, *Courier-Mail,*
21 November 1997

Murdoch's comments are more complex than they first appear: his reference to 'intruders' is an interesting metaphoric shadow of the very past he wishes to deny; and one need not disagree entirely with his notion of the incommensurability between Aboriginal and European senses of time and space, only with his purpose.[17]

It was still like this as late as the 1950s and 1960s. In fact, the general histories produced to meet the growth in university and other study of Australian history had minimal Aboriginal content.[18] These were the histories through which Australia's current national leadership was educated. In them, as Tom Griffiths has discussed, the conflict between settlers and indigenous people in the past was elided, suppressed, forgotten or viewed as so long ago that we in the present have no connection with those people or those events. None of our ancestors were individually involved in conflict with Aboriginal societies. In any particular place, violent conflict is denied — 'there were no Aborigines here', the people might say. The Aboriginal people simply 'disappeared', faded away and died out, at the hands of the mysterious forces of colonisation, not the agency of real people.

The return of the repressed: new Aboriginal histories

Yet this claim to the land, by right and history, did not go uncontested. Just when it seemed that Aboriginal prior occupation had all but disappeared from Australian consciousness, several developments led to a new interest. Political concern with racism in its local and international manifestations increased, along with a growing protest movement seeking equality and social justice for Aboriginal people. And in a broader cultural sphere — in fiction, painting, photography and film — interest in indigenous people had never really gone away. As many cultural critics have noted, representations of Aboriginal people outside academic history continued to be endless, abundant and innumerable, much like European exoticism and Orientalism, ranging from sympathetic to hostile, sometimes achieving considerable understanding, more often a white-centred form of appropriation and ignorance. It was in history and in thinking about the immediate past that it was especially difficult to come to terms with a prior and continuing indigenous presence.

In this new climate, those who crossed disciplinary boundaries were the first to resurrect historical knowledge of Aboriginal–European relations — in archaeology, art history, ethnohistory and political science. In the 1970s, some young historians were influenced by new left critiques of racism arising from opposition to South African apartheid, racial segregation in the United States, opposition to Australian involvement in the war in Vietnam, and from an emerging Australian civil rights movement. Some of the new histories that emerged at this time had a Marxist emphasis on the destructiveness of capitalism in a colonial context, and focused on its drive to exploit both land and labour, racial ideology and the institutionalisation of Aboriginal people. Sometimes these new histories, in their enthusiasm for uncovering and naming a brutal colonial past, risked portraying Aboriginal people as outside history, passive victims in a tragic narrative of destruction and despair. During the 1980s, as Bain Attwood notes in his chapter, some historians set out to redress the balance, drawing attention to examples of accommodation and more positive interaction. Others began to place greater emphasis on indigenous peoples' perceptions, understandings and active responses to colonisation.

By the late 1990s, the issues had shifted again. On the one hand, historians and their audiences began to tire of histories that homogenised Aboriginal people and societies as the victims of the past; on the other, historians began to wrestle with the 'genocide' issue, stimulated both by *Bringing Them Home* and an expanding international debate about genocide and modern history. It is time to return to the genocide question, this time evoking these wider contexts. The great twentieth-century Polish–Jewish jurist Raphaël Lemkin (1901–59) is generally regarded as having defined the term in his 1944 study, *Axis Rule in Occupied Europe*. His definition became the basis of the 1948 United Nations Convention, although that convention significantly altered his original formulations. Lemkin proposed in 1944 the new concept of 'genocide', deriving the term from the Greek word, *genos* (tribe or race), and the Latin, *cide* (killing, as in tyrannicide, homicide or fratricide). In Lemkin's definition, genocide signified a coordinated plan of different actions aimed at the destruction of the essential foundations of the life of national groups, with the 'aim' of annihilating the groups themselves. Genocide was to be considered as manifold and wide ranging, a composite of actions rather than one single defining act or mode by which the destruction of a nation or group's foundation of life was to be secured. It certainly could involve direct mass killing, but was not confined to it. For Lemkin, destruction of the essential foundations of the life of a group could occur in many ways. It involved consideration of the political, social, legal, intellectual, spiritual, economic, biological, physiological, religious and moral. The new crime was to be defined as a two-fold process, as Lemkin explained: 'Genocide has two phases: one, destruction of the national pattern of the oppressed group; the other, the imposition of the national pattern of the oppressor'. Genocide meant that one national pattern was to be destroyed, to be replaced by the imposition of another.[19]

The definition of genocide adopted in the UN Convention, now the basis for international law, was narrower and the requirement of proven intent was made stronger. Even so, the convention defined genocide as including:

> any of the following acts committed with intent to destroy, in whole or in part, a national, ethnical, racial or religious group, as such:
>
> Killing members of the group; Causing serious bodily or mental harm to members of the group; Deliberately inflicting on the group conditions of life calculated to bring about its physical destruction in whole or in part; Imposing measures intended to prevent births within the group; Forcibly transferring children of the group to another group.[20]

Whether we follow Lemkin's or the UN's definition, it is clear that genocide has a meaning far beyond direct killing and that it describes the destruction of the identity and ways of life of one people, and their replacement by another.

Several authors have pursued the question of whether colonialism is inherently genocidal. The purpose of colonisation in settler societies, after all, was to destroy the 'national pattern of the oppressed group' and to impose another in its place. Native American historian Ward Churchill argues that the greatest series of genocides ever perpetrated in history occurred in the Americas. From the outset, entire civilisations were eradicated. The pattern of destruction inaugurated by Columbus continued as the pattern of genocide for the Americas, where a population estimated to have been as great as 125 million was reduced by something over 90 per cent. He goes on to argue that settler-colonies around the world established during European expansion post-1492 in the United States, Canada, Australia, New Zealand, South Africa and Argentina, are inherently genocidal. In order for a settler-colony to be a settler-colony it requires 'wholesale displacement, reduction in numbers, and forced assimilation of native peoples'.[21]

In his remarkable book, *'Exterminate all the Brutes'* (1997), Sven Lindqvist traces the genealogy of the idea that extermination of entire peoples, later renamed genocide, was inevitable and necessary. In this search, examples from Australian history, at first seemingly irrelevant, gradually acquire major importance. Lindqvist traces the growth of the idea of extermination, or genocide, as the inevitable byproduct of progress, reminding us of what every Australian historian knows, that so great was the death rate of indigenous people in all the British colonies of settlement that the House of Commons established a select committee in 1837 to enquire into the impact of colonisation. Its eventual report recognised the rights of indigenous people to land and recommended that steps be taken to stop the slaughter.

Despite the attempts of British colonial authorities, and of non-government Aborigines protection societies, both in Britain and in the colonies, in the 1830s and 1840s, the slaughter continued. British observers were especially mindful of the destruction in Tasmania. Lindqvist draws attention to the attractions of new racial science which, by the 1850s, depicted these huge population losses as the result of inevitable processes whereby the higher races displaced the lower, bringing civilisation and progress to the world. In these circles, as Lindqvist puts it, 'the Tasmanian [case] became the paradigm, to which one part of the world after another yielded'. When the Anthropological Society debated the extinction of the so-called lower races on 19 January 1864, the opening speaker reminded his listeners of the fate of the Tasmanians, and predicted the next to depart the world stage would be the Maori. Indeed, so fixed had this idea of the complete extermination of the Tasmanian Aboriginal people become, that it was only with the rise of the Tasmanian Aboriginal movement in the second half of the 1970s, along with the publication of Ryan's book *The Aboriginal Tasmanians* in 1981, that most people learned there were indeed descendants. Genocide had taken place, but it had not been complete.[22]

Fears of expulsion, again

In the light of histories that recognise that colonisation of Australia produced population losses on a massive scale, it is a little curious to find today such strong reaction to the idea that the concept of genocide could be applied to the Australian colonial past.

Such strong reactions prompt an inquiry into their social, cultural and psychic basis. It seems to me that beneath the conservative critics' angry rejection of the 'genocide' label in particular, and the 'black armband' view of history in general, there is a fear of being cast out, exiled and made homeless again, after two centuries of securing a new home far away from home. There are fears of both a direct loss of land if Aboriginal land claims succeed, and a symbolic loss, of the legitimacy and permanency of the non-Aboriginal Australian's sense of home. In this phenomenology, if we fully recognise indigenous claims to the land and to a history of invasion, if we have a sense of living in someone else's country, we are, in a metaphorical if not a literal sense, in danger of homelessness again, of having to suffer yet again the original expulsion from the British Eden.

In the rejection of a history of land seizure by force, we have a white Australian version of *ressentiment* — Nietzsche's 'triumph of the weak as weak' — described by Wendy Brown as the 'moralising revenge of the powerless'. Brown argues that in contemporary society, in which 'individuals are buffeted and controlled by global configurations of disciplinarity and capitalist power of extraordinary proportions, [and] are at the same time nakedly individuated, stripped of reprieve from relentless exposure and accountability for themselves', *ressentiment* will abound. As unprotected yet individually accountable spectators in an uncontrollable world, white Australians see themselves as battling courageously against enormous odds. They construct for themselves a past that allocates the land as won through suffering, and therefore theirs.[23]

And so it is that in Australia, as in other settler societies, the trauma of expulsion, exodus and exile obscures empathetic recognition of indigenous perspectives, of their trauma of invasion, institutionalisation and dispersal. The self-chosen white victim finds it extremely difficult to recognise what he or she has done to others. The legacy of the colonial past is a continuing fear of illegitimacy, and therefore an inability to develop the kind of pluralist inclusive account of the past that might form the basis for a coherent national community. Debates over the numbers killed on the frontiers (and these are important debates to have) are for all these reasons not simply debates about numbers, or about empiricist versus postmodernist or Marxist or any other philosophy of history. They are, inevitably, no less than debates about the moral basis of British settlement in the past, and of Australian society in the present.

The author wishes to thank John Docker, as usual, for his intellectual input.

1 This chapter rehearses, at the request of the editors and in a substantially revised form, some of the arguments advanced in my earlier article, 'Whose home? Expulsion, exodus, and exile in white Australian historical mythology', *Journal of Australian Studies*, no. 61, 1999, pp. 1–18.

2 Andrew Lattas, 'Aborigines and contemporary Australian nationalism: Primordiality and the cultural politics of otherness', in Gillian Cowlishaw and Barry Morris (eds), *Race Matters: Indigenous Australians and 'Our' Society*, Aboriginal Studies Press, Canberra, 1997, pp. 234–5; Ross Gibson, *South of the West: Postcolonialism and the Narrative Construction of Australia*, Indiana University Press, Bloomington, 1992, pp. 173–4; Ken Inglis, *Sacred Places: War Memorials in the Australian Landscape*, Melbourne University Press, Melbourne, 1998.

3 There are of course many other migrant settler narratives in Australia, narratives of progress of the mainly European but sometimes Asian and Pacific communities that also memorialise the hardship and sacrifice of their first generation. Such immigrants, especially those from northern Europe, may be quite easily incorporated into, and made part of, the Anglo-Celtic narrative. Or they may, especially if from southern Europe or Asia, have their own quite separate stories of struggles and hardships that have less to do with the land and indigenous people and more to do with the ethnocentric and racist Anglo-Celtic majority itself. The complexities of 'whiteness' are a subject for further research.

4 See Benedict Anderson, *Imagined Communities: Reflections on the Origins and Spread of Nationalism*, Verso, London, 1983, pp. 11–16.

5 See Edward Said, 'Michael Waltzer's Exodus and Revolution: A Canaanite reading', in Said and Christopher Hitchens (eds), *Blaming the Victims: Spurious Scholarship and the Palestinian Question*, Verso, London, 1988, pp. 161–78.

6 Regina Schwartz, *The Curse of Cain: The Violent Legacy of Monotheism*, University of Chicago Press, Chicago, 1997, p. 6.

7 Sacvan Bercovitch, *The American Jeremiad*, University of Wisconsin Press, Madison, 1978, p. 47.

8 Deborah Bird Rose, 'Rupture and the ethics of care in colonised space', in Tim Bonyhady and Tom Griffiths

(eds), *Prehistory to Politics: John Mulvaney, the Humanities and the Public Intellectual*, Melbourne University Press, Melbourne, 1996, pp. 200, 205.

9 John Hirst, 'The pioneer legend', *Australian Historical Studies*, vol. 18, no. 71, 1978, pp. 316–37.

10 *Ibid*, p. 337.

11 Margaret Atwood, *Strange Things: The Malevolent North in Canadian Literature*, Clarendon Press, Oxford, 1995, p. 19.

12 JW Gregory, *The Dead Heart of Australia*, John Murray, London, 1906, p. 159.

13 Alan Moorehead, *Cooper's Creek*, Hamish Hamilton, London, 1962, p. 200.

14 Peter Otto, 'Forgetting colonialism', *Meanjin*, vol. 52, no. 3, 1993, pp. 545–8.

15 Frantz Fanon, 'Concerning violence', in Fanon, *The Wretched of the Earth* (1961), Penguin, Harmondsworth, 1973, pp. 39–40.

16 Galarrwuy Yunupingu, Speech to the National Press Club, Canberra, 13 February 1997.

17 Cited by Bain Attwood, 'The past as future: Aborigines, Australia and the (dis)course of history', in Attwood (ed.), *In the Age of Mabo: History, Aborigines and Australia*, Allen & Unwin, Sydney, 1996, p. xii.

18 Max Crawford, *Australia*, Hutchinson, London, 1952, had a brief chapter on Aboriginal life before the arrival of the Europeans, and of the later history noted only that the relations between squatters and Aborigines had been little studied. Gordon Greenwood (ed.), *Australia: A Social and Political History*, Angus and Robertson, Sydney, 1955, had virtually nothing; while AGL Shaw, *The Story of Australia*, Faber, London, 1955, had little more, and articulated the increasingly common view that there was no serious resistance from 'the aborigines with their primitive culture'. In the next decade, Douglas Pike, *Australia: The Quiet Continent*, Cambridge University Press, London, 1962, spoke on its first page of a 'native people in stone-age bondage' and little else. Marjorie Barnard, *A History of Australia*, Angus and Robertson, Sydney, 1962, Manning Clark, *A Short History of Australia*, Heinemann, London, 1963, and Russel Ward, *Australia*, Prentice-Hall, Englewood Cliffs, 1965, all contained little more than a few scattered references. Even in the 1970s, Frank Crowley's widely used university textbook, *A New History of Australia*, Heinemann, Melbourne, 1974, omitted Aboriginal history entirely.

19 Raphaël Lemkin, *Axis Rule in Occupied Europe: Law of Occupation, Analysis of Government Proposals for Redress*, Columbia University Press, New York, 1944, p. 79.

20 United Nations, *Convention on the Prevention and Punishment of the Crime of Genocide*, Article II, United Nations, 9 December 1948.

21 Ward Churchill, *A Little Matter of Genocide: Holocaust and Denial in the Americas 1492 to the Present*, City Lights Books, San Francisco, 1997, pp. 1, 84–8, 97, 129, 403.

22 Sven Lindqvist, *'Exterminate all the Brutes': One Man's Odyssey into the Heart of Darkness and the Origins of European Genocide*, The New Press, New York, 1997, pp. 122–41.

23 Wendy Brown, *States of Injury: Power to Freedom in Late Modernity*, Princeton University Press, Princeton, 1995, p. 66.

Graeme **Davison**

Conflict in the museum

National museums are now among the hot spots in a historic settling of accounts between indigenous people and European settler societies. Not only in Australia, but in South Africa, the United States, Canada, New Zealand and in Europe itself, where the formerly colonised have migrated to the metropolis, the material legacy of colonisation, exemplified by the collections of the great museums, has become a bone of contention. In the 1970s and 1980s, these disputes centred on the return of objects acquired through colonisation. Now the debate has shifted to how those objects are displayed and interpreted.

Since the nineteenth century, Benedict Anderson has argued, the museum has been a key site in the process of nation building.[1] At the end of the twentieth century, the museum remains a major educational and leisure industry as well as a focus for national pride and identity. The national museum is where the nation is publicly on show, both to locals and increasing numbers of international visitors. Distance and colonial dependence have long made Australians especially nervous about the impression that they make on the rest of the world; indeed it sometimes seems as though we are incapable of validating our sense of national selfhood except through the approving eyes of others. For all these reasons, it was likely that the version of the national past presented in the National Museum of Australia would receive critical scrutiny, especially by those fearful that the national self was somehow under threat. And it was likely that its presentation of the history of the relationships between Aborigines and Europeans would be a subject of special interest.

This issue has only recently come to the boil, but it has been quietly simmering for some time. The question of relations between Europeans and Aborigines has been at the heart of the National Museum's mission since the early 1970s when Geoffrey

Blainey and John Mulvaney wrote the pregnant 13 pages of the Pigott Report that became effectively the Museum's charter. It was they who mandated a Gallery of Aboriginal Australia (now the First Australians gallery) and who said that Aboriginal people should themselves have a large hand in deciding how that story should be told. 'The museum, where appropriate, should display controversial issues', Blainey and Mulvaney wrote. 'In our view, too many museums concentrate on certainty and dogma, thereby forsaking the function of stimulating legitimate doubt and thoughtful discussion.' Theirs was a generous and imaginative vision that has generally stood the test of time. It carefully balances the inspirational against the critical, the entertaining against the educational, the local against the international.[2]

Misadventures of a historical adviser

When, late in 1999, I was invited to serve as a historical adviser to the Museum I saw myself as upholding that generous vision. Only someone who had never read the Pigott Report and was ignorant of the long gestation of the Museum's exhibiting policies, could claim — as Keith Windschuttle did in a recent issue of *Quadrant* — that I am 'one of its intellectual architects'.[3] Even stranger is his suggestion that I am the author of the postmodernist philosophy animating the historical interpretations in the Museum. Having also recently been attacked by at least one reviewer of my book, *The Use and Abuse of Australian History* (2000), for my deep hostility to postmodernism,[4] you will understand how difficult it is to recognise myself in Windschuttle's lurid account of the Museum's gestation.

Like his book, *The Killing of History,* Windschuttle's article reveals him as a relentlessly adversarial critic.[5] He approaches history as a battleground on which good historians armed with facts rout bad historians misled by theory. Twenty years ago he was a Marxist, tilting his lance at the citadels of bourgeois hegemony. Now he is an anti-Marxist, but he has yet to shake off some of the bad intellectual habits of his youth. In Windschuttle's vision there are no shades of grey, no middle ground. If you are not an empiricist, you must be a postmodernist. Australian historians, as he portrays them, are a craven lot, all too-ready to dance to the tune of their pied piper, Henry Reynolds. Important disagreements among Australian historians over the extent, character and motivation of Aboriginal resistance are ignored in order to reinforce the idea of an academic conspiracy, and bolster his own image as a historical whistleblower.

Considering the weight that Windschuttle gives to facts, it is surprising that he is so careless about chronology. Only in July 1999, when the National Museum was well down the track towards completion, did I give the paper on national museums that Windschuttle sees as its postmodernist blueprint.[6] In this paper, I review developments in a number of European and American history museums. Half way through the paper I summarise, in a neutral way, the trends in what I call 'the new museology'. Windschuttle says I 'commend' and 'endorse' these trends, although I actually go on to make a number of critical observations about them. He thinks that the Museum's Council was 'taken in' by my postmodern interpretation, even though most members of the Council would have had no opportunity to read my views until the Museum was already open. I saw no sign whatsoever that the Council was of a mind to be taken in by anyone, least of all by me. On the contrary, members were briefed in detail on the exhibits and vigorously debated the selection of themes and objects. One member, David Barnett, even sought and was granted the opportunity to comment on the labels of exhibits. Towards the end of 2000, after many months of discussion, the Council finally decided — correctly in my view — that it should leave the detailed execution of the exhibits to the curatorial staff, and confine itself to the formulation of policy on the content of exhibits. It was only then that it ratified a revised version of the guidelines on content that I had drafted some months before. These guidelines were written in consultation with my fellow advisers, Geoffrey Bolton and John Mulvaney, and restate and expand the principles of the Pigott Report, often using similar words. By the time they were adopted by the Council late in 2000, the exhibits were effectively complete. Windschuttle nowhere quotes these guidelines — the only blueprint I ever wrote for the Museum — but misquotes and misconstrues my conference paper, which the Council never saw.

It was also at about this time that I was asked by the Chair of the Museum's Council, Tony Staley, to respond to Barnett's criticisms of the labels he had been reading. As an adviser I had previously read some thousands of words of labels, often commenting very critically on them. A former editor of *Quadrant,* Peter Coleman, writing in the *Adelaide Review,* suggested that I was asked to examine Barnett's criticisms because I had been recommended by Geoffrey Blainey, having previously recommended myself by writing a 'eulogy' of him for *The Oxford Companion to Australian History*.[7] This suggestion is as insulting to Geoffrey Blainey as it is to me, and could only be made by someone who thinks that there is no way of telling good history from bad except on ideological grounds. I was unaware that Blainey had been consulted until I had already agreed to act; knowing he had been consulted would not have influenced my acceptance one way or the other.

As it happened, I found almost all of Barnett's criticisms to be ill-founded. This was not because I thought that the Museum's work was beyond reproach; simply that his particular criticisms were not consistent with factual information or scholarly opinion on the matters he raised. I responded to every one of the criticisms in detail, often quoting my authorities. If Windschuttle thought that my advice was biased, he could easily have checked for himself, since both Barnett's critique and my reply were later published in full on the *Sydney Morning Herald* website.[8] I should also add that in my role as an adviser and reader of labels for the Museum exhibits, I specifically declined to deal with detailed issues in the First Australians gallery, because I considered Aboriginal history to be a field beyond my expertise. So it was not until opening day that I actually saw the Contested Frontiers exhibit that Windschuttle criticised in *Quadrant*.

Thus, in relation to the National Museum, I have not played the roles or asserted the influence that Windschuttle has ascribed to me. Specifically, I did not contribute to the exhibit on contested frontiers, and have no vested interest or previously stated opinion to defend. I am, however, deeply interested in how museums, especially national museums, interpret the past, confront controversial issues and contribute to matters of contemporary debate.

Conveying the message

Historians and journalists often begin with a view of museums as something like an illustrated history book. As wordsmiths ourselves, we pay special attention to the textual element of the museum — labels, documents and the like — and we expect the design of the museum to reflect the kind of narrative logic that we are so familiar with ourselves in books and journal articles. But of course museums are not like books at all. The amount of interpretative label text in the whole of the

Museum is less than in a short monograph. I am among those who would like labels to be longer but I have to admit that I do not always read them all, and that reading text, especially if the conservation staff control the lighting levels, is harder work than reading a book. If we treat museums as though they were illustrated texts, and bring the same expectations to them as we do to a book, we will inevitably be disappointed. We will also miss out on some of the things that museums are much better able to do than books.

Museums must choose those themes, episodes and ideas that can be most effectively communicated through objects and visual display. I think that it is insufficiently appreciated by critics of the Museum how relatively short has been its collecting history and how slender have been its acquisition budgets. In telling the story of frontier conflict, it has one or two iconic objects — such as the coatee of the explorer Captain Patrick Logan[9] — and others, such as muskets and spears that illustrate the terms on which armed combat between Aborigines and Europeans took place. But relics of specific conflict episodes have seldom survived.

Judging a museum exhibit by examining the labels alone is a bit like sitting in the cinema with your eyes closed, listening only to the soundtrack. Reading all those thousands of words of labels gave me only the vaguest idea of what the actual experience of the Museum would be like. The juxtaposition of objects, the use of space, light and ambient sound, the relative size of labels, and the use of various authorial voices all contribute to an experience that is more powerful than the information contained in the labels alone.

Visitors enter the Museum's exhibit on Contested Frontiers after leaving a complementary display illustrating the early history of attempts by Governor Arthur Phillip and others to 'conciliate [the] affections' of Aborigines. At the threshold, we pass this label summarising the theme of the exhibit:

> It soon became apparent to the Aboriginal people around Sydney Harbour that the British intended to stay. As the frontiers of colonisation expanded, Aboriginal groups resisted. Guerilla wars were fought along a rolling frontier for a century and a half. Today the names of resistance leaders such as Windradyne and Jandamarra are virtually unknown outside their communities.

The label encapsulates the main threads of what has now become the standard interpretation of frontier conflict: that Aborigines actively resisted European colonisation; that conflict was prolonged and violent; and that in memory, if not in formal history, Aboriginal communities still honour those who led that resistance.

The exhibit follows a similar narrative line to other recent museum exhibits on frontier conflict. Here, for example, is the introductory text to the exhibit Scars in the Landscape in Museum Victoria's Aboriginal gallery, Bunjilaka:

> '… men, women and children are shot wherever they can be met with …' Henry Meyrick, 1846
>
> Following the arrival of the British in Victoria, Aboriginal people suffered extreme violence. Many were killed directly. Others died from European diseases.
>
> In western Victoria, Aboriginal life was dramatically affected from 1834. The Hentys arrived from Tasmania and introduced sheep into country they regarded as rich pastoral land.
>
> Squatters took land from Aboriginal people by whatever means necessary:
>
> '… the best way [to procure a run] is to go outside and take up a new run, provided the conscience of the party is sufficiently seared to enable him without remorse to slaughter natives …' Niel Black, 1839
>
> Travelling through the district, GA Robinson, the Chief Protector of Aborigines, documented many atrocities committed against Aboriginal people. He wrote 'this would not be allowed in civilised society'.
>
> Aboriginal people resisted these actions and endured.

While the general story-line is similar, each museum has distinctive emphases. While Contested Frontiers exhibit emphasises a two-sided conflict, Bunjilaka emphasises Aboriginal suffering and dispossession and European atrocities; while Contested Frontiers emphasises heroic resistance, Bunjilaka emphasises survival.[10]

More powerful than the words of these labels, however, are the visual forms and atmospherics of the displays. One wall of the Contested Frontiers exhibit is defined by a large contemporary sculpture, *Annihilation of the Blacks,* by Fiona Foley, a Butchulla woman. The sculpture is inspired, the label tells us, by her mother's account of massacres of Aboriginal people in the Maryborough area, although it is apparently influenced by a ceremonial sculpture from the Aurukun region of Cape York,[11] and bears some resemblance to representations of American lynching parties. The mood of the exhibit is set by the mournful background sound of a solo cello. The idea of a rolling frontier and a long series of 'guerilla wars' is given visible form and persuasive force

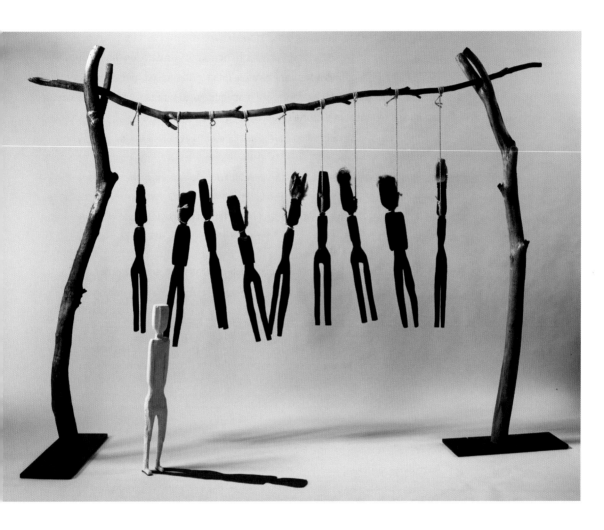

Fiona Foley
Annihilation of the blacks, 1986
sculpture
National Museum of Australia

by projecting the gradual spread of European settlement on a map of Australia, with flashing lights indicating the location of each episode of conflict. The image of frontier conflict as a long 'guerilla war' with its own unsung heroes challenges the belief that Aborigines were the passive victims of European conquest. One might argue, however, that the image of a continental map endows these intermittent engagements with the purposeful and continuous character of a national liberation struggle.

Scars in the Landscape adopts a simpler, but effective, interpretative approach. In a large-screen presentation, colour photos of Victorian places associated with frontier violence alternate with the voices of contemporary observers drawn from their journals, especially the most famous of the Aboriginal protectors, George Augustus Robinson, whose words also provide the motto of the exhibit: 'This would not be allowed in a civilised community'. The background sound, whispering voices interspersed with sounds of gunshot and death cries, is more confronting than the National Museum's mournful cello.

Getting it right

Windschuttle's criticisms of the Contested Frontiers exhibit concentrate on the factual accuracy of texts that accompany these displays and effects. He claims that the exhibit presents as historically accurate a popular account of the so-called Bells Falls massacre which seems to date only from recent times. According to this account, in the early 1820s, Aboriginal women and children were pursued by troopers to the edge of Bells Falls near Bathurst and forced to jump to their deaths. It is a vivid and shocking image of colonial brutality. We have only to recall alleged episodes of refugee children being thrown overboard in the Timor Sea to recognise the strong emotional pull of such images. Windschuttle says that the Museum failed to take account of David Roberts's research, published in *Australian Historical Studies* in 1995, which demonstrated, according to Windschuttle, that this story was a 'fabrication'.[12]

The exhibit, he continues, contains other fabrications as well. The murderous placenames projected onto the floor — Slaughterhouse Creek and Massacre Bay — are allegedly not real places but have been 'invented for this display'. A companion display on the so-called Bunuba uprising in Western Australia is said to be erroneous because the Museum's label wrongly claims that men apprehended for killing or stealing cattle in the Kimberley in the 1890s were 'imprisoned, transported to Rottnest Island in the south or executed'. This account, he insists, defames the Western Australian justice system and is not in accord with the evidence contained in the prison lists at Rottnest, which show that those incarcerated were mainly convicted of serious felonies against other Aborigines rather than cattle theft.

These are not trivial points of detail. However, judgements of the interpretative validity of the exhibit do not turn on these points of factual detail alone. The First Australians gallery is not like a house that must fall to the ground if one or two bolts are loose. Nor, for that matter, is any interpretation sound just because every factual bolt is secure. Because the objects and episodes are chosen to represent a broader theme or historical truth, a critic must attend to the validity of the general theme as well as the factual accuracy and appropriateness of the illustrations.

Let us begin, however, with the accusation of factual inaccuracy: first, that the placenames projected onto the floor of the exhibit were 'invented for the display'. In fact, those displayed are the names of actual places recorded in standard registers of placenames such as those of the Australian Surveying and Land Information Group and Macquarie University's Australian National Placenames Survey. For example, there are six Slaughterhouse Creeks: four in New South Wales, one in Queensland and one in Victoria. Massacre Bay is located near Colac in Victoria. There are several other titles with the word 'Massacre' in Australia, although the link with Aboriginal killings is tenuous in some cases. Attack Spring is near Moree in New South Wales, and there are other places, such as Attack Bay in Western Australia (now renamed Herald Bight), associated with incidents of conflict between Aborigines and Europeans.[13]

Second, the label mentioning the incarceration of Aboriginal 'cattle thieves' at Rottnest Island is concerned with Aborigines caught stealing cattle in the Kimberley, not with the origins of all Aboriginal prisoners at Rottnest Island. Windschuttle appears to be justified in his objection that no Aborigines are recorded as having been 'executed' for the offence, although some were probably shot by settlers in retaliation without ever facing the courts. This label could, and should, be amended without affecting the general interpretation presented in the exhibit.

Windschuttle's strongest accusations relate to the presentation of the so-called Bells Falls incident. As Roberts argues in his chapter in this volume, Windschuttle's characterisation of the story as a 'fabrication' is a crude summary of the complex interplay between oral tradition and documented historical events. Nowhere in the display does the Museum actually affirm the popular story of women and children being forced over the edge of the falls, name the place 'Bells Falls' or use the word 'massacre'. The general label covering the episode refers only in a general way to 'an exterminating war' being conducted in the Bathurst area in the early 1820s. The words that Windschuttle attributes to the Museum — 'This is a place of great sadness. Our people still hear the echoes of the women and children who died here' — are clearly attributed to a present-day Wiradjuri elder, Bill Allen. Curators of the exhibit argue that it is designed to convey the voices and beliefs of present-day Aborigines, not to endorse the historical truth of a story, which, as Roberts shows, has been documented in written sources only since the 1960s.

Reading a museum exhibit

A bystander may feel that both critic and defender give too much weight to the literal truth of the labels, and too little to the overall interpretation they support. Instead of asking 'Is every label literally correct?' let us approach the issue of interpretation in a different way. Imagine two typical visitors to the Museum. One is a tourist, perhaps visiting Canberra for the weekend, who moves through the Museum fairly rapidly, pausing occasionally to look closely at particular exhibits but responding mainly to the overall feel or atmosphere. Compare this casual visitor with a secondary or tertiary student who is researching a project or essay on frontier conflict. This visitor spends half an hour or more in the Contested Frontiers exhibit, reading each label carefully, making notes and asking questions of the Museum staff.

What conclusions is our casual visitor likely to form from the Contested Frontiers exhibit? He will approach the exhibit via the long gallery dealing with the character of traditional Aboriginal life in various regions of Australia, and through a larger display entitled To Conciliate Their Affections which illustrates processes of accommodation and pacification. Later, he will move to sections of the gallery dealing with the mission experience, the movement for Aboriginal rights and the celebration of contemporary Aboriginal culture in music and sport. The recess occupied by the Contested Frontiers exhibit is a dark passage in a longer narrative, the overall thread of which is more celebratory than dismal.

Our casual visitor will be strongly influenced by those themes and ideas that are reinforced by light, sound and strong images. While the Museum curators may be right in saying that Bill Allen's statement 'This is a place of great sadness' is clearly identified as that of a present-day Wiradjuri elder, it is reinforced by its prominent display in large white type, by a large (although unlabelled) colour photo of Bells Falls, and by the ambient sound of the mournful cello. Textual material from contemporary European sources, such as Governor Sir Thomas Brisbane's proclamation, which confirms that a war was in progress, but makes no specific reference to an incident at Bells Falls, and, on one possible reading, throws doubt on its occurrence, is displayed in smaller black type at the bottom of the display cabinet. Whatever the labels may actually say, the overall design of the exhibit tends to elevate recent Aboriginal tradition over the more equivocal material in contemporary written sources. Unless the visitor already knows the Bells Falls story, the exhibit will not validate it. But casual visitors are likely to leave with the impression that some sort of massacre of Aboriginal women and children took place in the Bathurst region. They will not have been seriously misled about the general truth — that life on the frontier in the 1820s was often violent and that Aborigines were killed by settlers — but they may have been misled into giving more credence to the Bells Falls story than the contemporary evidence supports.

Now let us look at the display from the vantage point of the student who stops and reads the display more carefully. She will probably stop and press all the buttons on the display below the illuminated map, giving brief details of conflict incidents across the continent. Through the excellent displays of Aboriginal and European weaponry, she will gain an insight into the tactical terms on which adversaries fought along the frontier. If she stops and reads all the graphics and labels of the Bells Falls exhibit, she will be led to ask some probing questions. For example, she will note the strong language of the *Sydney Gazette* reporting the proclamation of martial law in the Bathurst area, including the assertion that 'an exterminating war' was raging. But she may be puzzled by the statement in an accompanying text repealing martial law in December 1824: 'During the four months that Martial Law prevailed not one outrage was committed under it, neither was a life sacrificed or even blood spilt'. How is this statement to be reconciled with Bill Allen's more prominent statement that martial law was 'an excuse for soldiers to go out and kill hundreds of Wiradjuri men, women and children'? Is our student likely to be challenged, or just confused, by these

The Contested Frontiers
exhibit in the National
Museum of Australia
Photograph by George
Serras

dissonant voices? Is it enough for the Museum to say 'we just allow the voices to be heard'? If so, does not the prominence of one label, and near invisibility of the other, subtly tilt judgement in favour of one interpretation rather than the other? Should the Museum have taken a firmer editorial position of its own, even if it was to make clearer that the student was being invited to consider the relationship, in this instance, between documented history and popular memory? If visitors are being encouraged to think about these issues, what more could the Museum do — perhaps through supplementary material, guidebooks, student kits and so on — to enable them to pursue their inquiries?

How should the Museum respond to the critics of the Contested Frontiers exhibit? Windschuttle would like us to think that the flaws in the display invalidate the general interpretation, that the loose bolts jeopardise the entire structure. I am more inclined to think that the flaws are a product of attempting, within very limited space, to convey too many complex messages. Originally, I understand, the Contested Frontiers exhibit was expected to occupy a much larger space in which it might have been possible to convey fuller information and clarify some of the dissonance that currently detracts from the exhibit. If the objective was to convince visitors of the reality of European violence towards Aborigines, then other episodes such as Myall Creek or Coniston might have been better examples, assuming that the Museum could obtain artefacts to illustrate them well. In justification of the choice, however, it must be said that the exhibit does help to illustrate a symbolically important point: that violence between Aborigines and Europeans occurred from the crossing of the first land barrier, the Blue Mountains, in the 1820s. If, on the other hand, the Museum's primary objective was to invite visitors to consider the interplay of history and popular memory in the record of frontier conflict, I suspect that a more explicit and skilful approach to the labelling of the exhibit was required. It is for the Museum's curatorial staff to decide how best to respond to the criticisms made of the Contested Frontiers exhibit. At the moment, careful re-organisation and re-labelling seems more justified than wholesale revision or scrapping of the exhibit.

In its guidelines on exhibition content, the Museum pledges itself to 'challenge visitors to reflect upon the nation's past and ponder its future. It should stimulate legitimate doubt and thoughtful discussion. It will not avoid the presentation of controversial or painful issues, but will refrain from partisanship'. It also seeks to promote 'informed debate on issues of national importance'. It is clear from the other contributions to this volume that the Museum is already fulfilling that promise. Doing it better does not require a retreat from the idea of interpretative pluralism towards some imagined national orthodoxy. Pluralism is really the only practical approach in a society where people of goodwill remain divided on important issues. 'The contested frontier' is a nice metaphor, not only for a 'controversial and painful' episode in our history, but for the way in which the National Museum of Australia might itself advance that national debate.

1 Benedict Anderson, *Imagined Communities: Reflection on the Origin and Spread of Nationalism*, revised edition, Verso, London, 1991.

2 *Museums in Australia 1975: Report of the Committee of Inquiry on Museums and National Collections*, Australian Government Printing Service, Canberra, 1975, pp. 72–3.

3 Keith Windschuttle, 'How not to run a museum', *Quadrant*, vol. 45, no. 9, 2001, pp. 11–19.

4 Chris Healy, 'A foreign country', *Australian Review of Books*, vol. 5, no. 4, 2000, pp. 16–17, 27.

5 See Graeme Davison, 'A premature post-mortem?', *Agenda*, vol. 2, no. 3, 1995, pp. 381–3.

6 Davison, 'National museums in a global age: Observations abroad and reflections at home', in Darryl McIntyre and Kirsten Wehner (eds), *National Museums: Negotiating Histories Conference Proceedings*, National Museum of Australia, Canberra, 2001, pp. 12–28.

7 Peter Coleman, 'A stampeding herd of journalists', *Adelaide Review*, 22 August 2001, p. 18.

8 *Sydney Morning Herald*, 5 June 2001.

9 Logan's coatee was borrowed from the National Army Museum, London. In early 2002, it was returned and replaced by a replica.

10 Bunjilaka is arguably the harder-hitting story, although perhaps rather more tendentious. For example, it would be more accurate to say that 'many' Aborigines died from European diseases and 'others' were killed directly.

11 Luke Taylor (ed.), *Painting the Land Story*, National Museum of Australia, Canberra, 1999, pp. 10–11.

12 David Roberts, 'Bells Fall massacre and Bathurst's history of violence: Local tradition and Australian historiography', *Australian Historical Studies*, vol. 26, no. 105, 1995, pp. 615–33.

13 I am grateful to Nancy Michaelis for this information.

Index